VENICE

A thousand years of culture and civilization

D0088355

Endpapers: A mosaic of the life of Christ in San Marco.

Overleaf: 'The Tempesta' by Giorgione.

Peter Lauritzen

VENICE

A thousand years of culture and civilization

ATHENEUM NEW YORK
1978

For my wife
Rose
and our son
Frederick
born in Venice

Library of Congress Cataloging in Publication Data

Lauritzen, Peter.
  Venice.

    Bibliography: p.
    Includes index.
    1. Venice – Civilization. I. Title.
DG675.6.L38 1978   945'.31   78–2690
ISBN 0–689–10897–4

Contents

List of illustrations

Author's Note

I have written this study of Venetian culture and civilization for the general reader; the illustrations have been chosen to show something of what has survived in Venice despite the tremendous work of destruction and dispersal wrought after the collapse of the thousand-year Republic in 1797. I hope this book will interest the widest possible audience, although it may well have a special appeal for those who have already visited Venice, or who read it while they are there.

Much that is finest in the achievements of many European peoples can today be conveniently studied in museums, but what the Venetians created is best seen in Venice itself. One of my intentions was to reconstruct the proper historical context for the vast and complex legacy that Venice bequeathed to Europe. This contribution of the Venetians to western culture was of course only incidental to the evolution of their civilization. Until the last century of the Republic's existence they employed their artists and their craftsmen primarily to embellish their own city, and what they exported was usually a response to the demands of foreign markets.

I have no pretensions as a scholar or even as a student of all that I have touched on in this volume. My particular advantage is that I have lived in Venice for over a decade (long enough to have been accepted as a *cittadino* under the Republic) and I have thus come to feel at home in the extraordinary setting of Venetian culture. At first I found myself fascinated by the monuments and minor souvenirs of history that surrounded me. I then became curious about Venice's vanished role as gateway to the East and capital of a vast and amorphous sea-borne empire; and finally I found myself anxious to discover what it was that was peculiarly Venetian in all her arts. To satisfy such speculation adequately would be the work of a lifetime rather than a mere decade.

Living with and within Venetian history one cannot help being curious about the Venetians of the past: from the doges and the patriciate, the Great Chancellor and the *cittadini*, to the volunteer galley oarsmen, the master glass-blowers and the *Arsenalotti*. Informed people today – many Venetians included – maintain that there are no true Venetians left, that there is no one today who may justifiably lay claim to the inheritance of a millennial civilization. It is my hope that this limited survey will succeed in conveying an impression of the Venetian of the Republic and of his world.

In preparing this study my memory has been jogged by all sorts of unrelated reading, but certain specific studies proved fundamental, and these are fully listed in the select bibliography; the works of Horatio Brown, Pompeo Molmenti and Giulio Lorenzetti in particular still provide excellent guidelines, as do the more recent three volumes of Perocco and Salvadori's *Civiltà di Venezia* and the first of John Julius Norwich's projected two-volume history of Venice.

Much of the feeling for Venice that I may have been able to convey should be credited to my Venetian friends who have shared with me their own profound and often passionate understanding of the Republic. I was particularly encouraged in attempting to deal with this vast subject by a chance remark of Prince Clary, whose knowledge of European history is unequalled in my experience, and whose familiarity with Venice over seventy years has afforded me hours of fascinating conversation. I have also been singularly fortunate in the help given me in the final preparation of the manuscript by Ray and Carol Jacques, who have devoted many hours of their busy days to help correct what I have written. A felicity of phrase, a clearly made point or accurate spelling can often be attributed to them. For errors of historical interpretation or dating and attribution I am afraid I have only myself to blame.

This book could not have been written at all without the patience and support of my wife, who put up with bursts of conceit and confidence alternating with diffidence and despair. In the very midst of it all she excelled herself by producing a splendid son, who I hope will one day be pleased and proud to discover his name on the rolls of the city of Venice.

P.L.L.

Preface

Generations of connoisseurs, art historians, museum directors and their disciples have conditioned us to think first of Florence when we consider the extraordinary achievements of Italian culture in the long history of Christian Europe. The Florentine Renaissance was indeed a period of astonishing fecundity and artistic creativity, and no one should attempt to set the history of Venetian culture against it. Yet today the two cities seem to stand in contrast to each other. Florence has become a bustling and vital modern city. Whilst it may no longer nurture Michelangelos and Botticellis, there are native Florentine painters of international renown. Its ancient craft of leatherwork plays a distinctive role in contemporary fashion, and Florentines have effectively revived the old skills with stuffs and dyes and organized their distribution on a scale which dwarfs the network of the once ubiquitous Medici banks.

Venice instead is apparently a city belonging only to her past, an empty shell of former glories. Its native population diminishes constantly, deserting the island for the industrial wasteland that threatens to destroy what is left of millennial grandeur. Its last remaining industry makes baubles for the tourists who come in droves to stay on a statistical average of about eighteen hours, to mill about and to gawk at the remaining relics of the *Serenissima*'s magnificence. Many are disappointed that the shops are so poor, so provincial, that the city is so difficult to get around and that so often they are overcharged. And yet there are also very many, mingling with the disillusioned, who feel quite differently. The discriminating, the connoisseurs and the devotees sense the peace of Venice and its supreme beauty.

Venice remains one of the world's most magical and enchanting visual experiences. The expanses of water on all sides make it an island city of constantly shifting horizons – apparently close at hand in the crystalline light of autumn, and again infinitely distant in the mysterious muffling winter fogs. The broad ribbon of the Grand Canal stretching through the centre is a rippled and reflecting surface; its small tributary canals thread multi-faceted light between dark canyons of brick and stone-faced wall. Light, with its reflections and refractions, is essential to Venetian art. The palaces along the Grand Canal are tall, marble-sheathed and encrusted façades meant to be seen across and in the water; the mosaics of San Marco were carefully laid to catch and reflect the light that penetrated that *sanctum sanctorum* of the state. The city glistens with gilded carving and richly veined marbles, with the silvered surface of Murano mirror glass; and of course light glows in the colours of Venetian painting. From the pure, rich dyes of Renaissance robes to the smoky, stormy atmosphere of Tintoretto's visions; from the golden ground of the Byzantine heaven to the pale blues and pink-tinted clouds of Tiepolo's clear skies: man and nature are transformed by the Venetian love of light.

The paintings have been scattered throughout the world, and are the most widely known part of the Venetian legacy. There are famous Titian Venuses in Florence and his great portraits and mythologies in the Prado; Veronese's largest canvas is in the Louvre; Bellini's luminous portrait of a doge hangs near a room full of Crivelli's work in London; Vienna, New York and Washington all guard treasures of Venetian painting. Some of these represent the dispersal of the Venetian patrimony after the collapse of the Republic in 1797, whereas many recall the dominance of Venetian taste and culture over several centuries of European history. In Spain the king commissioned vast canvases from Titian while his courtiers drank from glasses blown at Murano; in Florence the Medici who displayed Venetian paintings acquired from Urbino bought as much Burano lace as they could afford; the princes of Europe, draped in Venetian velvets, ordered their bronze cannon and golden trinkets from the Republic while, much as earlier generations had treasured illuminated manuscripts and incunabula, the scholarly among them collected Aldine editions bound in Venetian tooled leather. For four centuries Venetian artists took their taste abroad. In the thirteenth century Venetian mosaicists were called to decorate the baptistry in Florence; Gentile Bellini was sent to Istanbul to paint for the sultan; the greatest emperor of the Holy Roman Empire was represented as stooping to pick up the paint brush Titian dropped; Gian Battista Tiepolo spread his vast and airy heavens over the stair hall of the prince-bishop's residence in Würzburg, and above the throne in the royal palace at Madrid; and

Canaletto painted for Englishmen while his nephew recorded the Baroque cities of Central Europe.

Venetian culture has exerted an influence beyond the court treasures of the past and the museums of today. Modern diplomacy, beginning with the idea of resident embassies in foreign countries, had Venetian practice as precedent, and the isolation of ambassadors in Venice herself is practised today at Peking and Moscow. While the Florentines can claim the dubious credit for inventing modern taxation, it was on the Rialto that double-entry book-keeping, giro-banking and other mechanisms of commerce and exchange were pioneered while the Republic's great market area became synonymous with world trading. Venice's immense wealth and enterprise was also based on its industrial centre at the Arsenal, where assembly-line organization was so efficiently applied to almost every aspect of naval construction, outfitting and armament that as long ago as the sixteenth century its dockyard matched the ship-a-day goal of World War Two shipyards.

As with any great civilization, the ultimate legacy of Venetian culture is to be found in the lessons to be learned from her history. The insights and inter-pretations of individual historians may be idiosyncratic and perhaps misleading in themselves, but they often force us to examine some of our own assumptions in a more critical light. The incredible efficiency of the Arsenal shipyards became so ossified that the Venetians continued to build antique galleys well into the age of sailing ships and broadside naval battles. Their bureaucracy was complex and incorruptible, but in the end the very people supported by this welfare state sought to overthrow the government which kept them. To compound further the irony of a governing aristocracy turning on itself, it was the Venetian working classes alone, and especially the *Arsenalotti*, who spon-taneously took up arms when the moment came to defend the millennial ducal government against the specious egalitarianism of the French Revolution. One of the Venetian institutions often misunderstood out of its local context is that derived from the Venetian word *ghetto*. It was indeed the area in the city where the Jews lived and worked and where they were closed in at night. Today the word has horrific connotations and emotional overtones, but to the Venetian of the Republic it was merely a local place name, and the Jews were no more segregated or ill-treated than were the Turks, the Persians and the Germans, or even the foreign ambassadors, all of whom lived a restricted life in their own compounds.

Many of the products of Venetian culture and civilization that are familiar today will be better understood if the conditions that helped produce them are taken into consideration. The Titians in a museum, the lace in a Medici portrait or the Vivaldi concerto in a concert hall should be approached bearing in mind the environment that produced them. Titian, for example, lived in a time crucial to Venice's survival as a European power, and his commissions reflect his country's policies and alliances. The lacemakers of Burano depended on the protection and encouragement of the government to compete with the craftsmen of Brussels and France; and Vivaldi, whilst evocative of the Rococo spirit of the Republic's final years, was composing in the context of one of Europe's oldest and most important musical traditions. Much that is distinctly Venetian in western culture and civilization will not be overlooked if such masterpieces are looked at in this light, and today's visitor to the treasures that Venice herself still preserves will understand better the great and long life of the Republic that gave birth to so much beauty.

I

The Flight
from the Barbarians
315-815

Vast millennial movements of the earth's surface produced the peculiar combination of mountains, plains, coast and land-locked lagoons that distinguish the northern end of the Adriatic sea. In the centre of one of the lagoons, equidistant from the marshy shoreline of the mainland and the thin strips of sand-banked littoral that act as a bastion against the sea, cluster a group of small mud-flat islands. With the statistical precision that became an obsession with the later settlers there, we can say that there were and are one hundred and seventeen of these islands. The channels between the islands were only a few metres wide, but currents, both from the sea tides and the freshwater rivers that emptied into the lagoon from the mainland, kept these channels deep enough to be navigated by shallow-bottomed craft. Still, these islands must have seemed inhospitable. Little would grow on them; they were suitable only for fishermen; and the early man who wanted to fish in the lagoon, protected as it was at all times from sea storms, would have had to settle there to learn and pass on to his descendants the secrets of the complex canals, the treacherous sandbanks that lay just beneath the high tides and the locations of those deep pools that attracted the bigger fish. No one can date the arrival of the earliest settlers. They left none of the traces of a culture or organized way of life as did the Euganian and Veneti tribes of the prehistoric settlements on the mainland but, just as they passed on the secrets of their livelihood to their descendants, they have bequeathed to today's inhabitants of these same islands traditions that have not died out. They probably built shelter for themselves and their boats in much the same way as did the fishermen described by Cassiodorius in the sixth century. Larchwood poles cut from the Lido forests, sharpened and sunk in the mud, half in water and half on the land, provided walls between which the boat could be beached and above which a platform covered by a pitched roof of wattle and reed housed the fisherman and his family. The fishermen of the lagoon still build these shelters for their boats and nets; they are called *cavane* in the local dialect.

Some time after the isolated fisherman settled to make his living from the brackish waters of the lagoon must have come the few men who realized that, by damming and controlling the flow of those same waters over the shoals, salt could be removed from the lagoon, and also that the clay substance of the more solid islands could be fired to make good bricks. These two products of a primitive industry could be loaded on rafts made from the trees of the littoral and floated up the rivers that flowed into the lagoon to the more urbanized settlements of the mainland. The rafts themselves were then broken up and sold for building material, so that even the means of transport provided a profit. The legacy of these early lagoon dwellers was immense. The thousands of buildings later to rise on those hundred-odd islands rested on those same pointed larchwood pilings, their walls were brick made from local clay, and the wealth that created this extraordinary and unique civilization – at times held to be the richest in the world – was based on maritime commerce and the ability to turn a profit with transport and local industry. During the golden age of this metropolitan culture, the finest artists of the day were commissioned by the government to paint the pageant of their city's rise from lagoon settlements to a great imperial power; and these same artists were paid their handsome fees by magistrates who controlled the vast resources, almost one thousand years after the founding of their city, of the state monopoly of salt.

But we are getting ahead of our story. The salt that was mined and the clay that was transported by river were sent to Roman settlements. In their beginnings they were military outposts of the legionaries, built not necessarily on the rivers which flowed down to the virtually empty lagoon, or to the hostile Adriatic sea, but built on the straight stone roads that followed the military advance to extend the sway of the great urban civilization and imperial power that was ancient Rome. These roads by-passed the fishermen of the lagoon and only in a few cases did the conquerors settle where ancient tribes had gathered together. It is not difficult to establish that trade with the scattered fishermen of the lagoon existed in Roman times. Not only would the Roman use their clay for his bricks, their timber for the beams of his houses and temples and their salt for his table, but after several generations of descendants of the legionaries had established themselves as the new people of the Venetia-Histria district, their craftsmen would seek the fine sand of the Adriatic shore with

which to make the ornaments and vessels of glass which represented a refinement from the capital that eventually reached and was produced in the
provinces.

Though it is virtually impossible to date and document these exchanges, we
are well into the realm of recorded history. The Via Annia, which stretched
to the north and brought corn from Roman Pannonia to the capital, was built
in 131 BC. Settlements developed only much later, but by the first century before
the birth of Christ temples to the Roman gods were built in towns like Atestum
(Este), Patavium (Padua) and Aquileia, the provincial capital. Not much of
these buildings survives *in situ*, but the ruins that do remain, scattered
triumphal arches or gates, suggest a high degree of artistic accomplishment
and a sophisticated provincial culture. The scale of a survival like the arena
of Verona illustrates the prosperity and size of cities that had developed in a
short space of time from military outposts to commercial entrepôts of primary
importance.

The legacy of imperial Rome to the various city cultures of medieval and
Renaissance Italy is well known: the plan and elevation of the basilica was taken
from Roman buildings as the model for most early Christian churches; later
the widespread use of the dome and the arch can be traced to Roman building
practice; the medieval cloister and the arcaded courtyard of the Renaissance
palace derive from the early Benedictine penchant for reconsecrating pagan
places of worship by settling their communities in the peristyled precincts of
Roman villas and temples. The influence of the Roman triumphal arch or the
bays of the Colosseum on High Renaissance architecture is a commonplace
of architectural history. Bits and pieces of Roman buildings and forums were
used and re-used in churches and palaces throughout Italy, and the statues
of tutelary deities and cult images as well as mere decorative sculpture found
their way into the private collections of princes, popes and connoisseurs of the
beautiful and rare in antiquity.

In the Veneto this legacy took a slightly different form. After the edict of
Constantine in AD 314 declaring Christianity the official religion of the entire
Roman empire, important buildings were erected everywhere to house the new
cult. In Aquileia, not far from the lagoon, the local bishop was further dignified
by the oriental title of patriarch. Ranking high above other bishops of the state
Church, and owning and administering vast territories that stretched north to
the lands of the empire's barbarian allies, the Patriarch of Aquileia owed both
temporal and spiritual allegiance to the emperor who had moved the capital
and thus the entire imperial administration to the Greek town of Byzantium
on the Bosphorus. Although his dignity and authority emanated from Constantinople, as the new capital had been christened, the Patriarch of Aquileia
adopted western and more specifically Roman buildings to suit his needs. He
built a great cathedral on the lines of a basilica: a tall central nave separated
from two lower side aisles by an arcade of columns. The whole ended in an

apse behind the altar where the patriarch and the serried ranks of his clergy sat enthroned. But the most Roman aspect of the cathedral church of Aquileia is the great floor mosaic in *opus tesselatum*. Hundreds of compartments framed in geometrical mosaic motifs contain animals, birds, full-length figures, heads and, appropriate to a setting so near the sea, hundreds and hundreds of fish. One section depicts lively fishing scenes; the boats are manned by what seem to be pagan cupids or *amorini* until one realizes that these are Christian angels, saints and disciples fishing, according to Christ's instruction, for men. When the fishermen and merchants of the lagoon islands wished a rich decoration for the floor of their patron's chapel, what could have been more natural for them to adopt than this legacy of Rome that had been preserved and elaborated by the patriarch who governed the church of their mainland?

But long before such a church was built on the lagoon islands, the Bishop of Aquileia was forced to flee his city. More than once Aquileia was deserted by its inhabitants as hordes of barbarians poured over the northern borders of the empire. By the time the Visigoths arrived early in the fifth century the Romans of the mainland towns from Aquileia to Padua must have wondered if the old imperial order would ever return, if a stable peace and prosperity could survive the passage of tribes living off the land, consuming the crops and making exorbitant demands on the urban populations. Initially the barbarians did not set out to destroy the towns and country they passed through and the local inhabitants probably did not have to flee. It was simply more comfortable to move out of the way, to move off the roads that all led to Rome. So they moved towards the lesser evil: the inhospitable but safe lands that bordered the lagoon. In the seventy-five years from the early Gothic invasions to the fall and systematic looting of the capital at the hands of the Vandals they had time to take what they needed with them. In the twenty years after the arrival of Alaric many of the mainland dwellers must have made a firm choice in favour of peace and safety nearer the lagoon. Some sought shelter among the fishermen who inhabited the one hundred-odd islands in the centre. And, since they would be settling on mud-flats with little save the local building materials, they first returned to their native cities to dismantle their public buildings, what remained of their pagan temples and forums, and to bring them to the islands where these relics of their ancient and civilized past would distinguish them and their descendants from the rude folk among whom they had chosen to live.

By AD 416 a church dedicated to the archangel Raphael was built on one of the westernmost of the cluster of islands where refugees from Padua had settled. Five years later a church dedicated to James the Apostle was consecrated in the very heart of the island group. A site was chosen not far from the high banks of the broad canal that described an S curve through the centre of the mud-flats and which gave its name to the settlement that grew up around the church of San Giacomo: the Rialto or *rivo alto*, the high bank. According to later chronicles and collections of legend the *Città di Rivo Alto*, as Venice was first known, was founded on the Feast of the Annunciation, 25 March AD 421, at noon. For centuries this feast marked the first day of the Venetian calendar year. But another two hundred and seventy-five years were to pass before the first doge in a thousand years of Venetian history was elected, and not until the beginning of the ninth century could the islands in the centre of the Venetian lagoon be regarded as a seat of government and commerce; nor was it until that time, four hundred years after the legendary founding of Venice, that the citizens of the primitive Venetian confederation were to be forced to seek safety from their enemies by fleeing *en masse* to the rialtine islands.

The history of the intervening period, that is to say from the legendary founding of Venice in AD 421 down to the transfer of the ducal capital to the rialtine islands in about 810, is confused and ill-documented as far as the lagoon settlements are concerned. The history of this period belongs still, both culturally and politically, to the mainland. In AD 452 the Huns of Attila swept into northern Italy, and the town of Aquileia fell to them. The patriarch and his clergy fled the city once again; they settled in the town of Grado which had been founded as the sea port of the patriarchal capital. With the arrival of Attila's hordes there was an ever greater influx of refugees to the lagoon settlements further south and in AD 466 maritime tribunes were elected in Grado to govern, in the name of the Roman emperor at Constantinople, the twelve communities that had established themselves in the Adriatic lagoons. Later Grado was the permanent seat of the patriarch who governed the Venetian church while the ancient cathedral of Aquileia was presided over by a puppet bishop of the Arian Longobards. As the constant controversy between Aquileia and Grado over their respective investiture and jurisdictions intensified, their importance as cities began to dwindle.

It was clear by the end of the fifth century that Ravenna would supplant them both in the politics and culture of northern Italy. Since the three-year siege of the capital city and the murder of Odovacer, Ravenna had been the capital of the Ostrogothic kingdom of Italy under the great Theodoric. He hoped to stabilize the confused mixture of peoples and traditions that existed in his kingdom and make of it an independent state that could withstand the attempts of the Byzantines to bring Ravenna, and with it Italy, again under the suzerainty of the Roman emperor at Constantinople. Theodoric's concern for the disparate customs of his subjects, the Roman population and his own West Goth tribesmen, was responsible for one of the greatest artistic legacies to western culture. Churches and baptistries were built where the Arian rite was celebrated for the Visigoths, while separate buildings were used by the orthodox clergy. Both sets of churches were built on the basilican plan, like those of paleo-Christian Rome and Aquileia, but details began to emerge that signalled the growth of a local school of architects, builders and stonecutters.

On the exterior of the brick walls a frieze of small blind arches broke up the flat surfaces near the roof line; the outer wall of the apse was often polygonal rather than round; the baptistries were octagonal with squinches making the transition to a domed roofing. The decoration of these buildings led to details that were even more distinctively Ravennate. The capitals of columns were carved with trellis or basketwork patterns; at Ravenna these capitals did not directly support the spring of the arch: an impost block carved with geometrical patterns or religious symbols was placed between the capital and the masonry work of the arch. *Transennae* or pierced carved slabs of marble used as screens in window openings were also typical, and provided patterns for stone carving in Venice for hundreds of years. Besides fostering a local school of architects and stonecutters, Theodoric encouraged a revival of the mosaic work that had been done in the time of Galla Placidia, wife of the Emperor Theodosius II and sister of the emperor who had earlier moved the western capital of the empire from Milan to Ravenna. Theodoric's mosaics were on a vast and ambitious scale. Immense figures of the saints on a golden ground lined the length of the basilican naves. These were stiff, hieratic figures draped with heavily outlined folds of cloth. The mere scale of these compositions is entirely different from the scenes, animals and small figures of the floor mosaics at Aquileia or the Hellenistic mosaic lunette of the Good Shepherd in the so-called Mausoleum of Galla Placidia.

Despite Theodoric's determination to maintain the independence of his western realms against the claims of the eastern emperor, the predominant influence in the mosaics of Ravenna is Byzantine. The artistic riches of Theodoric's Ravenna did not reach Venice in any significant sense until further historical developments acted as a catalyst to the emergence of the Venetian settlements as an autonomous culture. In the meantime we are given a picture of the primitive lagoon settlers by Theodoric's secretary, Cassiodorus, who wrote to the military tribunes governing the island settlements:

There lie your houses built like sea-birds' nests, half on sea and half on land ... For the solidity of the earth is secured only by wattle-work; and yet you fear not to place so frail a barrier between yourselves and the sea. Your inhabitants have fish in abundance. There is no distinction between rich and poor; the same food for all; the houses all alike ... All your activity is devoted to the salt-works, whence comes your wealth ... From your gains you repair your boats which, like horses, you keep tied up at your house doors.

This remarkable description makes it clear that the lagoon dwellers were not yet prosperous or sophisticated enough to appreciate the refinements of Theodoric's capital.

In the middle of the sixth century the great Byzantine general, Narses, came to reconquer Italy for the Roman empire and for his emperor, Justinian. Legend has it that two years before he defeated the Goths and established the Exarchate of the Eastern Emperor at Ravenna, Narses had vowed to build two churches in the islands of the lagoon. Both were built, not up the Grand Canal in the heart of the city like San Giacomo di Rialto, but near the basin of deep water where a large battle fleet could anchor. Both these churches have disappeared, but their names remain, redolent of the long period of Veneto-Byzantine culture: one was dedicated to San Geminiano and was built facing the other, dedicated to the Byzantine patron of Venice, Saint Theodore.

The political link that Theodoric forged between Ravenna and the Venetian lagoon was reinforced by Narses and successive exarchs who governed on behalf of the emperor. The emperor's presence in Ravenna was symbolized by the mosaic portraits of Justinian, Theodora, their courts and clergy in the sanctuary of the great octagonal church dedicated to San Vitale. If the exarchate's control over a crescent of territory around the head of the Adriatic to Istria was one catalyst in the emergence of Venetian culture, the second was a negative, if not destructive, agent.

In AD 568 the Longobards swept down on Italy from Pannonia, the land that had supplied Rome with grain and where Attila's hordes had grazed their horses. The Longobards did not come to seek confederation with the mixed peoples of northern Italy. They came to conquer: to sack and loot and destroy. The patriarch fled again from Aquileia to Grado; the Bishop of Padua sought sanctuary with his flock at the Lido settlement of Malamocco; the Bishop of Latin Concordia fled to the sea at Caorle and the Bishop of Oderzo established his seat on the Lido at Eraclea. All these heirs of rich benefices took their treasures with them just as their people transported whatever they could of their belongings and even their buildings. The scattered sanctuaries from the Longobard onslaught would be their new homes; permanent buildings were soon begun with the grandest projects undertaken by the Church. The Patriarch of Aquileia built a cathedral and an octagonal baptistry on Ravennate lines at Grado, while the floor paving was in a mosaic reminiscent of his more ancient seat. The Byzantine emperor Heraclius immediately recognized the spiritual and political primacy of the See of Grado by sending the throne chair of Saint Mark to Primigenio. The gift was not only a token of imperial recognition and protection, it was to inspire far greater consequences by sanctioning the legend that the evangelist had indeed visited the lagoon and had seen there a heavenly vision in which it was foretold that he would find rest in this very part of the world.

In the same year that the Longobard Rothari captured Oderzo, a cathedral church was consecrated on the island of Torcello where refugees from Altinium had settled. The original church has been enlarged and built over in later centuries, but there is little doubt that, in its earliest form, it was of Ravennate basilican form. The ancient Roman columns and corinthian capitals, as well as the fact that duplicates were later carved of these capitals, suggest the importance of stone salvaged from the Longobard invasions. In front of the present cathedral are the remains of the original seventh-century round baptistry, and

set in a wall of the church is a stone tablet that recalls the dedication and con-
secration of the church in the year AD 639; the names of the bishop and the
exarch are included in the inscription which is the oldest authentic document
of Venetian history. Further towards the centre of the lagoon, on an island
where the inhabitants had planted an olive grove, a church was built and dedicated to the eastern saints, Sergius and Bacchus.

By the end of the seventh century a certain coherence in the scattered settlements begins to emerge; the rich from many mainland cities pooled their prosperity and their responsibilities in order to organize a profitable means of survival, and in AD 697 they elected a single leader, a duke later to be known as
the doge. Their political allegiance was to the exarch, whose capital at Ravenna
was on the same sea coast to the south and whose jurisdiction in Italy was almost
entirely coastal. Beyond the sea touching the coastal lands of the exarch lay
the vast domains of Byzantium. However the first threats of Islam engaged
the emperor in the hinterland of his empire: the sea to the west as far as Venice
was free for the uninhibited development of trade and commerce.

The early struggle of the empire against Islam produced a curious paradox
in Byzantine policies when in AD 727 the Emperor Leo III proclaimed icono-
clasm as an official programme of the state religion. The Old Testament pro-
hibition of graven images was revived to counteract the extremely persuasive
Muslim arguments against religious images. The whole question of the divine
presence in images or icons and pedantic arguments over differing degrees of
worship which so characterized much of Constantinopolitan theology were
quite foreign to the western Church. The Bishop of Rome and the Longobard
king of Italy, Liutprand, opposed the eastern emperor's policies – the one on
theological grounds, the other for political reasons. Typically the second doge
of the Venetians temporized and succeeded in making trade agreements with
the Longobard kingdom of the mainland, while professing loyalty to the Exarch
of Ravenna. The exarch rewarded Venice with the trading privileges which
became the object of almost all her future policies and negotiations. But in
AD 751 the exarchate collapsed under the siege of Ravenna by the Longobards.
This meant the virtual closure of all the workshops in Ravenna and in all prob-
ability some of the stonecutters, mosaicists and architects, as well as refugee
artists from the iconoclast controversy, found their way to the traditional sanctuary of the lagoon islands. Certainly at Torcello the vault mosaic in the dia-
konion (one of the two subsidiary apse chapels characteristic of churches of
the oriental rite) depicting the *Agnus Dei* is a copy of mosaic in San Vitale,
even if it was not actually executed by Ravennate workmen.

From the fall of Ravenna onwards Venice remained the principal outpost
of the eastern empire in northern Italy, although the hostility of the Longobards
to Byzantine Venice made only the central islands of the lagoon seem a sufficiently secure haven. At the end of the eighth century the king of the Franks
came down on Italy from the north to conquer and incorporate the Longobard

The presence of the Byzantine emperor in Italy is represented in this sixth-century mosaic in San Vitale in Ravenna showing Justinian (527–565) and his retinue.

The eleventh-century cathedral of Torcello stands on the site of a church consecrated in 639. The mosaics show characteristics of the Ravenna workshops while the liturgical screen is made of beautifully carved marble slabs or *transennae* presumably made in Constantinople.

territories. With the benediction of the Bishop of Rome, Charlemagne was recognized throughout northern Italy as emperor of a resuscitated western empire based on Rome. Obeisance and its concomitant, tribute, were offered on every side save from Venice which remained staunchly legitimist in her allegiance to the emperor at Constantinople. Twice in the first decade after his coronation in Rome, Charlemagne's armies attempted to conquer the Byzantine outpost of Venice. His attacks on the Lido settlements very nearly succeeded in their purpose, but the principal families of the confederated communities and their duke managed to lead the population to the central islands for safety. The shoals and shifting channels of the lagoon provided an impregnable defence against invasion. When in AD 814 a treaty of mutual recognition was signed between the emperors of the East and West, Venetian representatives were included in the negotiations and in the end the treaty of Ratisbon represented a tacit recognition of Venice's political existence.

There is no doubt that the emperors themselves appreciated the commercial role Venice might play in both their empires. Charlemagne is supposed to have always worn a Venetian tunic, and his courtiers found the only robes worthy of their dignity were those brought to the market fairs at Pavia by Venetian merchants. In the second decade of the ninth century the Byzantine emperor, Leo v, sent the Doge Giustiniano Partecipazio the relics of the father of John the Baptist for the foundation of the church of San Zaccaria. This ancient church, one of the first Benedictine communities in Venetian territory, and thus a seat of western monasticism, was well endowed with lands in the islands including an orchard that would one day become the Piazza San Marco.

Down to the year AD 820 the communities in the Venetian lagoon had elected ten of their number to be doge for life. The first doge, Paoluccio Anafesto, was elected, according to the virtually sacrosanct traditions of Venetian historiography, in AD 697. The Republic which the doges governed came to an end exactly one thousand one hundred years later with the abdication of the one hundred and twentieth doge, Lodovico Manin, in 1797. In this millennial period, longer than the historical life of either the eastern Byzantine empire or the western Holy Roman empire, Venice produced one of the greatest civilizations and cultures in the world and contributed some of the masterpieces of western art to the long history of Christian Europe. By the beginning of the ninth century the stage was set for the emergence of Venice on the European scene. The cultural legacies of imperial and paleo-Christian Rome as well as the civilization and arts of Byzantium and the exarchate were combined in the next centuries with Venetian skill in commerce and navigation to make the contributions of her unique culture felt throughout the known world, from the Viking north to the court of the Great Khan.

2

The Arrival
of Saint Mark
815-1097

The events of the ninth, tenth and eleventh centuries of Venetian history are better documented than the earlier period and represent centuries of consolidation for the Venetian republic. Much was done for the arts in this period and many buildings were constructed, but unfortunately evidence of the latter is to be found only in scattered references. Little building survives from before the middle of the eleventh century and that little was so often overbuilt, enlarged and elaborated that it takes a considerable effort of imagination to see what it must have looked like to contemporary Venetians. Still, the evidence of these three centuries is crucial to any consideration of Venetian culture and civilization because it was in this period that Venice began to establish her sphere of influence beyond the limited boundaries of her tiny cluster of islands and her only marginally larger lagoon.

These few islands in the lagoon and the approaches to them were the strength of the young city state. There was no need for the Venetians to be on the defensive. The treaty of Ratisbon and the failure of Pepin's armies to take Venice for his father's empire virtually guaranteed her independent status in the West. Venice was, of course, technically the vassal of the Byzantine emperor, but with the disappearance of the exarch, the emperor's control over her was as remote as Constantinople was distant. The doges who ruled Venice after the fall of Ravenna and who gathered the scattered peoples of the lagoon together to bring them to the safety of the innermost islands began to rule like independent sovereigns with the help of procurators or ducal assistants. It was Angelo Partecipazio, elected in AD 811, who brought about the amalgamation of the lagoon peoples. His family and two others supplied Venice with the next seventeen doges who ruled over the state for two hundred years. Three times in the Partecipazio family alone a son succeeded his father as doge, while the succession from father to son in the Candiano family lasted for four generations. As much as these leaders did to assure the internal stability of the community which elected them, they also presided over the commercial expansion of Venice beyond the lagoon. In the early ninth century Venice had taken her trade in local timber as far as the coast of north Africa and in AD 822 laws were enacted to regulate this commerce. Mention has already been made of the role of Venetian merchants as the distributors of rare materials deemed fit for the western emperor and his courtiers. The earliest coasting galleys, probably a legacy of Roman shipbuilding, had already established reciprocal trade with the Levant.

There is an apposite symbolism in the story of the arrival of Saint Mark's relics in Venice. The legend of Saint Mark's visit to the lagoon (his resting place is said to have been near the present church of San Francesco della Vigna) is the only link between that part of the world and the apostolic age of Christianity. The political and spiritual primacy of the patriarchate of Grado had been emphasized by the gift from the Roman emperor of Saint Mark's throne. Now, thanks to her expanding commercial contacts in north Africa and the Levant, especially Alexandria in Egypt, Venice was to assert her political and even her spiritual primacy in Venetia-Histria by stealing the relics of the evangelist and bringing them home. The words of Saint Mark's vision, in a sense justifying the theft, would be carved on every representation of the Marcian lion: *Pax Tibi Marce Evangelista Meus*. But so that the theft did not seem to have been a policy of the government, it was said that the crime was carried out on the pious initiative of two of the lagoon's many fishermen – not merchants, but fishermen representing Venice's aboriginal inhabitants. And symbolically too, one was said to have come from Torcello, one of the first settlements in the centre of the lagoon, and the other was said to have come from Malamocco, the Lido settlement which, as the seat of the dominant Partecipazio family, finally triumphed over the others. In any case, Saint Mark's body was not brought to either of the two fishermen's homes, but directly to the place where the Partecipazio decided to establish the ducal government, and the third of the family to reign as doge built a chapel to house the precious relics. Archeological research has established that this first chapel of San Marco was probably a small cruciform building with a cupola, built on the lines of the churches of Contantinople that were set aside to house the bodies of martyrs. The church stood next to the chapel the Byzantine general, Narses, had dedicated to Saint Theodore.

There are in the present basilica of San Marco a number of carved capitals and also some extremely handsome *plutei* (the bas-relief carved marble slabs that stood between columns to make a railing or the screen of an iconostasis) that were undoubtedly carved by Ravennate sculptors some time after the fall of the exarchate in the late eighth century. There is also in the cathedral treasury a copy of the Gospels with an encrusted and enamelled binding probably made in Constantinople at the time the evangelist's relics were brought to Venice. But it is impossible to know for certain when these two examples of eighth- and ninth-century craftsmanship reached Venice. Venice was beginning to be rich enough to have commissioned either or both, but since in later centuries the Venetians collected so many treasures of the earliest periods to enrich the shrine of their patron, it is virtually impossible to know the precise provenance of any single item.

From about AD 830 to 870 the small Venetian trading fleet encountered two enemies that were to be factors in Venetian maritime history for the next eight hundred years. Pirates in the upper Adriatic sailing out of bases in Istria, Croatia and especially on the Narenta river in Herzegovina forced the Venetians to establish defensive bases on the shores opposite them. In more or less the same period the Byzantines called on the Venetian navy to sail as their ally against the Saracens who threatened their colonies in Sicily and in ancient Magna Grecia. The Venetians emerged from these engagements more confident of their role in the Mediterranean, first as an expanding commercial power which could guarantee the safe transport of goods and secondly as the defensive arm of the greatest empire in the known world. With every victory on behalf of the Byzantines the Venetians were rewarded in the only coin that had any enduring value for them: trading concessions and privileges.

Venetian expansion was not restricted to the activities of her fleet alone. Commercial treaties were made with Lothar I in AD 840 which guaranteed Venice a role in the markets, fairs and river commerce of the mainland. Venice's cultural contacts with the mainland were represented by the number of Benedictine monastic foundations established in the lagoon and its immediate territories. These communities were virtually autonomous and self-sufficient and in Venice they owned orchards, salt-pans and their own water supply. A well-head carved in the ninth century still survives in Venice; its decoration with paleo-Christian motifs and interlacing patterns is typical of the European Carolingian style that could be found anywhere from the south of France to Dalmatia. These monasteries not only housed skilled craftsmen, relics and treasures, they also extended the traditional sanctuary of the lagoon to those fleeing the enemies of religious orthodoxy. In AD 855 Pope Benedict III sought refuge at San Zaccaria from the forces of the current anti-pope. On 13 September the doge of the day came in state to welcome the eminent refugee and thus inaugurated the series of annual ducal visitations peculiar to the Venetian calendar of festivities. While offering comfortable and presumably even splendid sanctuary to a reigning

pontiff, the Venetians were capable of producing gifts worthy of the most sophisticated sovereign. In AD 886 the Doge Orso Partecipazio sent the Emperor of
Byzantium twelve bells which created a sensation in Constantinople. Only
shortly after this highly novel and successful gift was made, the Venetians began
to build their own great bell tower which was probably completed early in
the following century and which stood for a thousand years. The Campanile was not then or even later a part of the ducal chapel. Its bells tolled
the working hours of the day in terms of the breviary offices – matins, nones,
compline, vespers – but different sized bells were rung at different times to
call the people together to vote by acclamation, to arm in time of danger or
simply to begin their working day. And when completed the bell tower served
as a beacon to ships at sea and as a watch-tower for the guardians of the Republic's safety. The bell tower was then as much connected with commerce
and local industry as it was with the Church.

The solidity of Venice's commercial expansion was reflected in the wide acceptance of her coinage in the second half of the ninth century, although, at
the same time, Venetian territorial ambitions did not go unchallenged. Towards
the end of the ninth century the Hungarians became hostile to Venetian
attempts to establish bases in Dalmatia in order to rid herself of the pirate threat
in the upper Adriatic. This link between the Hungarians and the peoples of
Istria and Dalmatia, first encountered in the earliest years of Venetian expansion, was to remain a source of irritation and actual menace for many centuries
to come. The Venetians felt threatened enough for their Doge Pietro Tribuno
to build Venice's only defensive walls in 906. These pirates found their way
into Venetian legend and were enshrined in the calendar of ducal ceremonies.
In the winter of AD 944 a group of young Venetian maidens, gathered for a
betrothal ceremony, were kidnapped *en masse* by a party of Narentine
marauders who succeeded in penetrating the lagoon's defences. Their infuri-
ated young men immediately set off in pursuit and succeeded in overtaking
and defeating the pirates at Caorle where the maidens were freed. February 2
became a festal date in the ducal ceremonies when the doge and his suite visited
the church of Santa Maria Formosa in state to commemorate the defeat of the
raiders.

From the middle of the tenth century trading privileges on the mainland
were confined or renewed in the Venetian favour by Berengar II, King of Italy,
and by the Emperor Otto I. Liutprand, Bishop of Cremona, makes mention
of the silk brought by Venetians from Constantinople for the Emperor of the
West in AD 968. Venice's role as bridge between the East and the West was
already widely recognized and Liutprand's reference establishes an early date
for Venetian trade in oriental silk. Although her political, cultural and even
spiritual allegiance was to Byzantium, Venice's early maritime trade was not
exclusively with territory allied to Constantinople. As early as AD 971 the imperial court on the Bosphorus registered an objection to the Venetian trade

in her local wood along with iron and arms (swords and cross bows) from middle Europe with the infidel Saracen enemy. A certain arrogant independence seemed to be the spirit of Venice at about this time, a spirit that was personified by the Doge Pietro of the fourth generations of Candiano doges. Pietro put aside his first wife in order to marry the sister of the Marquis of Tuscany, Hwalderada, who brought with her a large dowry of lands in the Friuli, the Trevisan marches and the Ferrarese. With this personal wealth to back him, and foreign guards to protect him, Doge Pietro seemed bent on making the ducal office the hereditary prerogative of the princely Candiano family. The Venetians rose against him, set fire to his palace and murdered the doge himself.

Pietro Candiano's successor was elected by the ancient practice of popular assembly. It was this doge, the first of the Orseolo dynasty, who undertook the rebuilding of the ducal palace and started work on the reconstruction of the fire-damaged palatine chapel. Neither of these two important building projects survives, but the hostel or hospital which he began and which bore the name of the Orseolo stood in the Piazza until the sixteenth century. The façade of the Orseolo hospital was flush with the bell tower, and its arcades marked the southern boundary of the small cleared area in front of the palatine chapel that was then known as the Piazza San Marco. The western border of the Piazza was the rio Baratari, with Narses's chapel dedicated to San Geminiano built on the opposite shore facing the adjacent chapels of San Marco and San Teodoro across the Piazza. The ground floor arcades of the Orseolo hospice lined one side of the Piazza from the bell tower to the rio. This made of the Piazza in part a colonnaded atrium to the ducal chapel, an intention that never disappeared from either the plan or the function of the Piazza through the many centuries of its enlargement or remodelling. Like so many doges after him, Pietro Orseolo is remembered for his embellishment of the shrine to the evangelist. Precious *cloisonné* enamelled plaques were ordered from Constantinople to decorate the altar of Saint Mark. At least fifty-six of the many plaques of the present *Pala d'Oro*, or golden pallium, can be dated to the late tenth century and may therefore be part of his original contribution to the shrine. In whatever way and at whatever particular time they reached Venice, these plaques represent a contact between Venice and one of the richest periods of Byzantine cultural history.

The end of the tenth century was reached with the reign of Pietro's son. The western emperor, Otto II, was forced to sign a treaty recognizing Venetian autonomy and the eastern emperor published the first of many imperial Chrysobulls granting privileges to the Venetian fleet and to the Venetian merchants trading in the capital and throughout the empire. These various acts of public recognition by the imperial powers were mere preludes to acknowledgement of Venice's virtual sovereign independence. On the eve of the millennium the doge and a formidable fleet set sail to protect their client lands in Dalmatia from yet more harassment by Croatian and Narentine pirates. The day of their weighing anchor was the Feast of the Ascension, ever after a particularly sacred day in the Venetian calendar; and on their triumphant return the doge's adoption of the style *Dux Dalmatiae et Chroatiae* represented a political reality. The ancient Adriatic sea was effectively the Gulf of Venice. The dukedom of Dalmatia was technically a Byzantine investiture as Dalmatia was part of the empire. Venice was acting in her capacity as defender of Byzantium in freeing Dalmatia of the Narentine menace, but she was also obtaining secure ports of call for her coastal trade with the Levant. The merchant convoys of the eleventh and later centuries were composed of oared galleys that sailed only by daylight in calm weather near the coasts; safe ports of call were essential to any such fleet hoping to establish its hegemony over maritime commerce and transport. The Dalmatian ports also represented opportunities to trade and barter as well as loading points for any raw materials a lagoon-locked city-state might require. Otherwise Dalmatia was a primitive outpost of distant Constantinople and such remnants of civilization as existed were either imported from the capital or were the remains of Roman settlement. Of the latter, it has often been thought that Venetian familiarity with the great seaward portico of Diocletian's villa at Spalato (Split) had a considerable influence on some of the distinctive features of the so-called Veneto-Byzantine palaces of the twelfth and thirteenth centuries.

In the first year of the new century, Venice presented to the Emperor Otto III a trophy of the conquest of Istria and Dalmatia: the ivory throne of Bishop Maximian of Ravenna, one of the outstanding masterpieces of Byzantine art. The throne chair was taken by the Venetians from the church of Santa Maria di Pola in Istria which had been founded by the missionary bishop from Ravenna five hundred years earlier. The Venetians recognized the exceptional artistic value of Maximian's throne even though their own craftsmen did not practise the bas-relief carving of ivory plaques that had been a Byzantine tradition since the period of the so-called consular diptychs. The presentation of the throne not only symbolized Venice's intermediary role between the empires of the east and west, but the throne itself illustrated cross currents of artistic influence to which the Venetians were exposed through their contacts with Byzantium. The hands of four master sculptors have been recognized in the sixth-century carving: one familiar with the conventions of Asiatic and Anatolian sculpture; one whose Hellenistic echoes suggest the Alexandrian school; the third who seems to have been Egyptian; and the fourth whose work is identified by the borders and decoration of vine-leaf motifs, perhaps derived from Syrian carving. At different times individual pieces of carving from each of these traditions were brought to Venice, so that by the time a distinctively Venetian style in the arts begins to appear, echoes of a Levantine background may often be discerned.

The early years of the eleventh century saw the continuing self-confident expansion of the young state. The Venetian fleet gained a signal victory over the Saracen enemy of Byzantium at Bari in 1003. By this time, too, the Venetian fleet was trafficking in grain, wine and oil from the southern province of Puglia. From her local salt-pans the Republic had established a virtual monopoly of the manufacture and sale of salt. A monopoly of this sort, where the Venetians owned the means of both production and distribution combined with their role as sole shipper to and from ports on either shore of the Adriatic, led to the gradual establishment of staple rights over the northern end of the Adriatic. According to these rights shipments between Dalmatia and Puglia, for example, would be permitted only in Venetian ships. Staple rights became the subject of later Venetian legislation and enforcement, but the ground was laid for such a development already.

Between the year of the millennium and the first years of the twelfth century over fifty churches were built or enlarged in the lagoon islands. The most important survival of this period is the cathedral church of Torcello. Its famous bell tower was built along Ravennate lines: that is to say the walls of the square shaft are divided into low relief vertical zones by pilasters that are linked at the top by brick blind arches. These elegant slim arches of a stilted Byzantine type are repeated in the four light-openings of the bell chamber above. The façade of the enlarged cathedral is also decorated with a Ravennate motif of brick pilasters and blind arches. The widening of its nave, the laying of a wonderful *opus tesselatum* floor of multi-coloured patterns in tiny marble cubes, the re-use of capitals and columns from the seventh-century building: all these elements go beyond the traditions of the Exarchate of Ravenna to the earlier paleo-Christian churches of Aquileia. The raised chancel, the apse and throne, on the other hand, may well be a result of the recent Venetian dominion over Istria, since the Eufrasian basilica of Parenzo could easily have been the prototype for these particular details. The ambo and the iconostasis are certainly made up of imported pieces of carved marble, while the plutei of the screen separating the nave and the sanctuary are carved with Byzantine motifs of a quality that suggests the workshops of Constantinople herself. It has often been thought that the four alabaster columns now supporting the ciborium or canopy over Saint Mark's tomb might have arrived in Venice during this period when individual pieces of fine carving and examples of primitive Christian iconography, such as in the throne of Maximian, were highly prized. Obviously in such an early period as this, matters of taste in collecting are as difficult to document as are actual commissions.

By the middle of the century the prestige of Venice's many churches was well established in western Christendom and in 1054 Pope Leo IX made a special pilgrimage to Venice to visit the shrine of Saint Mark. That same year, Michael Cerularius, the powerful anti-Latin Patriarch of Constantinople, provoked a formal break with Rome, thus ensuring the autonomy of the eastern Church and his own office's absolute supremacy within it. It is interesting in the light of the Great Schism that the final rebuilding and enlargement of the church of San Marco should have followed eastern rather than western lines. The earlier church of the Orseolo was not a western basilica but rather an eastern martyrion, a centrally planned church of a type developed at Constantinople to house the relics of martyrs. In enlarging San Marco, Doge Contarini used the sixth-century Constantinopolitan church of the Holy Apostles as his model for several reasons. It obviously suggested itself as it was the shrine built for Saint Mark's fellow evangelist, Luke, as well as housing relics of the disciples Timothy and Andrew. The Aposteleion was also where the emperors lay in state and where several of them were buried; its function was similar to San Marco which, in addition to being the city's principal shrine and the church of the state, was also the private chapel and burial place of a number of her doges. The plan of the Aposteleion also made it suitable for the enlargement of the centrally planned Orseolo chapel; domes were added over the crossing and over each of the four arms of the Greek cross. The foot of the cross was enclosed in an exo-narthex, traditional in the ancient church for the catechizing of the unbaptized but used in Venice for ceremonial processions. In extending the arms of the transepts, part of the ancient chapel of San Teodoro was incorporated in the new walls. As at Torcello, individual elements of the decoration that can be dated to this period often reveal the very mixed sources of artistic inspiration the Venetians were willing to use in their major buildings. The small windows lighting the crypt beneath the raised chancel suggest that stonecutters trained in the northern Romanesque traditions were not unknown in Venice. The shell-crowned niches over the central door to the church from the narthex go back to Byzantine ivory plaques or even to paleo-Christian sarcophagi; the *transennae* across the niches containing the earliest ducal tombs, also in the narthex, are purely Ravennate, as are many of the columns with basket capitals and carved impost blocks. Just as the cathedral at Torcello housed a valuable collection of columns salvaged from Roman temples on the mainland, the state church displayed precious marble shafts brought to Venice from every part of her growing world of commercial influence. So many were there that some of the oldest merely stand as trophies supporting nothing save richly carved capitals that betray diverse origins and dates. In 1071 the walls of the third and final building of San Marco were complete.

The Doge Domenico Selvo, who had married the niece of the emperor of Byzantium, commissioned the decoration of the great church. At first this meant sheathing the brick walls of the interior with slabs of precious veined marbles; then a few small mosaics were laid in the most important positions. Those still surviving from the late eleventh century include the Madonna and saints over the central inner door of the church. San Marco was then and would remain for the next two hundred years a much more Byzantine building than the eclectic basilica we admire now. The vast mosaic decoration was begun only a hundred years later and the original programme took over two hundred years to complete. The façade of the ducal chapel consisted of five broad and deep archways each framing an entrance doorway into the narthex. On the level above were five smaller arches with the low profile of the brick cupolas rising behind. The principal façade was of brick, although marble slabs and some coloured marble columns may have already been placed as a lower order between and within the large receding entrance arches. In the upper order the smaller arches were either brick filled or pierced by small stone window frames and intricately carved screens.

During the last two decades of the eleventh century Venice began to assert her independence within the sphere of the empire. The Venetians were still firm allies and on more than one occasion their armed fleets sailed to protect the western territories of the Byzantine emperor from invasion by the Normans. After the first of these successful sorties, the Emperor Alexis Comnenus gave a pair of magnificent damascened doors for the principal entrance of the ducal chapel. Each of the doors' panels has a single figure of a saint outlined in the same stiff style that was typical of some later Venetian mosaic work. A year later the famous Chrysobull was published at Constantinople exempting Venetian merchants from all dues and customs within the empire. This extension of traditional trading privileges has been called the death warrant of Byzantium, and perhaps in the long run it did encourage Venetian greed and rapaciousness in the far-flung trading ports of the Levant. Nearer Venice the effect was even more immediate. The Chrysobull meant that Venice was licensed to enforce a system of staple rights over the whole northern Adriatic and in fact in 1085 the empire recognized the doge's style and authority as Duke of Dalmatia; within ten years Byzantium had renounced her claims to Croatia as well and Venetian merchants were granted extensive and exclusive trading privileges within Constantinople itself.

In this same century, the city of Venice began to assume some of the features still associated with it. Streets were traced among the clusters of houses and along the banks of the small canals, and documents speak of them by their distinctively Venetian names: *calli* and *fondamente*. Parish borders were drawn up in the same year the emperor's doors were given to San Marco, and in the last decade of the century documents make mention of a glass industry and of the small shallow-bottomed craft suitable for private transport, the *gondola*. Individual prosperity was still most conspicuous in the case of the doge, the sovereign ruler of the state. Domenico Selvo, the doge who had personally ordered the decoration of the palatine chapel, was the first to be given a state funeral. Of course, his wife was a niece of the Byzantine emperor and the earliest chronicles speak of her luxurious tastes (Saint Peter Damian reprimanded her for the affectation of eating with a fork instead of with her fingers) and the impression they made on the Venetians. Selvo's successor invited the emperor of the west to be godfather to his daughter, and although Henry IV agreed and came in person to Venice, it was more to honour Saint Mark, whose mislaid relics had been rediscovered, than to flatter the personal pride of the doge.

The potential abuse of the ducal office had been recognized by the powerful families of Venice in the early years of the century. In 1032 it was decreed that the doge could no longer nominate his successor. This brought an apparent end to the virtual dynastic succession of ducal families. In that same year two councillors were appointed to assist the doge in matters of policy, and additional advice was sought from a council (*i Pregadi*, later the Venetian designation for senators) expressly convened when major decisions were debated.

The assertion of Venetian autonomy against the feudal claims of the eastern empire and the restriction of ducal powers may both have represented a tendency towards western values where nation states and delegated authority were beginning to evolve. But in the arts, and therefore in the culture and civilization of Venice, western influence was minimal. In the last years of the eleventh century the church of Santa Fosca was built at Torcello along completely eastern lines. It is a Greek cross martyrion with truncated arms and a large dome on squinches. The dome was never completed and it has been argued, significantly perhaps for understanding Venice's role as bridge between east and west, that the Greek workmen who began the church deserted the job, leaving behind only local masons who were not competent to construct the dome; the external decoration of the apses at Santa Fosca was influenced by western taste and represents one of the rare examples of Romanesque workmanship in the islands. Nonetheless the appearance of Santa Fosca is eastern, especially in the porch arcade of stilted Byzantine arches. Those of Santa Fosca are the best and earliest example of the kind of arcade arches that became traditional for the openings on the canal or principal façade of the earliest surviving Venetian palaces. The other great island church of the late eleventh century is the church of Santa Maria e San Donato at Murano. The foundation is supposed to be due to a visit paid to Venice by the emperor of the west, Otto the Great, in the preceding century. The plan and the brickwork of the façade is that of a Ravennate basilica, but the remarkable feature of the cathedral of Murano is the apse with its Romanesque decorative brickwork inlaid with marble and ceramic plaques, and a round-arch arcade with oriental *plutei* between some of the columns.

At the very end of the century the area near one of the oldest churches in the middle of the city was set aside to be the trade and exchange centre of Venice, the Rialto market. And in 1099 the Venetians in their role as the primary shippers to Levantine ports were given a small, auxiliary role to play in the establishment of that epochal bridgehead between the civilizations of the east and the west that was the First Crusade.

3

Crusades
and Commerce

1100-1199

The Crusades to the Holy Land have given their name to forceful and high-minded undertakings in every western language. The root of the word is the Cross of Christianity, and it must not be forgotten that the specifically Christian and religious nature of their enterprise was supposedly uppermost in the minds of the Crusaders – at least in the minds of those who set off in response to the preaching of Peter the Hermit at the end of the eleventh century. The Crusaders were to make the holy places of their religion safe for pilgrims. It is often forgotten how popular pilgrimages to the Holy Land were before the time of the First Crusade. Doge Pietro Orseolo had established a hospice or hostel for pilgrims in the very centre of Venice and a similar hospital existed, one among several then, in Jerusalem itself, which was served and administered by Europeans who eventually became known throughout the Christian world as the Knights of Saint John. The Venetians had also seen to it that the churches of their city were well endowed with important relics of the saints that would attract the pious to Venice on their way to the Holy Land.

The Crusaders of the First Crusade did not pass through Venice: some did find their way to the Levant aboard Venetian ships, but the largest numbers went overland through the Balkans. It is not the purpose of this book to describe the movements or the motives of the Crusaders, but rather to consider briefly

the role of Venice in these epochal undertakings. At first the Venetian role
was peripheral, but it must have soon become obvious to the Crusaders that
they needed Venetian assistance. They were, after all, soldiers from northern
Europe, and the sophisticated and subtle ways of Constantinople where they
hoped to find arms and assistance, as well as the hostile climate and races of
the Levant, must have sorely taxed their patience and their resources. The
Venetians, on the other hand, were at home in this part of the world. They were
familiar with Byzantine ways, indeed by their culture they were a product of
Byzantium. And since the earliest days of their commercial expansion they had
traded profitably with the infidel Saracens themselves. As good businessmen
they were determined, if cautiously at first, to invest in success. Caution meant
that support of the Crusades was not immediately a matter of state policy, but
of individual initiative. In the first year of the twelfth century Venetian entre-
preneurs firmly allied themselves with the Crusaders. The Venetian base in
Jaffa was gained by conquest, but the terms for the Venetian presence in the
Holy Land were commercial and not military. There was no talk of fortifications or armies to be maintained by Venice. Instead they were granted trade
privileges throughout the Frankish states; a church and a market were assigned
to them in every town held by the Crusaders and in addition they were to receive
a full third part of every town they helped to capture.

To ensure that these privileges amounted to a virtual commercial monopoly
in the east, the Venetians kept up their more ancient alliances with the Byzantine emperor as well. The principal case in point was their defence of Byzantine
interests in Rhodes which were, in that same first year of the twelfth century,
threatened by the fleet of the Pisans. For the next two centuries these twin considerations determined Venetian policy in the Levant: commercial privilege,
if not monopoly in port or on land, and a recognized pre-eminence over western
rivals at sea. The foundation of the Arsenal shipyard is usually assigned to these
years; its name was derived, significantly, from the Arabic. The purpose
of the Arsenal was to concentrate, control and protect shipbuilding activities
in the city. With a firm footing in the Fertile Crescent guaranteed under the
patronage of the Crusaders, the Venetian government turned to supervise the
construction, maintenance and protection of its principal line of communica-
tion to its commercial outposts – in other words, its armed convoys or merchant
fleet. And to ensure the passage of pilgrims through the city, the Venetians
continued to enrich their churches with relics. Legend ascribes the arrival of
the body of the patron of fishermen and sailors, San Nicolò, to Venice in 1104.

The following year the city was once again scourged by fire – the perennial
threat on an island where the majority of buildings were still built of wood.
The Pala d'Oro, which must then have resembled a reliquary, was exposed,
and credited with subduing a conflagration that had already done considerable
damage to the fabric of the doge's chapel. It was only after this fire and an
earthquake that destroyed Malamocco in the same year that the domes of San

Looking across the Piazza San Marco to the third of the palatine chapels built to house the relics of the Republic's patron Evangelist. The thousand-year-old bell-tower-beacon stands near the arcaded building begun by Scamozzi and finished by Longhena (1682) for the nine Procurators or administrators of the Marcian patrimony.

Marco were completed; their shape, now hidden by the lead-covered cupolas, was the result of Venetian familiarity with Byzantine-derived Muslim architecture. In this same first decade of the twelfth century a less persistent artistic influence again appeared in the city, this time in the cloister of Sant'Apollonia which was built in the ancient area between the ducal palace and the convent of San Zaccaria: with its architecture of double columnettes it is the only surviving northern Romanesque building in Venice. It was contemporary with the stupendous cycle of mosaics in the chancel of the palatine chapel which recount the stories of Saint Peter, prince of the apostles, and Venice's own patron Saint Mark, and which show an emergent local style of mosaic work: generous golden spaces separate vividly narrated scenes peopled with simply outlined figures.

These sporadic appearances of Venetian taste in the arts are reflected in the frequent brusque alterations in Venetian policies as the state attempted to define its own independent role. The constant struggle to preserve her possessions in the Adriatic is typified by Doge Ordelafo Falier, who died asserting his claims as Duke of Dalmatia in the re-conquest of Zara from the Hungarians in 1117. In the next decade Venice played an active part in the taking of Ascalon and Tyre as she had earlier in the capture of Acre; these victories were part of the Venetian partnership with the Crusaders, whereas their alliance with Byzantium turned sour when the Emperor John II refused to renew the traditional Chrysobull in their favour. As a reprisal the Venetians took the island of Rhodes, the port of Modon in the Morea or Peloponnese and the island of Cephalonia, in addition to stealing Saint Isadore's body from the island of Chios. Yet in 1148 the Venetian fleet gained a signal victory at Corfu as ally of another emperor of Byzantium, Manuel Comnenus, whose territories in the west were threatened again by the Normans under Roger II.

The renewal of alliance with Byzantium suggests an explanation for the presence of Greek workmen in the Venetian mosaic workshops at Torcello and Murano. The elongated figures of the Madonna in the apse mosaics of the Assunta and Santa Maria e San Donato belong to this period and are ascribed to Byzantine taste. At the same time the central cupola of the Pentecost in San Marco was decorated with mosaic figures of the apostles in Byzantine style, while the contemporary mosaics of the chancel cupola are clearly Ravennate in inspiration. The Murano floor mosaics in *opus tesselatum* dated 1140 and those of the same period in the atrium of San Marco, show western influences not so much derived from Aquileia as based on the geometric patterns in coloured stone popularized by the Cosmati workshops in Rome. The co-existence of these potentially incompatible artistic influences in two major decoration schemes illustrates Venice's basically eclectic taste and her receptivity to all cultural currents. Venice was as much an entrepôt of artistic influences as she was of commerce and trade and the city was constantly being enriched by both these functions. So rich was she that her government bore the cost of lighting some of the main streets at night with small oil lamps and one of the administrators of the ducal chapel, the Procurator Leone da Molino, could personally commission a pair of silver damascened doors for San Marco in imitation of those donated previously by an emperor of Byzantium. The extravagant marble sheathing of the chapel's interior provided a richly veined and colourful base for the patterned translucence of the golden mosaics above. By mid-century the shaft of the bell tower was completed to its present height and topped with a gilded roof to catch the sun's rays and act as a beacon to the ships at sea. Documents of the period tell us that cloth of gold and silver was produced in Venice in the early part of the century and by 1157 banks are mentioned as established on the Rialto.

By the middle of the twelfth century Venice found herself preparing to assume again the role of middleman, negotiator and deviser of compromise: not between east and west this time but between church and state as the virtual arbiter of spiritual and temporal jurisdiction. In the city's parishes, the Venetians had evolved a system whereby the laity selected their priest from among the local clergy and their nomination was sent to the bishop for approval. At this time there were two episcopal seats in the lagoon: the most ancient was at Torcello and the more recent was established on the island of the olive groves in the ancient church dedicated to Saints Sergius and Bacchus. (The island of Olivolo was subsequently known as Castello from the fortifications built there and the cathedral church rededicated to Saint Peter.) The two bishops of the lagoon were under the metropolitan jurisdiction of the Patriarch of Grado, who by tradition was always a Venetian. Just as much as the parish priest or the bishops of the lagoons, the patriarch's political loyalties were thoroughly Venetian and there was little conflict in matters of episcopal investiture. On the widest scale, however, conflicting claims of civic and ecclesiastical jurisdiction had involved the pope and the emperor in bitter quarrels. In Venetian territory the antagonism was rooted in local history with the furious jealousies of the neighbouring patriarchs of Grado and Aquileia. The former ruled the lagoon churches while the latter was a great territorial magnate whose people marched with the empire. In 1162 the Venetians, defending the primacy of their own Patriarch of Grado defeated Ulrich, Patriarch of Aquileia, and brought him and twelve of his canons of Venice to watch a pointedly humiliating spectacle in the Piazza where a bull and twelve pigs were baited and killed. But beyond this local intervention the Venetians did not for the moment join fully with either of the contenders in the fierce controversy. They provided financial aid to the Lombard League, the League of Communes who tried to protect their independence from the emperor's armies, but otherwise Venetian attention and their resources were fully taxed by the rebellion of their subjects in Dalmatia.

This time rebellion was incited by the Byzantine emperor himself. A measure of the crisis precipitated by their former ally came in March of 1171 when

Manuel Comnenus ordered all Venetian goods seized in Constantinople, all commerce with the lagoon city stopped and all the Venetians resident in the capital arrested. As a result of these threats to her commercial existence, obscure factions formed in Venice and the doge himself, Vitale Michiel, was murdered. But typically the Venetians came to their senses quickly enough. Unlike other Italian cities where a faction in opposition could retreat to a stronghold in the surrounding country and either bide its time or seek alliance to force its return to power, Venice was an island with impenetrable defences. Political life was only possible within the community. The avoidance of faction by legislation or general agreement soon became an essential characteristic of Venetian civilization. A codified system of administrative checks and balances had to evolve if the city were not to fall prey to a tyranny. Thus the so-called Venetian constitution was developed. In 1172 this meant the organization of a deliberating body which would broadly represent various local points of view to the doge and his councils. But since it was immediately recognized that the doge and his councillors, from henceforth six in number, might represent a self-serving factionalism, his election was to be by specially appointed commission and no longer by acclamation. The first of these commissions numbered eleven men who chose the forty ducal electors from among the newly organized greater council. The electoral system chose Sebastiano Ziani, one of the most important and influential of Venice's many doges.

During his reign the two great columns on the Molo were put in place, a feat of engineering that became legendary. It was said that the successful engineer, Nicolò Baratari, asked to be allowed a gambling concession between the columns as reward for his achievement. The council granted his request, but ever fearful of financial ruin for any Venetian, the government decided to make the same restricted space infamous for misfortune – the public executions would be held there. These great monoliths had arrived in Venice as ballast in the galleys of the Levantine trade, just as hundreds of rare marble columns of smaller dimensions were taken from temples and buildings throughout the east and brought to Venice as decoration for the ever richer façade of the palatine chapel. The administrators of the chapel, known as the Procurators of Saint Mark and, like the doge, chosen for life, built for themselves offices and residences facing the Orseolo hospital on the Piazza. The small canal that marked the boundary of the old Piazza in front of San Marco was filled in, the church Narses had dedicated to San Geminiano was pulled down and the area of the Piazza extended to approximately its present length. It was at this time too that the ducal palace was rebuilt. There can be only hypothetical reconstructions of what the Ziani palace looked like, but from the nature and extent of the later building certain facts do emerge. What we now call the Doge's Palace was then a complex of three buildings, each of whose different functions was referred to by a separate name in contemporary documents. There was a building along the small canal which was the residence of the doge and his councillors; of this ducal palace virtually nothing of the original architecture survives. On the other hand the wing on the Molo has traces of a tower at the end nearest the Rio del Palazzo. This has suggested a Venetian type of palace, commonly called Veneto-Byzantine, of which examples survive from early in the following century. Their common characteristics included a long flat waterfront façade, two storeys high, with a stilted arch arcade running the length of the façade on both the ground and first or principal floor. The open arcaded façade was flanked at either end by slightly taller towers of solid masonry; the whole was crowned by a decorative parapet. The motif of the seaward side arcade flanked by towers can be supposed to have been adopted from the same features of Diocletian's palace at Spalato in Dalmatia. But whatever their origin, these features were typical of the earliest Venetian palaces and were very likely typical of Sebastiano Ziani's rebuilding of the old moated and fortified seat of the Venetian government. It was in the *palatium consilium* on the Molo that the meetings of the councils were held. Facing the Piazzetta was a wing housing the various magistracies of the government and known as the *palatium justitia*. Whatever improvements Ziani may have made, it is certain that the complex of building contained within it the essential elements of the Venetian government: the executive's residence, reception rooms and offices, the meeting rooms of the legislative branch and the courts of the judicial branch.

The constitution of Venice represented by the government and its doge had acquired a considerable international reputation by the third quarter of the century. The island had offered shelter to yet another refugee pope, this time in the person of Alexander III fleeing the troops of a hostile emperor. As the pope's ally, the Venetian fleet had helped defeat Frederick Barbarossa at Legnano in 1176 and in the following year it was decided that the end of the bitter papal-imperial quarrel could be negotiated at Venice. Only Venice and her doge were sufficiently respected by both parties to stage the formal reconciliation of the pope and the emperor. This episode proved one of the most popular in Venetian legend and iconography. On the Feast of the Ascension in 1177, the pope and the doge proceeded in ceremonial barges to the Lido where the doge cast into the sea a ring given him for the occasion by the pope. This ritual marriage of the sea was completed by the formula recited then or added later to reinforce the ceremony's nuptial solemnity: *Desponsamus te mare in signum veri perpetuque nostri dominii*. The *Sposalizio da Mar* was repeated annually as part of the ducal ceremonial.

The formal reconciliation of the pope and the emperor took place on 1 August of that same year and was endlessly repeated in the official iconography of Venetian history, playing a prominent part in the several cycles of historical paintings commissioned by the state for the decoration of the ducal palace. The various stages of greeting and encounter between the pope, the doge and the emperor sometimes figure in surviving versions, but the most dramatic moment came when the emperor knelt in token submission before the pope in the doorway of the ducal chapel. According to legend, the pope placed his foot on the emperor's neck and recited a biblical verse punning on his gesture; the emperor quickly joined the learned repartee and the reconciliation was effected as the two attended mass in San Marco. The entire episode seems to have been a happy one and an atmosphere of festivity and celebration exists in all the contemporary accounts. The Venetians quickly exploited these events as a further attraction for pilgrims and assorted foreigners. In 1180 the city was crowded with visitors anxious to benefit from the papal indulgence the Venetians obtained for the annual Marriage of the Sea.

Venice was not only signally honoured by the events that took place in the chapel of her patron saint, but the doge also received invaluable tokens of recognition from both the pope and the emperor. The ducal regalia had consisted simply of robes similar to those worn by any government official, though made of cloth of gold for gala occasions; as a crown the doge wore a curious phrygian cap of indeterminate origin. Now the pope and the emperor granted the doge the right to be covered by a canopy or ceremonial umbrella; a faldstool and a sword preceding him betokened the sovereignty of his state; henceforth the Doge of Venice was to be addressed as Most Serene Prince, *Serenissima*.

As so often happens in history, such a high water mark of a state's prestige and prosperity coincided with events that put an entirely different cast on the future. In Constantinople the Venetian merchant still had an important role to play, but Byzantine suspicion of the exiguous westerners often strained the bonds of alliance. In 1182 there was a massacre of Latin merchants within the city. Although Pisans and Genoese were the principal victims, the emperor set out to placate the powerful Venetian colony in an increasingly explosive atmosphere. In 1183 the emperor granted indemnities for Venetian losses eleven years earlier, and towards the end of the eighties the Venetian quarter was enlarged on the condition of an obligatory military alliance with the empire. In 1187 the holy city of Jerusalem fell to the Saracens. The horrified reaction of the Christian west to this epochal disaster resulted in the Third Crusade and the capture of Acre and Jaffa, important cities for Venetian trade. By that time the power and pre-eminence of Venice was undisputed in the west and her commercial role in the eastern Mediterranean was seen as essential to European civilization and culture.

The last decade of the twelfth century and the first of the thirteenth were periods of intense artistic activity in Venice. The extension of the vast scheme of mosaic decoration of the ducal chapel resulted in one of the keystones of Venetian culture. There is much evidence and a certain concordance of scholarly opinion that the mosaics completed in this period represent the development of a self-confident local style of mosaic work. All the diverse elements that had contributed to this characteristically Venetian art form – both political and artistic – make ever more elusive appearances now, and the final result is increasingly something new and distinctively Venetian. Apart from the Roman legacy of work in glass and the tiny glass-coated cubes made for mosaics of the paleo-Christian basilicas and the development of this art in the late Roman, Ostrogothic and Exarchical periods of Ravenna, there were recollections of classical traditions recently introduced by links with Constantinople. In this period of Byzantine artistic history, mosaicists especially seem to have visited every corner of the ever diminishing, though still vast, territories of the empire to decorate the rich outposts of eastern Christianity. It is probable that with Byzantium obviously nervous of further offending the Venetians, some of her prized mosaicists may even have been sent to Venice to help in the continued decoration of the palatine chapel. The iconography of the decoration was completely Byzantine, and eastern liturgical considerations were obviously a part of a plan adopted from the Apostoleion in Constantinople. The programme for the principal mosaics is said to have come from the Apostoleion as well, though tradition also mentions a European, Gioacchino da Santa Fiora, as author of the overall scheme.

Differing treatment of individual figures and scenes is obvious in the mosaics done at this time and may represent different schools of thought about the relation of these illustrations to the worshipper in the church. In the north and south transepts arches were decorated with scenes from the Life of the Virgin, the Infancy of Christ and the Miracles of Christ with extremely large and forceful figures. But in the Acts of the Apostles in the great arch over the right aisle and in the arch between the crossing and the south transept, figures are set in very extensive gold ground and executed with an extraordinary delicacy, in part derived from Ravenna. Two different approaches to the instructive and artistic function of mosaic decoration are illustrated in these sections of the basilica. One where a clearly visible narrative content seems the principal concern and the other where the decorative, aesthetic achievement is primary. At the same time the cupola dedicated to Saint John the Evangelist was completed in a style reminiscent of the earlier Ravennate cupolas and the figures in the apse of the four patron saints of Venice – Nicholas, Peter, Mark and the Bishop of Torcello, Hermagoras – were remade over the older figures that were a part of Domenico Selvo's decoration of the chancel.

At the same time as this decoration was executed the government offices in charge of the Marcian patrimony, the Procuratie, were enlarged: treasurers or *camerlenghi* were elected to serve under the procurators. In the next four centuries the procurators would often be the foremost patrons of the arts in Venice, both as rich men elected to high office for life and constantly in touch with the artists retained by the state, and as officials of the Republic responsible for the embellishment as well as the maintenance of the fabric of the ducal chapel. The treasurers would also figure in the artistic commissions of the day. Another significant addition to the growing Venetian bureaucracy was made with the election of special judges for civil and commercial trials; the doge and his councillors retained their jurisdiction over criminal cases, but the doge's individual power was constantly diminishing and in 1192 the newly elected Enrico Dandolo was made to swear to the first *'promissione ducale'*. This oath was the result of a commission appointed on the death of a doge to examine his reign and determine any instances of abuse of the ducal powers and office. The newly elected doge was then made to swear in public to an oath which would prevent the repetition of such abuses. In time these promises became lengthy and fascinating in their detail.

But the introduction of the ducal promises is not the principal reason for recalling the election of Enrico Dandolo. The story of this extraordinary doge belongs to the following century although the end of the twelfth century saw the setting of the stage for his great role in the drama of Venetian history. In 1196 Zara and Ragusa rebelled against their Venetian masters; two years later Byzantine attempts to placate Venetian commercial demands resulted in the total restoration of Venetian privileges by the usurper Emperor Alexis III. In the same year, the forces of Christianity in the west gathered to hear the forceful preaching of Pope Innocent III. The west must rescue the holy places from defilement by the infidel. Another, a Fourth Crusade, must be mounted by Christian men in Europe to preserve Christianity in the rest of the world.

4

The Spoils
of Byzantium

1200-1299

The thirteenth century was the period in which Venice became a world power, the century in which she took part in an epochal conquest and ruled the territories which resulted from her victories. It was the century too in which her government evolved into its definitive form, in which all the elements of the Venetian constitution were present to make of this small island city-state the powerful and effective capital of a vast empire. Venice's victories and dominion were achieved in the east, yet they were accomplished through the agency of western alliances: the role as a bridgehead remained crucial to her power and prosperity. The pattern of Venetian culture and civilization remained much the same as in preceding centuries. Venice accepted and absorbed cross-currents of artistic influence from both the east and the west and used them for the embellishment of the few great buildings that symbolized the growing might of the state. The thirteenth century shows Venice at the apogee of the civilization she inherited from Byzantium at the same time as she acted as purveyor of the refinements of eastern civilization to the west.

In April 1201 the Crusaders gathered in Venice under the leadership of Boniface of Montferrat, Louis of Blois, Hugh of Saint Pol, Philip of Swabia and Baldwin of Flanders. Their immense fighting force has been said to number over four thousand knights, more than twice as many squires and at least twenty thousand infantry men. The Venetians and their doge, Enrico Dandolo, were every bit as wary of such a concentration of adventurers, soldiers of fortune and dedicated Christians as had been the emperors of Byzantium when earlier crusading armies demanded passage across the Bosphorus through the capital of Constantinople. Like those suspicious Byzantines, the Venetians kept the Crusaders at a distance while they negotiated passage and transport to the Holy Land. The armed forces of western Christianity were housed on the Lido at high cost to each knight and his entourage. An added expense would be the hire of the galleys needed to transport the entire force to the east. After five months at the Lido it became obvious to the Venetians that the Crusaders would never be able to raise the eighty-five thousand silver marks to pay for the journey. The doge and his councillors began to consider ways to cut their losses. It was finally agreed that part of the debt would be offset if the Crusaders helped the Venetians subdue their rebellious subjects in Dalmatia. In October 1202 the entire force sailed for Zara where the rebel city surrendered after a brief and ineffective resistance. There the Crusaders began to consider the next stage of the Crusade as much in their own interest as the Venetians had arranged this first stage to suit themselves. The presence of the pretender to the throne of Byzantium, Alexis, who was also brother-in-law to Philip of Swabia, determined to a certain extent the final goal of the Fourth Crusade.

In the spring of 1203 the Crusaders under Boniface set sail with the Venetian fleet for Constantinople. When their goal was known, Christian rulers on every side condemned the undertaking. The pope was especially enraged to think that his Crusade to rescue Jerusalem from the infidel might end in the siege of the Second Rome and a virtual civil war between Christians. But that is what came to pass and worse. The young Alexis was to be the Crusaders' pretext: his father, the Emperor Isaac, had been deposed in a palace revolution, blinded and imprisoned in Constantinople. Although details of Alexis' argument to persuade the Crusaders to restore their house to the throne are obscure, it would have been easy enough for Isaac's son to gain a hearing from the Crusaders through Philip of Swabia. Historians now believe that his arguments swayed the Crusaders' intentions only after the pacification of Zara and that, in good faith, the Crusade had left Venice with the Holy Land as its ultimate goal.

The presence of an imperial pretender among them might have moved the Crusaders to meddle in the internal politics of the empire, but they must have realized that this meant attacking the sacred city of eastern Christianity as well as its armies and inhabitants who were fellow Christians. But the Crusaders probably did not see their undertaking as either paradoxical or problematical. Once they determined to set aright the imperial succession, they were attacking a great city that had more than once in the recent past, and even more frequently in the remote past, failed in its promises of alliance with armies from the west. The earlier Crusaders had almost all received very ambiguous if not openly

hostile treatment from the emperors and armed forces of Byzantium. They
had been treated with suspicion and reluctant hospitality when the capital was
known to be overwhelmingly rich and when the westerners had undergone
tremendous hardships to reach the east and to help Byzantium against
her enemy. By restoring Alexis and his family to the throne of Byzantium, the
Crusaders undoubtedly thought they would secure lasting and profitable
alliances between the two great bodies of Christians, who could then move as
one to defeat the Mohammedans. The Venetians went along, as they did on
the First Crusade, to secure their own trading privileges in the Levant. This
time, however, they were ready and strong enough to take an active role along-
side the Crusaders. They were spurred on by their own recollection of recent
Byzantine hostility: of the seizure and arrest of Venetian merchants in 1171,
of the massacre of Latins in 1182 and of lengthy and often fruitless negotiations
with Constantinople to obtain the mere recognition and renewal of ancient commercial treaties.

However the blame may be apportioned, the Crusaders laid siege to Constantinople, entered the capital victorious and succeeded in restoring Alexis
and his blind father in the summer of 1203. The following winter local resistance forced the virtual reconquest of the city on 12 April 1204. Byzantine factions, shifting alliances and outright treachery left the westerners exasperated
with the officials and inhabitants of Constantinople and disillusioned with their
own puppet dynasty. Mutual suspicion and tension rose until the inevitable
reprisal occurred: Constantinople was sacked by the Crusaders. This event is
often described as one of the great crimes of Christendom; the Crusaders probably realized that what they were doing could and would be interpreted, especially by the pope, as sacrilege. But to them the sack of Constantinople was part
of the contemporary policy of punishment of a vanquished yet recalcitrant
enemy; outside the context of contemporary thirteenth-century warfare, or
even without a religious frame of reference, the sack of Constantinople was
a great crime against culture and civilization. It was a crime that would be
repeated, it is true, throughout the centuries and even down to our own day,
and it would be repeated with particular appropriateness but perhaps more
deliberation shortly after Venice herself fell in 1797.

Throughout the spring and summer of 1204 the Crusaders apportioned the
spoils. It was no longer a question of carrying off the loot and leaving the city
stripped of its treasure. The Crusaders were to remain and establish themselves
as the rulers of what history calls the Latin empire of the east. The Venetian
role in the division became more and more prominent. The Crusaders owed
the Venetians a great debt for bringing them to all these riches; and an even
greater debt to the magnificent leadership of the Doge Enrico Dandolo who,
though over eighty years old and blind, fought in the van of the soldiers who
breached the great walls of the city. A measure of his prestige among the Crusader barons was reflected in the legend of their offer of the crown of the empire.

He refused, and on 9 May 1204 Baldwin of Flanders was elected the first Latin emperor. His electors were twelve in number and the Venetians saw to it that six of this college were their own countrymen. The first Latin Patriarch of Constantinople was a Venetian, Tommaso Morosini.

In that first year of the conquest of Constantinople, the Venetians established the pattern of their vast imperial dominion. They did not covet great land holdings that their small island population could not hold; rather they sought to secure the ports that led to the richest trade routes or that could be used to protect the passage of their convoys in the eastern Mediterranean. The Latin emperor reconfirmed their possession of what was called the *Dominum Adriae* and to this was added the coasts of the Ionian Sea, islands of the Cyclades and key outposts on the Straits of Gallipoli and Rodosto; in August 1204 Boniface of Montferrat renounced the island of Crete in Venice's favour. This was to become one of the crucial possessions of the Venetian empire. Unlike other of their territories, Crete would be colonized and a governor sent out from Venice to administer the entire island. Otherwise Venice occupied only the key points of her new acquisitions: Durazzo in Epirus, Coron and Modon in the Peloponnese or Morea and the island of Negroponte. The rest was parcelled out to various Venetian families to be held in fief to the Republic; for example the family of the doge, the Dandolos, were to rule Andros while the Barozzi family governed Santorini.

The city of Constantinople as capital of the empire and as the principal trading entrepôt of the Levant obviously held many attractions for the Venetians. Basing their claim on the terms of ancient trading treaties they took a section of the town and a church as their own. But in the new circumstances resulting from the Fourth Crusade their section of the city gave them the right to the resounding title of Lord of a Quarter and a Half of the Roman Empire, and the church they were assigned was nothing less than Santa Sophia itself. In 1205 Doge Enrico Dandolo died and, with imperial solemnity, was buried in the Venetian church of the Holy Wisdom. In the same year the spoils of victory and of the sack of Constantinople began to reach Venice. Many of these reflected the virtually theocratic character of the ancient Byzantine empire and were therefore most appropriately housed in the ducal chapel. Much of the contents of the treasury of San Marco was lost and dispersed after its sack by Napoleon almost exactly six hundred years later, but many fine examples of Constantinopolitan workmanship can still be found in the city. Carved stonework in the form of *paterae*, *plutei*, capitals and columns of precious marbles were brought to the city in merchant galleys as ballast. *Cloisonné* enamel panels were taken from the Pantakrator monastery to enrich the famous golden altar screen or Pala d'Oro. Often these panels came from Byzantine bindings which were encrusted with gems, so the Marcian treasury also acquired ancient manuscripts and fine examples of the work of Byzantine gemcutters and goldsmiths.

These confiscations were not entirely the result of wanton looting, but were founded on political motivation, much as were Napoleon's, or Henry VIII's suppression of the monasteries. In Constantinople each church administered by regular clergy, and in the east almost all of them were, represented a potential haven of opposition and resistance to the Latinization of Byzantium. Monasteries, with their traditions of virtual autonomy and inviolate sanctuary, had to be either completely westernized or else closed. Once closed, their treasures could be sent elsewhere for safe keeping. But the greatest legacy of the fall of Constantinople and her culture were the Byzantine craftsmen, artists and architects who came to the lagoon city. Many of them worked in the ducal chapel and even more must have exercised their lesser talents on the minor Byzantine-style churches in the city.

Two treasures from Constantinople captured the imagination of the Venetians and were then and are still thought of as symbolic of Venetian culture and civilization in a way few other things in Venice are. The first is the *Madonna Nicopeia*, an icon of uncertain date, but said to have been the one that always preceded the person of the Emperor of Byzantium into battle. The second treasure was the four gilded copper-bronze horses from the arch of the Hippodrome which, on their arrival from Constantinople, were appropriately kept at the Arsenal as a trophy of the Venetian victory over Byzantium. Over the centuries an impressive provenance was devised to explain their evident quality as masterpieces of sculpture: the name of Lysippus is often mentioned, even today. Scholars now agree that these four splendid animals are of Constantine's period and thus masterpieces of Hellenistic Roman sculpture. In 1222 the horses were brought to the Piazza to stand over the central door of the narthex of the ducal chapel, on the terrace that had been extended at this time to include the two small arches supported by clusters of precious columns.

The central arch over which the horses stood was now embellished by a carved frieze in a curious mixture of Byzantine and Romanesque styles. On the north façade of the chapel the so-called Flower Gate was opened; as oriental as its name, it could be considered a seminal piece of architecture and carving in the history of oriental influence brought by the Crusaders to the west. The curves of the pointed arch of the gateway are sinuously eastern, but similar curves would later find their way into the vocabulary of Gothic stonecutters and masons. Inside the church the mosaic decoration was continued according to a predominantly Byzantine iconography expressed in an increasingly distinct local style. One of the most powerful mosaics of the interior, *The Agony in the Garden*, was probably completed just before the end of the century.

In this same period the Venetians were also occupied in the colonization of their principal territorial possession in the eastern Mediterranean, Crete. Two separate colonies were sent out composed of men from each of Venice's six *sestieri*. Knight's fiefs were granted to the nobles who went, and the rank of sergeant was bestowed on Venetians of the citizen class. So heavy was the

Venetian commercial investment in the east at this time, and so much did she see herself as the heir of Byzantium, that in 1225 the Doge Pietro Ziani who had been the first Duke of Crete actually proposed that the capital of the Venetian empire be transferred to Constantinople. Legend says that the proposal was defeated by a single vote.

Despite Venice's heavy commitment to her maritime trade and her far-flung possessions, she could not afford to ignore her position in the west. Only forty years before Venetian mosaicists were sent to the pope in 1218, Venice had been an ally of Pope Alexander III. In 1223 Ugolino, Bishop of Ostia, later Gregory IX, asked the Doge Pietro Ziani to build the church of Santa Maria Nova di Gerusaleme in Rome. Less well documented, perhaps, but no less indicative of Venetian religious and ultimately cultural links with the west is the supposed shipwreck of Saint Francis of Assisi in the lagoon in 1220. In another generation the first hint of the earliest Italian Gothic architecture was felt in Venice with the establishment of a Franciscan friary in the city, but in the meantime western building techniques apparent in Venice are still the infrequent works of a few Romanesque stonecutters. Several of the city's bell towers of the early thirteenth century were built by masons of the Romanesque tradition: their shafts are divided by pilasters capped by blind arches outlined in double rows of distinctive decorative brickwork. More sophisticated Romanesque carving is to be seen in the two grotesque preying beasts at the base of the bell tower of San Polo or in the hooded stone porch of the Carmelite church. Otherwise the greatest masters of this western style were sculptors at work in the ducal chapel. The second frieze carved in the arch of the main door is in the vigorous style of the Ferrarese school of Antelami and depicts the months of the year as well as virtues and beatitudes. The four great gilded angels standing high in the spandrels beneath the central dome are unmistakably Romanesque, as are the figures of four small prophets in the southern antechamber, now closed off from the narthex as the Zen chapel. The contemporary narthex mosaics, beginning near this chapel with the *Creation of the World* are Veneto-Byzantine in spirit, while the cupola of the Ascension is decorated in purer Byzantine mosaic style.

Veneto-Byzantine is a term used by historians of Venetian architecture to describe the derivation of her palaces. Typical elements of the Veneto-Byzantine style in the present Doge's Palace survive from the earlier palace built by the Doge Sebastiano Ziani, just as details of late twelfth-century building appear in the Palazzo da Mosto near the Rialto. However, the architectural historian is on firmer ground in the early thirteenth century. The palace built for Matteo Palmieri in 1225 still survives in a cold and heavy-handed nineteenth-century reconstruction which nonetheless illustrates characteristics of the early style and period. An arcade of tall, stilted arches ran the width of the façade on the ground and first floors; the whole was flanked by two towers and crowned with a decorative parapet. The Veneto-Byzantine palaces were generally built not

Jacopo de' Barbari's aerial view of Venice, dated 1500, was made of six immense woodcut blocks and remained the most accurate plan of the city throughout the Republic's history. The map shows clearly the extent of the Arsenal shipyards though the artist was instructed to leave out certain recently-built strategic buildings.

on the water's edge, but back from the canal. The sloping bank in front of the house was used to beach the lighters that brought goods from the merchant convoys anchored in the basin of San Marco or tied up near the pontoon bridge at the Rialto. The majority of these houses surviving today, probably the largest and richest of all those built at this period, are found near the exchange and commercial centre of the city on the Rialto. Because additional floors were later added above the original two storeys and many alterations made behind the arcades of the water front, it is now virtually impossible to know how they were arranged inside. Provision was undoubtedly made for the storage and perhaps distribution of the goods in trade managed by the owner of the house. In any case, the thirteenth-century Veneto-Byzantine façade became the prototype of all Venetian palace façades. The open arcade on the first floor was eventually reduced to a cluster of windows lighting the central gallery-hall known as the *portego* which ran the depth of the house. In later palaces the two lateral towers were widened to contain the living rooms flanking this hall; this invariable internal arrangement is reflected in the tripartite division of the Venetian palace façade.

By the middle of the thirteenth century Venetian maritime commerce was well organized and controlled by the state. The galleys of the merchant fleet were constructed in the Arsenal shipyards by workmen under the supervision of government appointees. The completed ships were auctioned and their ownership purchased by a rich merchant or by a partnership. Before the formation of a closed aristocracy at the end of the century, the merchants who were rich enough to afford such an investment probably also served in the councils of the state. Therefore the state supervision of Levantine trade had to be as efficient as possible in order to encourage and to permit this individual initiative to flourish. The investor-owner saw to the ship's commissioning and provisioning; a relation, a younger son or a man of his own class, was hired to captain and staff the galley. The oarsmen were recruited from parish lists of trained men who were partly supported by the state with pensions, rations and provisions, and with benefits for his family during his absence. A galley oarsman was considered to hold a good and honourable job and in the early days of Venetian commerce there were more than sufficient volunteers among the native population. Each oarsman had space allotted beneath his bench for the storage of his own goods which he could trade in the ports where the ship called.

The galleys that went in convoy to the east carried the more valuable trade of Venice and had to be protected; well-paid archers were put aboard each merchant ship. In wartime the Republic set up public targets for archery practice in the city's squares and required that all able-bodied men in the parish aged between eighteen and thirty-five report for training and practice with a crossbow. Eventually permanent fleets of state galleys were stationed overseas to protect the merchant ships coming out from Venice. In the Gulf of Venice, as the Adriatic was known, there was a fleet of six to twelve galleys; the Levant fleet was stationed at Candia in Crete or at Negroponte, and later there was another in Cyprus. The merchant ships these fleets were to protect were sent out in convoys of about fifteen or twenty twice a year. Since the use of magnetic compasses was understood only in the following century, the galleys proceeded first along the coast of Dalmatia by day and only in calm weather. If the winds were in the right quarter the huge single lateen rigged sail was hoisted and the galley sailed along its coastal route. Otherwise it was rowed, as it was when entering or leaving port. From Dalmatia to Crete the vessels would proceed via the ports of the Peloponnese and then on to Constantinople through the Cyclades, or else on the open run to Alexandria or across to the Crusader cities on the coasts of the Holy Land.

The merchant government of the Republic early realized the necessity of securing ports of call along this profitable trade route. This was the reason for Venice's constant preoccupation with the subjugation of Dalmatia. When, after the fall of Constantinople, Venice fell heir to numerous scattered territories in the Levant, the Venetians set about organizing an imperial administration. In Dalmatia the virtual autonomy of the tiny city-states was respected and local government was partly copied from the Venetian model. There was a *bailo* or *rettore*, assisted in his governing by an executive council and other councils dealing with specific problems. In later years a nobleman was sent out from Venice for two years as governor answerable to the Senate for his administration. Similar government on the Dalmatian model was followed in the ports and towns throughout the eastern Mediterranean where the Venetians were in charge of a substantial native population and not simply a fortified military outpost.

By virtue of its position in the eastern Mediterranean Crete became the crossroads of Venetian trade and her most important possession. In the first half of the thirteenth century numbers of Venetians were sent to colonize Crete. As a result of the earliest local resistance to Venetian colonization the Cretans were little represented in the councils of government and the richer of them were induced or forced to submit to the Republic. From the outset the whole island was governed by a duke who had his seat at Candia (present day Heraklion). He was assisted by two councillors and two magistrates and his finances were in the charge of three *camerlenghi*; in addition a captain had charge of the island's defences. The three principal cities of the colony were each governed by rectors and it was on this most local level that a much less representative version of the Dalmatian model of colonial government was adopted in Crete.

It is clear that Venetian imperial government was at the outset a fairly flexible and pragmatic affair based on local conditions. This continued to be the case because many of these administrations were set up before the Venetian government itself had evolved into its final form; their flexibility was also due to their relatively simple structure and to the brief tenure of the governors. The sensitivity of the colonial government to local conditions meant that Venetian culture was not imposed on the towns of their territories. Fortifications marked with the Marcian lion were ubiquitous, it is true, and were products of European military engineering, but the churches and houses built with local labour continued to be built on only slightly modified lines. Where the refinements of Byzantine culture had penetrated or where there were remains of Roman settlement, as in Dalmatia, the appearance of colonial towns recalled those elements found in Venice herself. But where there had been little medieval cultural flowering, such as in Crete, the Peloponnese or the islands, the Venetians did not impose their taste, but left the towns in almost as primitive a state as they found them. After all these were merely trading and military outposts. Such artists and local craftsmen as there were would be encouraged to come to the capital or else left undisturbed to pursue their traditional arts, such as the fifteenth-century school of icon painters which flourished in Crete. The cultural influence of Venice in the eastern Mediterranean was not very impressive. On the other hand the mere existence of these ports, outposts, territories and lands made Venice the richest and greatest city of the west. It is one of the paradoxes of Venice that, well preserved as she is, little or nothing survives today of the vast riches that must have accumulated in the city's churches, palaces and other buildings at the height of her power. The chapel of her patron saint and her doge is virtually the only reminder of this great period of her cultural inheritance from Byzantium.

By the middle of the century the first section of the atrium mosaics was completed in a forceful local style illustrating the Creation, the Flood and the stories of Abraham and Joseph. At about the same time the Venetians defeated the Genoese, their western commercial rivals, in a skirmish at Acre in 1256 and sent the two Syriac carved stone piers from the Genoese church that stand in front of the southern entrance to San Marco. Only five years later the rivalry with this same Italian commercial power became the first in a series of bitter struggles lasting over one hundred and twenty years and ending in the definitive defeat of the Genoese fleet on the edge of the Venetian lagoon. Otherwise the political links between Venice and the west were still somewhat tentative and intermittent. In the very early years of the century trade agreements had been made with the Patriarch of Aquileia, but only a few decades later Venetian trade on the mainland was blocked when the western emperor, Frederick II, seized Ferrara. It was only in the year of the Venetian victory over Genoa at Acre that the Republic renewed its principal western alliance in order to pursue a policy that foreshadowed her later expansion onto the mainland: in 1256 the Venetians joined with the pope in the war against Ezzolino da Romano for possession of territories in the March of Treviso.

In 1261 the Byzantine Emperor Michael Palaeologus reconquered Constantinople and the Latin empire of the east collapsed. Owing to skilful negotiation the integrity of Venice's possessions in Crete and in the Morea was

guaranteed by the restored emperor within the year. Four years later the
Palaceologus dynasty published a Chrysobull such as had not been issued for
over a century, granting the Venetians a favourable position in Levantine trade
with the customary extensive exemptions and privileges. This rapprochement
with Byzantium was again reflected in Byzantine-style mosaics, this time
depicting the recovery of the relics of Saint Mark. The inner stability of the
Venetian government, and its ability to cope with as radical a change in her
prospects as the resurrection of Byzantium represented, was seen too
in local improvements that were also gestures of self-confidence. The ducal
elections of 1268 were conducted according to a satisfactory formula that
endured until the extinction of the Republic. The centre of the city was put in
better order with brick paving for the Piazza; riding in the Merceria was forbidden and a permanent wooden bridge replaced the rafts used to cross the
broad Cannaregio canal. The population of the city at this time was said to
have been almost one hundred thousand people and many of them began
to organize themselves into corporations according to their trades. In the
last decade of the century the glass furnaces of the city were transferred by
law to Murano to diminish the danger of fire in the centre of the city. In
1282 the stability of Venice was further demonstrated by an event more
far-reaching and significant than any internal legislation or local improvement: the first golden ducat was coined. This coin quickly became the
currency of trade throughout the world, and thus one of the most important legacies of Venice to western civilization. Even more remarkable is the
fact that the coin's weight in gold was maintained for more than five
hundred years, from the ducat's first appearance to the final collapse of
the Republic.

By the end of the thirteenth century the most constant elements in the internal stability of the Venetian Republic had made their appearance. In 1297 the
closure of the Great Council determined one of the most remarkable features
of Venetian political and social life: the intricate relationships that existed
within the Venetian class system. The reorganization of the Great Council
was an attempt to render the Venetian system of debate and legislation
less cumbersome. It was the culmination of a tendency begun two hundred
years earlier when the traditional election of the doge by acclamation was abol-
ished in favour of a council or college of electors. When the first Great Council
was established to represent a broader selection of the city's merchants, bankers
and other notables whose commercial activities would either benefit from or
be hindered by the government's decisions, the criterion for membership was
not clearly defined. The need for such a criterion was felt long before the larger
numbers were admitted to the council after the conquest of Constantinople,
rendering the whole business of government too time-consuming for the
average busy merchant. The efficiency of short terms of office for the empire's
colonial administrators, and indeed for all the offices of the Republic save the

doge and the procurators, was already appreciated at home and much admired abroad.

When Venice closed the Great Council to all save men whose fathers and grandfathers had served the Republic, and registered these men's names, making membership hereditary to all their male issue, Venice created an aristocracy. Besides three generations of service to the council, the criterion was undoubtedly success in commerce and business. Venice was to be governed by an oligarchy, though as the centuries progressed this general description held less and less true. Members of the governing aristocracy lost their fortunes despite the Republic's attempts to protect prosperity, and members of other classes became enriched. Venice never restricted the opportunities for commercial success to her governing class. As can be seen even in the case of the galley oarsman who was encouraged to trade and barter, even the humblest had a chance to turn a profit from commerce; and anyone with capital could participate in partnerships and investment. Remarkably, in a supposedly closed society, this broad range of potential investors also included foreigners. By the first decade of the next century the nature of this inclusion was already codified by law. The Republic granted citizenship *'de intus'* to anyone who had resided in the city for twelve years and practised a craft or profession; a citizen *'de intus et extra'* was someone who after eighteen years residence in the city could become an independent merchant and engage in trade abroad. These legal definitions did not, of course, apply only to foreigners, but to the Venetians themselves.

The citizen class was of extreme importance in Venice. Though the *cittadini* had no voice or vote in the deliberations of the government or its councils, they played an important role in the history of the Republic. Like the colonial administrators, their function became more complicated with the passage of time, but the essential elements were present in the dispositions made at the close of the thirteenth century. It was the citizen class who staffed the chancery of the Republic; they were trusted with the job of recording the most secret debates and voting of the government as well as its day to day business. Whereas no doge or procurator could be elected from their numbers, they were already represented by a Great Chancellor in 1268. This office became the exclusive privilege of the citizen class and the man was chosen for life. In the ceremonial precedence and protocol which came to have more significance in the hierarchies of state, the Great Chancellor was granted, on all official occasions, a place above the highest officers of the Republic save the doge himself. In the later elaboration of his duties the Great Chancellor was required to countersign all the ducal decrees before they could be put into effect. This duty as countersignatory extended down into the lower ranks of the chancery with the secretaries countersigning the decrees of both provincial governors and commanding generals. The secretaries who had reached this level of their service to the Republic and who in later centuries also staffed various embassies, sometimes serving as *chargés d'affaires*, were members of what was called the Ducal Chancery; a lower rank of notary and other recording officials formed what was called the Order of Secretaries. Of course the citizens who thus served the Republic were specially trained for their duties as later provisions attest, but the majority of their class were more than content to make their living from the innumerable opportunities offered by a flourishing commerce with the east.

Such a man was Marco Polo, who had returned from his legendary sojourn at the court of the Great Khan two years before the closure of the Great Council. At first his tales of the fabulous riches of the Orient were not believed, but so insistent was he on the millions and millions of gold ducats rendered to Kublai that the Venetians referred to him as *Il Milion*. Marco Polo was treated as a crank by his fellow Venetians, not because his travels were so extraordinary, but precisely because they appeared at first to be simply an extension of the kind of trade most Venetian merchants engaged in. It took the appearance of Marco's written account of his travels to convince his fellow merchants that he had ventured further than they had ever dreamt of and seen more than they knew. More typical of his fellow citizens had been Marco's uncle and his father who had set out for the Orient in 1260 and who returned to the city as prosperous as was Marco, but with no fantastic tales to tell.

In the city the merchants of the Republic, both noble and citizen, were to be found at the Rialto where their *colleganze* or investment partnerships were formed. The *cittadini de intus*, who practised a craft or profession, were scattered throughout the city, although by the thirteenth century those of a common craft often settled in the same street or *contrada*. The street names of Venice still refer to these concentrations: the swordmakers (*Spadaria*), arrowmakers (*Frezzeria*), mercers (*Merceria*), blacksmiths (*Fabbri*) to name only the most familiar streets near the Piazza. These groupings of craftsmen sometimes led to the tentative formation of guilds. But the guild system never assumed political prominence in Venetian society, perhaps because the government had early showed an interest in controlling and protecting local crafts, so the guild was not needed for this function. The work of many of the craftsmen supplied government monopolies rather than individual clients, as in the case of the arrow and sword makers, not to speak of the carpenters, cordwainers, etc., who worked in the Arsenal shipyards. The *casseleri* or chestmakers have left a fine example of the varied purposes of their craft. Primarily they made chests to contain goods in trade and none of these has survived. They probably also made bridal chests, though these may never have been as popular with the rich Venetians as they were to be with Tuscan merchant families. The wooden chest made towards the end of the century to contain the relics of the Venetian nun, the blessed Giuliana Collalto, is decorated in a way that suggests another rare appearance of western decorative motifs in Venice, perhaps explained by Giuliana's Friulian origins or her vocation as a Benedictine.

The easy application of a secular craft to a religious purpose is typical not only of Venice but of this period throughout Italy. Just when the guild system was beginning to develop in other Italian city-states, devotional societies were introduced in Venice cutting across class and occupational boundaries in a way more consonant with the Venetian way of life. These confraternities probably appeared from Umbria, the cradle of the new Franciscan religious fervour. In Venice their popular combination of apocalyptic visions, corporal works of mercy, penitence and flagellation long survived in the *scuole* that grew out of them in the following centuries.

The *scuole* or devotional confraternities of Venice were one of the many links between the prosperous citizen class and the poor of the city. Their principal function was charitable and the poor members of a *scuola* were cared for by its collective prosperity. Otherwise the most cohesive body of the lower classes distinguishable in medieval Venetian society was the large number employed by the government in every aspect of her shipbuilding monopoly. Craftsmen such as carpenters were obviously the most highly rewarded for their talents, and their craft was passed on in particular families from generation to generation. These families were also members of the citizen class as were others in the Arsenal whose crafts were perhaps less demanding, but nonetheless required considerable skill. The mass of workers in the great Arsenal were known as the Arsenalotti and they were a highly respected work force. They were privy to many state secrets in the construction, arming and fitting of ships of the fleet and their importance to the Republic was recognized by the government in a way that was typically Venetian. The Arsenalotti alone were privileged to stand guard in the Piazza when the Great Council was in session. This was of course a symbolic duty, but it also implicitly recognized that the Arsenalotti could be called on to form a militia loyal to the government. In the following century that trust would be misused by a doge, but the traditional loyalty of the Arsenalotti proved itself incredibly staunch in the very last days of the Republic when they alone of all the various classes of Venetian society attempted to defend the millennial republic from destruction.

5

Medieval
Venice
1300-1399

Despite the absence of factional strife within the ranks of Venetian society there was a reaction to the government's attempts to order the various classes of her peoples. In the very first year of the fourteenth century a conspiracy was uncovered to overthrow the government and restore power to the people. Only ten years later a more widespread, yet equally abortive rising was led by the patrician Bajamonte Tiepolo and members of the Querini family against the Doge Pietro Gradenigo. The severity with which the Republic reacted to this threat and suppressed the rebellion acted as a warning to future generations of malcontents. The houses of the Tiepolo and Querini families were razed to the ground and later an inscribed column of infamy was planted on the site. An even more effective precaution was the formation within the government of a committee of public safety known as the Council of Ten. The Council of Ten's role in Venetian history has been much romanticized and exaggerated. It is true that the council had almost absolute powers, but these applied only to cases of high treason and subversion. The system of secret denunciations, and the lion's mouth letter boxes placed all over the city to receive them, did not in fact encourage anonymous accusations. It was made clear from the outset that a denunciation would set in motion a painstaking and extremely thorough investigation, in the course of which the accuser's identity would probably be discovered. Torture would be applied in such an investigation, but that was the accepted method of the day, and recent research has shown that few sentences of capital punishment resulted from secret denunciation. For whatever reason, the creation of the council and the suppression of the Tiepolo plot helped to ensure the internal security and stability of the state. As soon as the danger was past the Council of Ten was disbanded and not re-established until an even more alarming threat to the Republic arose in mid-century.

These events of the first decades of the fourteenth century illustrate a process of internal consolidation begun with the closure of the Great Council in 1297 and strengthened, despite intermittent crises, through the continual legislation. At the same time, the fourteenth century represented a new phase in the development of Venetian culture and civilization. Abroad the boundaries of the empire were well established, although the Venetian monopoly of trade in the eastern Mediterranean was now repeatedly challenged. Throughout the fourteenth century Venice was to find herself at war with the aggressive Republic of Genoa. These wars were no longer fought out between merchants over the boundaries in the commercial quarters of a remote Levantine city; they were full-scale naval engagements with armed fleets pursuing the advantage, making taunting raids and engaged in a concentrated struggle to the death all over the Mediterranean Sea. Although these battles resulted in new techniques of naval warfare, they were nonetheless a legacy of all that had gone before: of the earliest commerce with the Levant, of the decay and collapse of Byzantium and of the Fourth Crusade with its dependence on the maritime republics. The restored though debilitated eastern empire followed a subtle policy of weakening the west's commercial hold on the Levant by setting the western merchant republics at each others' throats.

In the fourteenth century, however, Venice was not exclusively concerned with the east, nor even with the threat to her commerce there by the Genoese. From the very first years of the century she found herself more and more involved in the politics of the mainland. At first this involvement consisted of the usual quarrels with the Patriarch of Aquileia over the coastal territories of the northern Adriatic. In 1304 the patriarch ceded his claims over Istria and neighbouring lands for the sum of four hundred and fifty silver marks. Five years later a different sort of quarrel broke out on the mainland; it involved Venice's traditional access to the river trade and markets of the mainland along the Po river which passed through Ferrara. This profitable and strategic route was blocked, not by rebellious Ferrarese nor by the troops of the emperor, but by Venice's erstwhile ally the pope, who reclaimed the fief of Ferrara and all its lands. So strong had the ancient commercial bond between Ferrara and Venice become that Fresco d'Este, son and heir of Azzo VIII, actually made a bequest of the city and its territories to the Republic. The pope contested the legacy, forced the issue to arms, and in 1309 excommunicated Venice. A ban of excommunication was among the most powerful weapons of the medieval papacy and no doubt the factions that rose against the government in the following year under Bajamonte Tiepolo knew that they could count on papal support if they succeeded in overthrowing the ducal government. But the Republic managed to weather all these crises; in the case of Ferrara the city was returned by treaty to the d'Este dynasty and the ban lifted.

Political involvement on the mainland produced few cultural echoes in the city. The most suggestive are those that involved the Tuscan influence already beginning to be felt in the Veneto. Giotto was at work on the stupendous cycle of frescoes in the chapel built by the Paduan merchant Enrico Scrovegni, but one of the earliest dated Venetian panel paintings, *San Donato with two Donors*, Podestà Memmo of Murano and his wife, shows little Tuscan influence. The influx of Lucchese silk weavers from 1307 onwards was of ultimately greater significance, although their role in the life of the Republic was commercial rather than artistic. It was not until late in the following century that the richest of these families would commission work in the latest Tuscan style for the church dedicated to San Giobbe. The early part of the century was still devoted to organizing or consolidating not only the efficient working of the government but also of Venetian crafts and industry. In 1303 a new area in the Arsenal was built enlarging the old basins within the fortified precinct where ships were constructed, fitted, armed, careened and repaired. Square-rigged cogs made their first appearance at about this time with the innovation of the rudder attached to the stern-post. The government appointed three patricians to be the first *provveditori all'Arsenale* in the same year, and it was presumably to them that a Tuscan presented his model for the construction of the first *tana*, the long building designed for rope weaving. Andrea Pisano, the Pisan stone-cutter-architect, was a native of another of the four Italian maritime republics where familiarity with all stages of ship construction was common to local builders. His name, like that of Giotto, presents a tantalizing glimpse of a completely different Venetian culture had the Venetians accepted Tuscan innovations on a broader basis. A generation later, when the Arsenal was again enlarged and over sixteen thousand men in thirty corporations worked there, bronze casters trained in the Arsenal were called upon to cast Pisano's first set of bronze doors for the Baptistry of Florence. The power and importance of the Venetian Arsenal impressed yet another Tuscan, the poet Dante Alighieri, who arrived in Venice as Orator of Ravenna in 1321 and saw the huge vats full of boiling pitch used for caulking which inspired a vividly infernal simile for his great epic poem.

Medieval scholasticism derived from Aquinas and thirteenth-century Dominican monasticism, was apparently a more congenial influence in early fourteenth-century Venice than were the innovations of the Tuscan proto-Renaissance. When the Doge Marino Zorzi died in 1312 he left money for the building of an orphanage and church to be administered by Dominicans; the building was completed five years later and its administration was absorbed

by the community of San Giovanni e Paolo. The prior commissioned a set
of illuminated antiphonals in memory of Zorzi which demonstrate yet again
Venetian eclecticism in the arts; there are traces of a local school of illumination
but Byzantine traditions are still very strong. This same mixture of styles is
evident in the *mariegole* or charters drawn up in 1307 and 1311 for the Scuole
di San Giovanni Evangelista and San Teodoro respectively. On one page of
the latter there is a Byzantine *Deisis* set with a Gothic throne.

The *mariegole*, although the charters of devotional societies, were primarily secular in intent. They were the constitutions of charitable institutions
set up by merchants, for the most part of the citizen class, to employ their
combined wealth in the corporal works of mercy. The expiatory intent of their
generosity is clear from the fact that the recipients of their charity were at first
expected to march in the processions of the *scuole* as flagellants. Their meeting-
rooms contained ecclesiastical furnishings and as they became richer they were
able to acquire the relics of the saints who were their patrons. They had their
own chaplains to direct their devotions and it is thus not surprising that the
illuminatory work on their charters was executed within ecclesiastical conventions.

As has been said before, the *scuole* were not guilds, although such institutions
did exist in Venice. Despite the fact that the guilds did not contribute to the
distinctive character of Venetian culture and civilization in the way they did
in Florence, the crafts and guilds were prominently represented in 1320 in the
iconography of the main arch over the central door of San Marco. Combined
with figures of the prophets these carvings represent the first prominent public
appearance of Gothic-style sculpture in Venice, an obvious instance of
early fourteenth-century links with the mainland. By the second decade of the
fourteenth century many crafts had reached a high degree of sophistication.
Mirror-making is supposed to have been introduced in Murano at this time
from the north, possibly from Germany, whereas from the south and more
significantly from Assisi, an important centre of Gothic architecture and
decoration in Italy, orders for stained glass were received. If the Germans
brought the art of mirror-making to Venice in 1317, it was only a year later
that there were enough German merchants, traders and perhaps even craftsmen
in the city for the government to allot a space near the Rialto for the construction of a *fondaco*, or warehouse-emporium, for the German colony in
Venice. These buildings, many times enlarged in later centuries, were both
residences and trading centres for foreigners who sought the advantages of collective bargaining with the Venetians and a convenient depot for their commerce with the east. The Germans represented one of the oldest and largest
of the groups of European traders who settled in the city. It is probably more
than coincidental that with the appearance of Germans in large numbers in
Venice the first signs of the northern or Gothic style of architecture, sculpture
and decorative work should make itself felt in the city.

In the second decade of the fourteenth century an artist appeared who is widely considered to be the founder of the Venetian school of painting and some of whose work survives in Venice. There is no question that Master Paolo the Venetian, Paolo Veneziano, is the first distinctive personality among the anonymous artists who had matured in the mosaic workshops of the ducal chapels or who had followed the conventions of the icon painters in the execution of devotional panels. Paolo is of the latter tradition as far as his debt to Byzantium goes, but his very Venetian talent for absorbing and adapting the cross currents of diverse artistic traditions, along with his native genius, gives him an immediately recognizable artistic personality. In the early panel often dated around 1324 the crowned head of the enthroned Virgin could be taken, despite its graceful and expressive inclination, from a Byzantine icon. The Christ child is not seated in her lap but is enthroned in a radiant mandorla which the Virgin holds; the Child inclines to bless the tiny kneeling worshipper protected by the Virgin's mantle. The head and face of the donor are strong and full of character, almost Giottesque in their expressiveness. But the distinctive quality of the panel is its Gothic lineature, the draping and the edges of the Virgin's fine robes, her graceful limp hand extending the folds above the worshipper's upturned head, and especially the billowing folds and lines of the material held behind her throne by two angels whose tunics are by contrast creased in stiff Byzantine folds. This panel contains the several traditions that helped form Paolo's style; in Venice there are later panels that more fully illustrate his mastery and his unique contribution to Venetian painting.

The traditional cultural influences of Byzantium were still important in Venice, and in 1325 the *Paliotto* or Pala d'Oro, that splendid collection of Byzantine enamel plaques, was placed in front of Saint Mark's tomb in the ducal chapel where it remained until the fall of the Republic. Of the three hundred and twenty-four plaques many were original Byzantine work dating to the tenth century and had been brought to Venice in various ways; a number of the plaques were probably local fourteenth-century copies of earlier mosaics in San Marco indicating a certain weakened artistic confidence of craftsmen who were once masters of the Byzantine idiom of enamel work and eastern iconography. The final bejewelled setting which took fifty years to complete was entirely western and Gothic.

The splendid extravagance of Venetian Gothic work in gold was the subject of government legislation in 1331 and goldsmiths were obliged to congregate on the Rialto island. Three years later even the dress of the wealthy Venetian came under government supervision and control. These sumptuary laws were a constant feature of Venetian life, especially those concerning dress. The Venetian patrician was obliged to serve the government and throughout the centuries he dressed in a long, large-sleeved gown or coat, coloured according to his office. In winter these robes were lined and the thin edge of fur that showed led to richer and richer furs being employed in the lining. Thus furs were among the few items of masculine attire subject to sumptuary laws; one other item was gold chain, the government early specifying the number, size and weight of links that could be worn. Otherwise personal sumptuary laws applied mostly to women, to their jewels and especially to the lengths of materials in which they draped themselves. The laws curtailing or forbidding trains were the most frequently repeated over a very long period, indicating that feminine cunning often outwitted the ponderous legislation of their menfolk as well as their inefficient attempts to enforce it. Sumptuary laws appeared in other Italian cities and states of the period, but in Venice the intention behind them was not just an attempt on the government's part to curb temporary extravagance but a very real part of Venetian civilization. The Venetian government early recognized that it had succeeded in creating a class structure that almost perfectly suited its island community. All the classes were given incentive to work for the state, from the lowliest who rowed or built the ships of the fleet to the merchants who traded in markets abroad; the citizens who were the archivists of Venice to the patricians who made the laws. In no case was a single family or individual to be given preference over the others. The *promissione ducale* saw to that in the most obvious case, that of the doge himself, whereas the sumptuary laws prevented all other Venetians from assuming an undue prominence through lavish display or even extravagant generosity. The size of dowries was the subject of some of the most often repeated restrictions, as was the expenditure on a wedding or other family festivities.

As the middle of the fourteenth century drew nearer signs of Venetian wealth and power took on ever more distinctive characteristics. Not only was society becoming organized under the government's supervision and control of the myriad details of daily life, but the city sought to establish claims over neighbouring territories now in the hands not of remote suzerains like the pope, emperor or patriarch, but of local tyrants. Padua had become a lordship or signory under the da Carrara, while the della Scala dynasty expanded its domain beyond the March of Verona to cover most of the Veneto. In 1336 the Republic declared war on Mastino della Scala and in the following three years lands in the Trevigiano, once taken by Venice from the Patriarch of Aquileia, were fought over and regained by the Republic. This political conflict with the rulers of Verona opened one of the most significant two decades in the history of medieval Venice.

The next twenty years produced an astonishing flowering of Venetian Gothic culture. The year 1340 could almost be called an *annus mirabilis* and there are many who consider the Gothic to be the Venetian style par excellence. Just as the epochal transfer of the ducal government from the Lido to the Rialtine islands coincided with the arrival in Venice of Saint Mark's relics, so the year 1340 is associated with an equally popular and frequently commemorated Venetian legend. It was said that on 15 February of that year a fierce storm arose in the lagoon and a poor fisherman huddled under the Ponte della Paglia

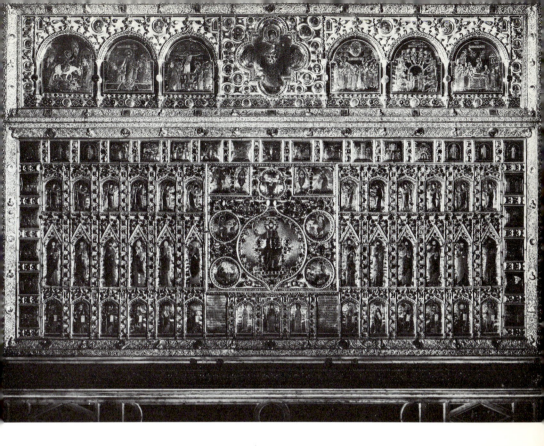

The *Pala d'Oro* or Golden Screen (detail, below right) composed of gold plaques decorated with exquisite byzantine enamel work dating from the tenth to the twelfth centuries and set in a bejewelled gothic frame in 1345. At the time of the Sack of Venice by Napoleon's agents, the Golden Screen (originally used as a frontal for St Mark's tomb) escaped being melted down because it was thought to have been made of merely gilded, base metal.

near the Doge's Palace to wait it out. A shadowy stranger approached him and forced the frightened man to row him across the storm-tossed basin to the island of San Giorgio, where they were joined by another mysterious figure who insisted on being taken to San Nicolò on the Lido. At San Nicolò a third dark figure climbed aboard and the three made the fisherman take his boat out to the open sea. Beyond the comparative safety of the lagoon they came upon a ship full of evil spirits. The terrified fisherman's passengers thereupon revealed themselves in a dazzling moment as the Holy Protectors of Venice, Saints Mark, George and Nicholas. The barque of malignant spirits on their way to savage Venice by storm was dispersed by the heavenly trio, and the astonished fisherman given a ring by Saint Mark himself to take to the doge.

By the fourteenth century the doge had become more a symbol of the Venetian state than a prince mediating between the controversies of the pope and the emperor, or a warrior duke sailing with his fleet or leading his troops through the breached walls of an enemy city. As a figurehead he represented the heaven-protected survival of Venice through her marriage with and dominion over the sea; in reality he was but one of a powerful council whose other members often took the initiative with far-reaching consequences. The number of the doge's circle of intimate advisers or privy council had grown and among their number were those called *savii* or wise men. In mid-December 1340 three *savii*, Nicolo Suranzo, Tommaso Gradenigo, kinsman of the doge, and Marco Erizzo, tabled a motion to decide within eight days whether to enlarge the meeting-rooms of the Great Council (which numbered some twelve hundred men by 1340) or to build anew the wing on the Molo known as the *palatium consilium*. The *savii* quickly decided to build a new palace and ten thousand ducats were voted for the project: the old building, part of the enlargement built under Sebastiano Ziani, was torn down. When completed the new wing determined the distinctive architecture of the entire palace as it exists today and as such it was early recognized as one of the most remarkable Gothic buildings in Europe. It is a unique and yet extremely Venetian building: the Doge's Palace represents an eclectic adaptation of much that had gone before.

The long pointed arch arcades on the ground and first floors were probably adapted from the Veneto-Byzantine stilted arch arcades of the Ziani palace. The solid mass above, which is considered such an extraordinary innovation by architectural historians, developed from two considerations: first of all from the need for an extra large room to house the Great Council. The arcaded front on the ground and first floors provided space for public access to offices housed on those floors: the nature of these offices mean the public would be expected to come and go very freely and frequently, whereas – and this was the second consideration – the council room had to be completely enclosed with a minimum number of easily guarded entrances. What more logical solution than to create this space with a solid curtain wall between the *torreselle*

The oldest surviving façade of the gothic Doge's Palace (begun 1340) is that on the Mole overlooking the Basin of San Marco. The quatrefoil tracery of the first floor loggia was copied to decorate Venetian gothic palace façades for over one hundred and fifty years. The distinctively patterned curtain wall enclosed the immense Hall of the Great Council.

or small flanking towers of the Veneto-Byzantine Ziani *palatium consilium?*
The upper floor housing the Great Council room was extremely tall but in
keeping with the importance of the room its height was to be emphasized by
a steep hipped roof supported by a ship's keel beam construction. Large pointed
arch windows lit the hall from the Molo, while above them rose windows providing light for the large areas of historical painting planned for the walls opposite. Indicative of the ties between Venetian and mainland Gothic building,
the tall hip-roofed council room was similar to an arrangement in Padua where
the Palazzo della Ragione had just been completed. The distinctively Venetian
features were the immense room's position on the second rather than the first
floor, the tracery of the arcades and the external wall decoration in patterned
red and white marble.

In the same year that work was started on the Molo wing of the ducal palace,
a new church was begun for the community of Franciscan friars who had settled
in Venice over a century before. At that time they had built a small church
in the *sestiere* called San Polo and now they wanted a building more worthy
of their immensely rich and powerful order. As was traditional in medieval
church building, they began by constructing the tall apses; eventually the new
Gothic building would engulf the old, but not until its plain brick walls had
risen to the great height of the apses and transepts. The tall apse walls with
their long, narrow pointed windows were well within the conventions of mainland Gothic architecture found at Verona, Padua and other cities of northern
Italy, while the tracery used at the ducal palace was a purely Venetian product.
This tracery, which much later became the most widely adopted of all Gothic
motifs in Venetian palace decoration, consisted of a round opening placed
directly above the column of the arcade; the opening was decorated with cusp-
ing of a four-lobe pattern and the interstices between adjoining quatrefoils were
filled with tiny lions' heads or rosettes. (The tracery of the six windows lighting
the great hall though more elaborate was less original and derived from trans-
alpine Gothic.) The capitals of the ground and first floor arcades were also
distinctively Venetian, not because of any specific innovation, but for the remarkable individualism of the details that were part of an iconographic programme devised for the seat of government. Some of these capitals were carved
with immediately identifiable subjects or a variety of faces and human types
serving to remind one that the offices behind these arcades were frequented
by Venetians of all ranks; the figure of a scale-bearing Justice was constantly
repeated in reference to the government's principal obligation to the people.

Only a few years after the work on the ducal palace was begun Andrea Dandolo was elected fifty-fourth doge of the Republic. Like his distant kinsman
the blind doge of the Fourth Crusade, Andrea was one of the most remarkable
men of his day. He was probably only about thirty-seven years old when he
was elected doge and for the previous seven years he had been a *procurator
de supra* in charge of the palatine patrimony in the half of the city where San

Marco was situated. Like most of the procurators before and after him, he was exceptionally rich; his branch of the Dandolo held vast feudal territories in Istria. But such riches and holdings were not exceptional in a ducal candidate: what made Andrea Dandolo remarkable was his learning and his patronage of the arts. According to the earliest chronicles he is said to have attended the university at Padua, the great *studio* which had been founded a little over a century before, one of the oldest universities in Europe. Tradition attributes to him the laurels of a doctorate and even a chair in Jurisprudence, but his close friendship with Petrarch and the poet's high opinion of Andrea's abilities and intelligence is sufficient testimony to his outstanding talents.

In his patronage of the arts Dandolo exemplifies a tradition that remained fairly constant throughout the Republic's history. As a procurator he was responsible for the fabric and decoration of San Marco and the properties owned by the ducal chapel in half of Venice. Shortly after his election two hundred ducats were voted to the office of his former fellow procurators to complete the Pala d'Oro. The work was entrusted to the Venetian goldsmith Gianpolo Boninsegna who would, over the next thirty years, produce a jewel encrusted Gothic setting for hundreds of Byzantine enamel panels. The completed screen is a complex and delicate fantasy on northern Gothic architectural themes of the sort used in the elaborate reliquaries and processional crosses of the day. In addition Paolo Veneziano was commissioned to decorate a wooden cover for the precious screen. Paolo's fourteen panels (the upper row a pietà with five saints and the lower depicting seven scenes from the life and miracles of Saint Mark) is one of the most important paintings of the Venetian *trecento*. It is signed by Paolo and his two sons and dated 1345. Byzantine influence is still very strong in this work, especially in the sorrowing Virgin and in the busts of some of the saints. The architectural backgrounds of the lower panels are rendered in a credible perspective while buildings depicted are for the most part of a striking simplicity. The most interesting panel in terms of the increasing realism of late Gothic art is the representation of the episode in which the ship carrying Saint Mark's body is about to be wrecked on the rocks when the saint arises, averts the catastrophe and the ship, an accurately represented fourteenth-century Venetian cog, slips safely between the rocks. Much of the iconography of this incident can be found in the twelfth-century mosaics of the chancel, but the ship passing through the space between the foreground and background rocks has been rendered with a naturalism and sense of pictorial depth unrealized until the fourteenth century.

In keeping with his former responsibilities as a procurator of Saint Mark's, Dandolo as doge made considerable alterations in the fabric of the chapel. He closed off a section of the southern atrium to make a baptistry which he then had decorated with an important and forceful series of mosaics depicting the life of Saint John. A number of the figures, such as the dancing Salome, are rendered with a freedom of expression and rhythm that can only be considered Gothic in spirit. On the other side of San Marco the doge built a chapel to house the recovered relics of Saint Isidore which had been brought to Venice from Chios in 1125 and then, like the relics of Saint Mark, lost in the various rebuildings of their chapel. The new building incorporated the last remaining vestiges of the ancient Byzantine chapel dedicated to the earliest patron of Venice, Saint Theodore. Little or nothing then remained in the city to remind the Venetians of Saint Theodore save the patchwork statue placed on top of one of the two great columns in 1329. The mosaics in the new chapel depicting the life and martyrdom of Saint Isidore are not only Gothic in style, but in the figures of mounted armoured knights represent the so-called *stile cavalleresco*. The spirit of medieval chivalry inspired several literary works in the same period, like Niccolò da Verona's Franco-Venetian epic based on the Carolingian romances. Although written in the courtly French of the International Gothic, it is a work often considered among the first examples of Venetian literature, and it is appropriate that it appeared in the reign of one of Venice's most highly literate early doges. The sarcophagus Dandolo commissioned to hold the saint's relics is a splendid example of the elaborate Gothic work of the de Sanctis workshops of Padua. When he died in 1354 the doge himself was buried in his baptistry chapel where another sarcophagus by the de Sanctis had been prepared for him.

The new wing of the ducal palace and the two chapels in San Marco were not the only important building projects of this period. The monastic orders, the great propagators of the Gothic in Italy, led the way in Venice. The Pietà, a hospice for abandoned children, was founded by a Franciscan in 1346; a Carmelite church was consecrated two years later while a church dedicated to Saint Christopher, later known as the Madonna dell'Orto, was begun in the northern part of the island on the designs of a Franciscan monk from Parma. In 1348 Venice was hit by an earthquake of such intensity as to empty the Grand Canal and leave it dry for fifteen days: this was the same year that the infamous Black Death ravaged Europe. Venice lost three-fifths of her population to the plague. The religious fervour that revived after these cataclysmic scourges perhaps inspired the three Venetian merchants to donate to Saint Peter's in Rome a large piece of rock crystal framed with Byzantine enamel medallions of the saints to keep safe the most precious relic of Christendom, the *Sacrarium* or Holy Veil of Saint Veronica.

On the whole, however, the almost severely puritan and penitential atmosphere that pervaded Italy after the holocaust of the Black Death did not appear in Venice. The spirit of the rest of the century continued to be a happy mixture of learning and sensitivity to the arts that marked the reign of Andrea Dandolo. In the years following the great doge's death Paolo Veneziano and possibly members of his workshop were engaged on one of the loveliest treasures of Venice, the *Coronation of the Virgin*, now in the Academy Gallery. In the small

One tempera panel of the cover for the *Pala d'Oro* painted by Paolo Veneziano and his sons and dated 1345 shows St Mark averting the wreck of the ship that brought his body from Alexandria to Venice in 828.

lateral panels of the great polyptych gracefully drawn and colourfully draped figures move around the figure of a Christ, whose robes are creased in gilded folds and whose head is modelled in Byzantine fashion. In the central panel, whose subject gives its name to the whole, Christ crowns the Virgin in a glistening golden paradise to the strains of a strumming, plucking and bowing orchestra of angels. The Virgin looks out at the spectator as if from an icon, while Christ's face, distinctly Levantine in cast, wears a softened Gothic expression. The great legacy of this painting, no matter from which tradition it may derive, is its richness of jewel-like colour, its effulgent gilding and the splendidly patterned robes which were every bit as familiar to the Venetian who knew the local work in silks and cloth of gold as were the conventions of Byzantine iconography.

While the rich delicacy and jewel-like radiance of Paolo's painting could be said to represent the cultural climate of Venice in the mid-fourteenth century and an emerging Mariolatry combined with Byzantine traditions might reflect the religious climate, the political situation was neither so subtle nor serene. There had been rebellion in Zara yet again, and in 1349 the Venetian fleet engaged the Genoese off Alghero in Sardinia in a battle where the first use of naval artillery in the Mediterranean was recorded. Several such battles were fought under the first of the great Venetian naval heroes, Niccolò Pisani, including his victory over Antonia Grimaldi in 1353 and that over the Genoese fleet of Paganino Doria off the Morea in the following year.

The internal stability of the Republic was briefly rocked to its foundations in 1355. In that year a conspiracy to overthrow the patrician government was uncovered and certain of the overseers of the Arsenal were found to be prominent in the plot. The conspiracy might have been mistaken as similar in intent to the thwarted popular uprising led by Mario Boccacini in 1300 were it not that the principal conspirator was known to every Venetian: he was none other than Marin Falier, fifty-fifth doge of the Republic. The story of the plot has become one of the best known of Venetian history. Byron wrote a tragedy based on it and Verdi made an opera from Byron's version while the black veil painted over the traitor doge's portrait is still pointed out to visitors to the Great Council Chamber. The story began when the doge was insulted by a young noble called Michele Steno whom he immediately had arrested and brought to trial. Steno's peers voted to punish the young man, but the doge felt the sentence inadequate considering the insult to his person and to the dignity of his office. At the same time as he was brooding over this slight, one of the overseers of the Arsenal sought out the doge to complain of an assault he had suffered at the hands of a haughty patrician. Falier thought these complaints sufficient to warrant ridding the Republic of an overbearing aristocracy. With the support of the Arsenalotti pledged by the overseers, the doge hoped to establish a monarchy in his own person. As the plot spread so did rumour; witnesses were questioned and within hours the principals were arrested. The

Doge's Palace was sealed off during the doge's arrest and speedy trial, and not opened again until 13 April 1355 when the populace were encouraged to witness the execution of their doge for high treason. Marin Falier was decapitated at the top of an external staircase that led at that time to the first floor of the new *palatium consilium*. And a lengthy Latin inscription referring to his sin of pride was written under his portrait already painted in the frieze around the hall of the Great Council. Only much later was his portrait painted out with the famous black veil and the inscription changed to read '*Hic est Locus Marini Falehri decapitati pro criminibus*'. The veil and the terse inscription were afterthoughts but indicative of the government's fear of treason and subversion. For similar reason a Column of Infamy was erected on the site of the Tiepolo houses in 1364, almost fifty-five years after the suppression of that conspiracy to overthrow the government. The immediate result of the treason of Marin Falier was the establishment of the Council of Ten as a permanent and powerful committee of the Venetian government.

The latter part of the fourteenth century found Venice still entangled in political struggles and warfare. The King of Hungary had invaded theTrevigiano and was at the same time inciting Dalmatia to further rebellion. There was also insurrection on the island of Crete, although the Venetians stamped it out with the combination of the able Admiral Domenico Michiel and troops under the *condottiere* or mercenary commander, Luchino dal Verme. The news of the submission of Candia reached Venice on 4 June 1364 and the resulting celebration was graphically described by Petrarch who, much in the spirit of his late friend Dandolo's reign, had been given a house in the city by the government. Petrarch gives a lively description of the garlanded victory ships and the anticipation of the crowds gathered on the Molo, as well as an account of the festivities in the Piazza which he witnessed seated on the doge's right hand beneath the golden horses. The Republic honoured Petrarch in many ways, though not with pompous ceremonial or pretentious boasting of their own englightenment. He was the doge's friend, honoured guest of the Republic and participant in Venice's joys and sorrows. When he decided to retire, the Republic allowed him to depart to the simple house in the Euganean hills donated by the government of Padua. Petrarch was grateful for Venice's hospitality that he left his most valuable possessions to the state. In 1362 he bequeathed to the Republic his precious collection of codices, incunabula and other literary treasures including manuscripts of Homer and Plato. His gift was of such importance that Venice established a state library to house the precious manuscripts. This was the famous Library of Saint Mark for which, two hundred years later, the most ornate public building in the city was built on a site opposite the Doge's Palace.

Petrarch's gift and his presence were signal contributions to Venetian culture in a period rich in improvements to the city's fabric. The bell towers of the Frari and other churches were monuments to the Gothic style in building. The octagonal bell chamber of the former is a reminder of what the great campanile's crown must have looked like when its low-pitched roof was gilded to catch the sun as a beacon to the ships at sea. Gothic bell towers of the period were finished either with a square or octagonal bell chamber or else topped by a cone-shaped spire covered with terracotta cobbles and known from its resemblance to a pine cone as a *pigna*. Bell tower shafts were distinguished by a rich variety of patterned brickwork decorating the blind arches or pilaster edges. The same sort of elaborate brickwork was used on the apses and transepts of the vast Dominican church in Venice, San Giovanni e Paolo. In the two great Gothic monastic churches begun in the fourteenth century, the apse and transept sections of the building were the most elaborate both in architectural and decorative detail. San Zanipolo, as it is known in the local dialect, has no fewer than five polygonal apse chapels which were finished in 1368. This elaboration made up for the fact that the nave and the lateral walls were generally of the utmost simplicity.

Venetian Gothic churches, like all the buildings of the city until the present day, were built of brick. Their walls, resting on soft or even shifting foundations, could not be too thick or heavy; nor could their Gothic vaulting be of excessive height or even of a very sharp pitch. With weight as the principal consideration of building on mud foundations, little stone was used save for supporting piers, and even the groins of the vaults were often of brick. With thin light walls buttresses were not needed, nor would they be wanted in a city where the space for a building was so very limited. In any case the possible shifting of the building's foundations and the subsequent stress on the vaults could be sufficiently absorbed by a system of tie beams; for even greater elasticity these tie beams were often in fact chains disguised in a beam-like sheathing. Vaulting may have been considered too problematical to be completely satisfactory to the Gothic builder in Venice: as a system of covering it hardly exists outside the city's churches and even then it was not used in many of the churches built in Venice in the fourteenth century. The Augustinian monastery of Santo Stefano is said to have been completed in 1372 and indeed its nave and side aisle plan are a fine example of fourteenth-century architecture. Although the beautiful ship's keel roof is a later solution to the problem of covering, the slender columns of the nave indicate that vaulting was never considered.

If Venetian Gothic architecture of this period was essentially simple and unadorned, the masters of her pictorial arts were adopting the decorative elaboration made popular in the so-called International School. Typical of the complex cross currents influencing the Venetian artistic experience is Guariento di Arpo, who as a Paduan was exposed to both the monumentality of Giotto and to the delicate lineature and fanciful elaboration of the International Gothic which came to northern Italy from France. Called to Venice to fresco the wall of the Great Council chamber in 1365, ten years after the execution of Marin Falier,

Guariento displayed an obvious debt to the Byzantine tradition still alive in the ateliers of the city. The subject chosen for the great fresco was an hieratic one that appealed to a taste for splendour and transcendent religious magnificence: the *Coronation of the Virgin*. Only fragments of the vast composition remain, but a sketch made before Tintoretto's immense *Paradiso* replaced it does exist, as well as a small panel version painted seventy years later by Jacobello del Fiore. The Virgin assumed a central role in official Venetian iconography: not the humble Virgin of the Nativity nor the maiden of the Annunciation, nor even the sorrowing Virgin of the Pietà. The Virgin of Venice was the enthroned and glorified Virgin crowned by Christ in paradise, or a solemn icon-like Mary holding the infant Christ popularized by the *madonnieri* or Madonna painters, or else the Virgin of the Renaissance enthroned and surrounded by saints in *sacra conversazione*. Of course many of these compositions are common to the artistic traditions of other Italian cities, but the feasts of the Virgin and her intercession on behalf of the Republic are constantly alluded to in the paintings commissioned by the government, and Lorenzo Celsi, the doge of Guariento's day, changed the ducal gala robes from red to white in honour of the Virgin.

The decade after the completion of Guariento's fresco found Venice locked in a struggle for survival with her fiercest enemy and rival commercial power, Genoa. The last Genoese war was fought mostly at sea, but at the same time Venetian forces were engaged on the mainland with the de Carrara of Padua and their allies, the Hungarians, as well as in warfare against the Austrians in Dalmatia. In 1377 the Genoese war was being fought on both sides of the Italian peninsula and the great Venetian admiral Vettor Pisani won a significant victory at Anzio the following year. However, shortly afterwards Pisani was defeated at Pola in Istria and the Genoese war was brought disastrously close to home when the Genoese captured Chioggia in 1379. The Venetians had never been so seriously threatened since the armies of Pepin had arrived on the edge of the lagoon more than five hundred years before. For a moment the government seemed to panic, and suspicion of treason and betrayal was rife. Vettor Pisani himself was cast into prison for the losses suffered under his command. This action has been ascribed to the fickleness of the Venetians, but render was always grounds for such suspicion. Indeed, it was often proved that composed of powerful committees which could examine the deporting of a general, admiral or governor at any time and demand his immediate detention if any neglect of duty was suspected. A major military or naval loss or surrender was always grounds for such suspcion. Indeed, it was often proved that negligence on one side contributed to a victory as much as luck on the other, and both factors frequently outweighed any occasional superiority of force or strategy. Whatever the truth behind the arrest of a prominent admiral, or later a mercenary commander or *condottiere*, in the case of the war of Chioggia the final Venetian victory was determined by the same set of circumstances that had defeated the imperial forces of Pepin. The flanking strategy of the Venetian fleet contributed to the victory, but the *coup de grâce* was given by Venice's natural defences. Under their admiral, Vettor Pisani, the Venetians used their knowledge of the lagoon to besiege the Genoese at Chioggia until they were virtually starved into unconditional surrender.

In 1381 peace between Genoa and Venice was mediated by Amadeo of Savoy. What began as a quarrel over commercial rights in the Levant ended with complicated negotiation over territories and possessions on the Italian mainland. Venice's vacillating mainland policies, her antagonizing of the emperor or the patriarch, her intermittent attempts to stem the expansionism of countless petty tyrants or suppress rebellion incited by Hungarians and Austrians, all combined with major defeats at the hands of the Genoese to limit Venice's bargaining powers. She was virtually forced to surrender her two oldest colonial possessions, Dalmatia and the Mark of Treviso.

Only a few years later, however, the Venetians seemed to have adopted a more determined attitude towards foreign policy. In 1386 Corfu became a subject territory of the Republic and two years later territory in the Morea, the ports of Nauplion and Argos, were acquired along with parts of the Albanian coast. At the same time Venice took her revenge on the da Carrara of Padua by joining a league with Gian Galeazzo Visconti of Milan; nearby Treviso and the strategic bishopric of Ceneda were allotted to Venice as a result of their successful joint campaigns.

In the very last years of the century a new spirit was introduced into the arts of the city. The painting of Paolo Veneziano was to retain its influence over the work of the next several generations of Venetian painters; the architecture of the Doge's Palace placed a distinctive stamp, not only on traditional Venetian building patterns, but also on certain elements common to the Gothic vocabulary throughout Europe; now it was the turn of sculpture. In 1387 two tabernacles were designed to be placed in the piers on either side of the chancel near the tomb of Saint Mark. They were Gothic compositions full of a curiously individual mixture of architectural and sculptural elements. They seem in fact to be stone versions of the thrones or architectural backgrounds of fourteenth-century painting, or else based on one of the elaborate gilded frames that often surrounded such altar pieces. The two tabernacles are suitably rich and very ornately decorated with pinnacles and niches. Six years later the same sculptor and his workshop completed the masterful series of large free-standing figures nearby: the Virgin, Saint John the Evangelist and the Twelve Apostles stand atop the long pillared screen that acts as iconostasis between the nave and the sanctuary of the ducal chapel. Each individual figure is a forceful rendering in stone of the monumental solidity and expressiveness that Giotto had introduced to the Veneto in his painting. The entire group is signed by the brothers Jacobello and Pietro Paolo delle Masegne and dated 1393. The commission, like so many others in the long history of the decoration of the ducal chapel came from one of the procurators or administrators of the Marcian

This exquisite small portrait statue represents Venice's sixty-second Doge, Antonio Venier (1382–1400). It is a masterpiece of Venetian gothic sculpture and has often been attributed to Jacobello delle Massegne. Originally the kneeling figure held the staff of the banner of St Mark and thus corresponded to the official iconography of the Republic's coinage.

patrimony, in this case Michele Steno. Jacobello also executed a commission on a smaller scale, only a fragment of which survives – the kneeling figure of the Doge Antonio Venier – a profound reading of personality that is dignified by a rendering of extreme simplicity. The delle Masegne family workshop received increasingly important official commissions in the following century, but perhaps their most easily recognized though little appreciated contribution to Venetian art was their 'Gothicizing' of San Marco. It was the delle Masegne who designed and supervised the addition of the myriad pinnacles, aedicules and kiosks that inspired Ruskin's elaborate comparison of the façade of San Marco with crystallized sea foam.

Just as these additions have given San Marco a characteristic fairy-tale appearance and enhanced its air of exotic richness, so too this final decade saw a large number of Gothic palaces built whose distinctive façades make Venice an essentially Gothic city for many visitors and connoisseurs. By this time the open arcade of the ground and first floor of the Veneto-Byzantine palace of the preceding century had given way to a more compact, more enclosed and more practical use of the limited building space afforded by the small mud islands. Not only were the palaces now built flush with the water's edge, but their façades followed the curve of a small canal to make use of all available space. Late fourteenth-century Gothic palaces illustrate the simple schema that will be much elaborated in the coming decades. At the back was a raised courtyard with a well-head over a cistern; against the back wall of the house an external staircase rose in two flights on pointed arches to the *piano nobile*. On the façade the central bank of windows was made with pointed arches which were quite simple and uninflected. Projecting balconies, once considered so remarkable, did not appear until the following century: at this time *plutei* of carved marble were inserted between the columns to make a solid balustrade, as had been done on the earlier Veneto-Byzantine façades. The late fourteenth-century palace façade was quite plain, with brick walls predominating and a single arch marking the water entrance. Ornament was supplied by occasional dentil or sawtooth moulding made of brick ends and by the carved stone used for capitals and rudimentary tracery. Inside, the Venetian Gothic house had a plan that became traditional in all later palace construction. A central hall ran the depth of the palace, lit by the bank of windows overlooking the water at one end and the courtyard or garden at the other. At this time the windows were unglazed and the hall gained the character of a gallery or portico, reflected in its traditional Venetian name, the *portego*. On either side were the living-rooms heated with their large hooded chimneys. On the ground floor the same layout was repeated with a central hall known as the *andron* or entrance from the water, flanked by smaller rooms used for storage or for the kitchens. The basic materials of the palace – and indeed of most Venetian buildings – remained constant from this time onwards. The building was erected on larch-wood pilings sunk in the mud, above which a raft of planks was laid. Blocks of white stone quarried in Istria made a damp course for the walls at the water line, and above that the principal building material was brick. Coniferous beams were used for the ceilings and crushed marble, which afforded some elasticity, was the traditional Venetian terrazzo flooring. There is a larger number of Gothic buildings in Venice than in any other city in Europe and in the first half of the following century, long after the Gothic style had gone out of fashion elsewhere, many of the most distinctive and characteristic of these Venetian buildings were built.

6

High Gothic into Renaissance
1400-1499

The fifteenth century can be divided into two halves in terms of Venetian culture and civilization. In the first half the spirit of Venetian Gothic reached its fullest realization in works of sculpture and in the masterpieces of painting that survive today. Politically this was the period of Venice's determined expansion on the mainland, and it was no coincidence that most of the family workshops of Gothic stonecutters who established themselves in Venice were of mainland origin. In the extraordinarily rich decade from 1450 to 1460 the most important workshops completed some of the city's finest Gothic palaces, while a new generation of painters was emerging from Byzantine and Gothic traditions to lay the foundations of the Venetian Renaissance. In the second half of the century the Lombardo family brought to Venice styles of architecture and sculpture, of carving and decoration that were to leave their unique imprint on all the arts in the city and to influence a generation of great painters as well as the engravers and the printers of the day.

New artistic influences were slow to make an impression on the conservatism of Venetian cultural attitudes. The Byzantine taste in painting and mosaic work survived longer in Venice than elsewhere in Italy, as did the succeeding Gothic style. There was an almost medieval devotion to the thought and teaching of Aristotle when Platonism and Humanist disciplines permeated *quattrocento* thinking elsewhere. This conservatism did not interfere with two other characteristics inherent in Venetian culture. The Venetians were at first collectors rather than patrons. While it is true that the individual doge or procurator commissioned splendid works of art for the embellishment of the ducal chapel or the public monuments, the merchants and patricians brought to Venice whatever they came across on their voyages that seemed to them rare and beautiful. The ancient necessity of importing building materials and the fact that the first such materials were often columns from the Roman buildings and ruins of the mainland meant that rare marbles, columns and capitals were a substantial part of their early collections. The multiplicity of columns on the façade of their patron's chapel which distinguished it from all other Byzantine buildings, the great columns on the Molo and the precious marble shafts imported to divide the *portego* windows of the Gothic palace façade, were all part of a widespread Venetian attitude. The other characteristic which developed from this collecting instinct was the eclecticism of their taste. The Venetians would use and re-use what they had; the Renaissance ambition to make anew, to build or else to camouflage a building according to pure Vitruvian criteria never gained wide acceptance among Venetians. Gothic decoration had been freely applied to the Byzantine San Marco in the previous century. The great Gothic masterpiece of the Doge's Palace used architectural elements that probably came from the Byzantine Ziani palace, just as the fifteenth-century masterpiece of Venetian flamboyant Gothic architecture, the *Cà d'Oro*, incorporates a water entrance taken from the Byzantine palace of the Zen family that previously stood on the site. Architecture is perhaps the most public of the arts and in some ways the most indicative of the general taste, but painting and sculpture in Venice adapted themselves to the same conservatism and eclecticism. The Venetians did eventually adopt the innovations the Tuscans introduced to painting, but only after these had been modified in a typically Venetian way. Colour and even gold ground remained more characteristic than the depiction of the current theories of space and perspective, foreshortening, musculature or anatomical structure. In sculpture this resulted in a curious irony. The free-standing and especially bas-relief sculpture produced by the Lombardo family at the end of the fifteenth century was in its lineature essentially a refinement of Gothic taste. Treating surfaces and outline with ever increasing sensitivity and delicacy they arrived at a moment when, paradoxically, their sculpture seemed closer to antique work than anything produced elsewhere in conscious imitation of antiquity. Their best carving approximated Greek work, which they could hardly have known, and not the Roman sculpture so much imitated throughout Renaissance Italy.

The first half of the century was a period in which Gothic sculpture seemed to characterize the most highly developed and distinctive elements of Venetian culture and civilization. Throughout Venetian history the arts were always at the service of the state and this was no less true in the early years of the quattrocento. In the first few years of the century Pier Paolo and his son Paolo delle Masegne carved the great Gothic centrepiece for the principal waterfront façade of the new *palatium consilium* that was its ceremonial balcony. The extremely elaborate pinnacled frame is not unlike the delle Masegne treatment of the tabernacles in San Marco, though at the Doge's Palace secular iconography crowns the composition. An enormous sword-bearing figure of Justice stands above the entire composition as a motif of official Venetian iconography that will become more and more popular. This part of the ducal palace housed the legislature, but beneath the hall of the Great Council and also adjacent to it were various magistracies that did serve to mete out justice according to Venetian law. As the Venetians extended their sway over mainland territories their direct administrative responsibilities grew greater. The subject cities of their commercial empire enjoyed a certain autonomy granted because of their great distance from the capital, but the cities of the mainland often had to apply directly to Venice for justice.

In 1403 the war against the da Carrara of Padua resulted in the acquisition of Vicenza, Feltre, Bassano and Belluno. In the next few years the Polesine and then Verona and its territory had become part of the Republic and finally Padua herself was forced to submit to the island city that was to be known throughout her mainland empire as the *Dominante*. There seemed to be no stopping the Venetian forces. Admiral Carlo Zeno won a signal victory over the Genoese at Modon, Zara was reconquered and Dalmatia re-acquired through a treaty in 1409. In the same year the Venetians declared yet another war on their old enemies the Patriarch of Aquileia and the King of Hungary over their claim to lands in the Friuli. With the expansion of Venetian political power on the mainland, her cultural contacts even further afield in Italy began to be of some significance. In 1403 the Doge Michele Steno, who as procurator had commissioned the iconostasis from the delle Masegne, made a formal request to the Signoria of Florence for the loan of Nicolò Lamberti, stonecutter; yet more than a decade was to pass before this Tuscan sculptor began work at the ducal palace. In the meantime there is evidence that Jacopo della Quercia worked in Venice, possibly as early as 1405, on the Gothic tomb of Paolo Savelli, a commander of the Venetian armies in the war against the da Carrara. Savelli's tomb in the Frari Church is the first example of an equestrian monument in Venice and one that established a precedent for the commemoration of the Republic's *condottieri* or mercenary army commanders. Another Tuscan presence that is even better documented than Jacopo's is that of Gentile de Fabriano who from 1409 until 1411 was employed on a series of frescoes in the Doge's Palace. As important as these frescoes may have been, especially in terms of enriching the local vocabulary of International Gothic conventions in painting, very little is known of them and nothing survives. Other evidence of Tuscan contacts does survive, although perhaps not as well documented as the painted history cycles commissioned for the rooms in the very heart of the government.

The year 1410 is frequently given as a late date for the beginning of the carving of the capitals of the palace on the Molo. The presence of workers from Lombardy is unquestioned and in some cases individual hands have been deciphered. Two stylistic tendencies are certainly evident. One represents the growing popularity of the International or Courtly Gothic and includes in a suitably conservative programme renderings of such favourite subjects as the months of the year, the signs of the zodiac, the various crafts and allegories of vices and virtues. Another hand, however, represents a more realistic or naturalistic approach to sculptural subject matter. Matteo Raverti, the architect of Milan's cathedral, is held by many to be responsible for the series representing the strongly marked individualism of Crusader portraits, women's heads and representations of the races and nations of mankind. Raverti is also credited with the two most important bas-relief groups carved in Venice at this time: the *Adam and Eve* at the corner of the palace nearest the Piazzetta and the group representing the *Naked Noah Covered by his Two Sons*. Both of these serve an allegorical function: the severity of good government represented by the punishment of Adam and Eve and the mercy of good government represented by the compassion of Shem and Japheth. The influence of Lombardy can also be seen in the architecture of the beautiful brickwork façade of the Madonna dell'Orto completed in the first decade of the century, but the Gothic aedicular niches of the aisle sections were filled with statues from the local delle Masegne workshop.

Venetian conservatism influenced the curriculum of the school established at this time for the aristocracy on the Rialto. Logic, metaphysics, natural philosophy and science were still taught, according to the medieval precepts of Aristotle, fifty years after Petrarch had advocated the Platonism which through the Humanists came to prevail everywhere else in fifteenth-century Italy. But abstract philosophy or poetic idealism never much appealed to the pragmatic Venetian patrician; besides shrewd businessmen, the schools of Venice trained historians and diplomats in later centuries but hardly any philosophers. The education available to the patrician was either the practical training of a merchant or banker or the experience gained from dedicating his time to the service of the state, or else a combination of the two as in the case of the man elected doge of Venice in January 1414.

The first of the seven doges of the Mocenigo family, Tommaso Mocenigo, had already filled important administrative and diplomatic offices and had been particularly distinguished by high military rank as well. At one point in his career he was appointed *Capitano Generale da Mar* and again *Provveditore in Campo* for the armies at war with the da Carrara of Padua. It seems he was several times involved in actions in the Genoese war: once with the battle fleet of Vettor Pisani at Pola in 1379 and again when one of his merchant ships was captured by the enemy on its return to Venice from Syria. According to Marin Sanudo, the great sixteenth-century diarist and historian, the discourses and orations of Mocenigo were especially impressive. Among his many qualities, it was undoubtedly this particular talent for logic and rhetoric which made him an influential figure in the councils of the government; his harangue delivered at the end of his career, which at once summarized the wealth of the Republic and was a warning against the ambitious policies of Francesco Foscari, remains one of the most often cited documents of Venetian history.

Coincidentally Mocenigo's tenure as doge represents another aspect of Venetian history that has intrigued recent historians. From the election of Mocenigo onwards for the next hundred and fifty years no doge was elected from the twenty-four ancient families of the Republic. This represents a departure from tradition as apparently significant as the eleventh-century legislation against inheritance of the ducal office, although some scholars believe this exclusion of the old families from the highest office was not the result of hidden factionalism but perhaps a case of mere coincidence. It is nonetheless true that the predominance of the new families in the government of the next century coincides with a general modification of traditional policy. The old families had brought Venice not merely to trade, but to rule in the east, a vast undertaking eventually challenged by their commercial rivals, the Genoese. With the very near defeat of Venice, the Republic had called on the patriotism and resources of some of its richest citizens, who contributed generously to the Genoese defeat. These newly rich families were admitted to the patriciate and thus entered the government. At the end of his life Mocenigo addressed the government advocating the traditional commitment to maritime commerce despite his own policies of mainland expansion. His nine-year reign was perhaps too brief for his policies to have been other than forced by circumstance, yet he remains one of the more interesting personalities of Venetian history.

The year after his election the Republic managed to defeat the Patriarch of Aquileia and his ally the King of Hungary. The whole Friuli was ceded to Venice, marking the effective end of the power of the richest prelate in Christendom after the pope, while in 1416 there were great celebrations in Venice for the defeat of the Turkish fleet at Gallipoli. Whereas the former victory was to all intents and purposes definitive, the latter was merely a prelude to interminable encounters with the Turks that would prove the undoing of the entire Venetian empire of the east. With the appearance of a Turkish war fleet in the eastern Mediterranean, the government's increasing commitment to a mainland empire and inevitable embroilment in the complicated alliances and politics of the Italian peninsula, Venice could be said to have entered a period of weakness and potential decline. Overseas the Venetians were now seriously on the defensive and on the mainland their territorial claims would soon be overextended. Yet the great age of Venetian culture was only just dawning.

The Doge Tommaso Mocenigo (1414–23), author of a remarkable summary of Venetian wealth and commerce, is portrayed by Gentile Bellini wearing the linen *camauro* or amice beneath the ordinary stiff gold brocade *corno* or ducal bonnet which was replaced on gala occasions by a jewel-encrusted *corno* of similar shape.

The Ca' d'Oro or Golden House, built for Marino Contarini in the early fifteenth century, was so-called for the gold leaf which was used to pick out the carved ornamentation of its façade. Though it represents the most elaborate gothic façade in Venice, several of the Ca' d'Oro's carved friezes and the watergate arcade are byzantine work.

Tommaso Mocenigo's reign saw the continuation of several projects that vastly enriched the city's fabric. The year 1415 is often given as the early date for the completion of the Gothic decoration of the Molo façade of the Doge's Palace: not only the series of capitals but all the tracery details of the windows of the great hall, where in 1419 the full Great Council met for the first time. Tuscan stonecutters at work on the palace were completing the Gothic decoration of San Marco as well. The numerous kiosks and aedicules designed by the delle Masegne workshops were filled with saints carved in the Lamberti workshop. Nicolò's son, Pietro, was responsible for the Gothic fascia carved to decorate the central upper arch which was opened as a great window after the Byzantine screen-work had been destroyed by fire in the previous century. In several of its details, execution and inspiration, the great fascia represents a Tuscan style of sculpture influenced by Ghiberti. Purely local Gothic traditions of architecture and stonecutting continued in the workshops of the Bon family, who carved the handsome floriate doorway for Santo Stefano in 1420. Venetian painting at this date was still an expression of International Gothic. In 1415 the greatest master of the style, Pisanello, was invited to continue Gentile's frescoes in the Great Council Chamber illustrating the history of the Republic, while in 1421 the most prominent local exponent of this highly elaborate and decorated style of painting, Jacobello del Fiore, painted a heavily embossed panel depicting the figure of Justice surrounded by archangels for one of the many Venetian magistracies.

In 1422 there occurred an incident that is extremely interesting in the history of private and state patronage in the arts and building of Venice. A fine of one thousand ducats had been established by the government to penalize any individual who attempted to alter any part of the ducal palace. Such a fine can be taken to indicate that the government through various committees wished to assume complete corporate control of the patronage for the decoration of the new wing on the Molo. But, as is usually the case with laws that attempt to prevent every eventual abuse, this one inhibited any improvement as well. Thus Mocenigo personally paid the fine so that the highly successful architecture of the Molo wing could be extended on the Piazzetta side to replace the old *palatium justitia* wing of the Ziani building there. The decoration of the new Piazzetta wing was almost entirely by Tuscan stonecutters. At the same time four large, handsome Hercules figures were carved for the northern façade of the ducal chapel. Their attribution to Jacopo della Quercia suggests yet another example of well-known masters imported to work with the Tuscan workshops already established in Venice as a permanent part of her artistic community. Some time in the year 1423 or shortly thereafter the principal sculptor-architect of the ducal palace, Pietro Lamberti, collaborated with Giovanni Martini from Fiesole on a commission for the Doge Tommaso Mocenigo's tomb. The sarcophagus which combines Gothic and early Renaissance motifs reveals its Tuscan paternity in the small corner statue of Saint

George, an almost exact miniature copy of the Saint George which Donatello carved for the Florentine *Orsanmichele* in 1416.

In 1423 Mocenigo died. After personally assuring the continuation of the magnificent state palace – only the public offices were rebuilt in this period – the doge made a public testament in the form of a deathbed oration delivered to a gathering of senators. It was a 'state of the nation' address delivered for political ends, but it is also one of the most important documents of Venetian history:

My Lords, by the weakness in which I find myself, I know that I am near the end of my life.... In my time four millions of debts have been paid off, and there are other six millions owing, which debt was incurred for the wars of Padua, Vicenza, and Verona; we have paid every six months two instalments of the debts, and have paid all my officers and regiments. This our city now sends out in the way of business to different parts of the world ten millions of ducats' worth yearly by ships and galleys, and the profit is not less than two million ducats a year. In this city there are three thousand vessels of one to two hundred *'anfore'* [Venetian measure of capacity] with seventeen thousand seamen; there are three hundred larger ships with eight thousand sailors. Every year there go to sea forty-five galleys with eleven thousand sailors, and there are three thousand ship's carpenters and three thousand caulkers. There are three thousand weavers of silk and sixteen thousand weavers of cotton cloth; the houses are estimated to be worth seven millions and fifty thousand ducats. The rents are five hundred thousand ducats. There are one thousand noblemen whose income is from seven hundred to four thousand ducats. If you go on in this manner you will increase from good to better, and you will be the masters of wealth and Christendom; everyone will fear you. But beware, as you would be of fire, of taking what belongs to others and of waging unjust war, for God cannot endure those errors in princes. Everyone knows that the war with the Turks has made you brave and experienced of the sea; you have six generals fit to fight any great army, and for each of these you have sea-captains, slingers, officers, boatswains, mates, and rowers enough to man one hundred galleys; and in these years you have shown distinctly that the world considers you the leaders of Christianity. You have many men experienced in embassies and in the government of cities, who are accomplished orators. You have many doctors of divers sciences, and especially many lawyers, wherefore numerous foreigners come here for judgment of their differences, and abide by your verdicts. Your mint coins every year a million ducats of gold and two hundred thousand of silver; it also coins yearly eight hundred thousand ducats' worth between *'grossetti, mezzanini, and soldoni'*. You know that the Florentines send us each year sixteen thousand pieces of cloth, which we make use of [in commerce] in Barbary, in Egypt, in Syria, in Cyprus, in Rhodes, in Roumania, in Candia, in the Morea, and in Istria, and every month the Florentines bring into this city seventy thousand ducats' worth of all sorts of merchandise, which amounts to eight hundred and forty thousand ducats yearly and more; and they take back French woollens, catalans, and crimson, and fine corded wool and silk, gold and silver thread and jewellery, with great advantage to the city. Therefore, be wise in governing such a State, and be careful to watch it and to see that it is not diminished by negligence. You must be very careful as to who is to succeed in my place, for by him the Republic may have much good and much evil. ... Many are inclined to Messer Francesco Foscari, and do not know that he is proud and untruthful; he has no principle in his affairs, he has an exaggerated disposition, he grasps at much and holds but little. If he be Doge you will always be at war; he who has ten thousand ducats will not be master of one thousand, he who has two houses will not be the master of one; you will spend gold and silver, reputation and honour, and where you are now the chiefs, you will be the slaves of your soldiers and men-at-arms and of their captains. I could not resist the desire to tell you this opinion of mine. God grant that you may elect the best man, and direct you, and preserve you in peace.

Historians have found Mocenigo's statistics and estimates to be remarkably accurate, but despite his warnings Francesco Foscari was elected doge. Mocenigo's references to his successor seem extremely polemical, especially following such a reasoned account of the state. In tone it might be a rhetorical device applied for political ends and indeed Mocenigo's pleading for peace on the mainland was given the lie by his own policy. Foscari was indeed to prove a hawk, but the role has been shown to have been forced upon him by the aggressive expansionism carried out under his predecessors. Either he had to defend the integrity of the Venetian mainland empire or lose it entirely. But the story of Foscari's foreign policy and even that of his private life, fascinating as they are, are less important to the overall legacy of Venetian culture and civilization than was the final flowering of the Gothic arts and the prelude to the extraordinary artistic achievement of the Venetian Renaissance which took place during his long reign.

In the thirty years of Foscari's rule a number of buildings were erected which embodied the most elaborate development, not only of Venetian Gothic architecture, which still followed typically conservative and conventional patterns, but of the sculptural decoration which enriched them. Two complementary schools of decoration have been distinguished: that bringing the current fashions in carving from Tuscany or Lombardy, and the local workshops such as that of the Bon family. The Golden House or *Cà d'Oro* built around 1425 for Marino Contarini can be taken as the most evolved example of the flamboyant Gothic style in Venice. Yet for all the extraordinarily rich elaboration of carved motifs on the Grand Canal façade of the Cà d'Oro – and it must have seemed even richer when the bas-relief carving was picked out in gold – the house still illustrates Venetian conservatism. The watergate was an arcade from a Veneto-Byzantine palace; the strips of carving inlaid on the façade were also taken from an older palace and used in a way reminiscent of the Veneto-Byzantine incrustation of two centuries earlier; and of course the plan of the Cà d'Oro is in keeping with local convention. The carved decoration of the façade, usually attributed to the Bon family, has its counterpart in the courtyard where Marino Contarini indicated to Matteo Raverti and his Milanese workmen an external staircase made a few years earlier for another Contarini palace to be used as a model for the one at the Cà d'Oro. From now on the precise role of the individual patron is more frequently documented. Contarini also commissioned Bartolomeo Bon to carve a well-head which still stands in the courtyard; there is no doubt that it is one of the most vigorous pieces of transitional sculpture in the city and with the Mascoli altar reredos in San Marco carved by Bartolomeo in 1430, the following year, it shows the increasing influence of the Tuscan taste on the workshops of Venice.

This influence is hardly surprising given the ever increasing commerce with Florence mentioned by Mocenigo in his summary of the state's finances. It must not be forgotten that Mocenigo was trying to prevent the election of his political rival. Foscari's policies included further commitment to mainland expansion possibly at the expense of overseas commerce. Party to his policies were the Tuscan ambassadors desperately seeking a military alliance with their fellow republic. When Foscari was elected a league was almost immediately formed between Florence, Venice and Amadeo VIII of Savoy against the aggressive Duke of Milan, Filippo Maria Visconti. Their league was highly successful in the next five years and the *condottiere* of the Republic's armies, Francesco Carmagnola, gained striking victories over Visconti which resulted in the surrender of much of the territory of Bergamo and Brescia to Venice.

This alliance between the two great Italian republics plus the added territories of Lombardy accelerated the cultural influence of mainland Italy on Venice. In 1425 the Florentine Paolo Uccello was working on the mosaics of the ducal chapel; five years later Andrea Castagno appeared in Venice on a similar commission, but by then the individual Tuscan was outnumbered by local masters who represent the evolution of a distinctively Venetian transition between the Gothic and the early Renaissance. Michele Giambono was still at work in the vocabulary of the International Gothic while Jacopo Bellini still employed the conventions of Byzantium. According to tradition all these men were at work in the thirties and forties on the mosaic decoration of San Marco, not engaged there on works of art that enhanced their individual reputations or demonstrated their mastery of the latest techniques, but contributing virtually anonymously to the continuation of an ancient programme of decoration dedicated to the glory of the state and her patron saint. The masters of the newest Tuscan style and technique in painting were invited to express their talents in the most ancient if not anachronistic Venetian art form, mosaic.

Teaching and education based on the classics which elsewhere in Italy became such an important source of the new Renaissance learning was still in Venice primarily dedicated to the service of the state. In the Chancery School established at the Rialto classical authors provided models, not for individual meditation or expression, but for the more elegant and thus convincing phrasing of treaties, diplomatic *relazioni*, despatches, the recording of debate and the wording of legislation. At the same time Venetian religious houses, engaged in extensive building or rebuilding programmes, also enriched their libraries with collections of manuscripts, incunabula and richly illuminated antiphonals and the like. One such collection attracted Cosimo de' Medici to Venice during his exile from Florence in 1433; so impressed was he by the library of San Giorgio Maggiore that he ordered his companion Michelozzo to design the Benedictines a building worthy to house their collection. The career of the Abbot of San Giorgio, who was Cosimo's host, provides another interesting glimpse of the potential though hypothetical development of a joint Tuscan-Venetian Renaissance. He was Gabriele Condulmer, a Venetian who was elected Pope Eugenius IV two years before Cosimo's arrival in Venice. It was he who presided over the Ecumenical Council held first at Bologna, then Ferrara and finally in Florence when a final attempt was made to reconcile the western and the eastern churches. The Council attracted an influx of learned orthodox prelates many of whom, such as those in the suite of the Emperor John Paleologus, passed through Venice in 1438. A number of these Greeks remained in the west to teach and thus to transmit the treasures of classical Greek literature and philosophy that had been lost to Europe during the so-called Dark Ages. To the Venetians these Greeks were not the harbingers of a new age and learning, they merely constituted a different order of the several ranks of Byzantine Greeks who had long since settled or traded in Venice. A sizeable Greek settlement is recorded in 1400 and the richest and most prominent natives of Crete had been accepted in the ranks of the patriciate since the time of the Genoese wars.

Venetian conservatism in matters of learning, in the survival of Byzantine traditions in painting and in her reluctance to adopt the innovations of Michelozzo or those of Donatello in nearby Padua ten years later can be illustrated in many ways. The Gothic churches built or rebuilt in the first half of the fifteenth century, Sant'Alvise, Sant'Elena, the Carità and its intentional duplicate, San Gregorio, are all of the plain brick single nave type with three polygonal chapels and no transepts. The starkness of their interior and the lack of ornament on their tripartite façades present a striking contrast to the elaborate work Contarini commissioned for his house only a few years before. The extravagant Cà d'Oro remained an isolated example of private lavishness whereas the simple lines of the Venetian Gothic church façade were adopted for even a grand and important church like the Frari which was completed in 1443. This ecclesiastical austerity was in keeping with such personalities as the saintly, ascetic Lorenzo Giustinian, who in 1451 was made first Patriarch of Venice, or with Ludovico Barbo, the zealous Benedictine reformer who was appointed inspector of San Giorgio by Eugenius IV. A number of monastic foundations underwent significant reforms at this time and the stricter or so-called Observant orders became well established in Venice. San Giobbe, for example, was founded with a charitable bequest made by a member of the ancient Contarini family late in the preceding century. It was dedicated to Saint

Job, a dedication deriving from the Byzantine tradition which canonized figures of the Old Testament (in Venice there are churches dedicated to Saints Samuel, Jeremiah and Moses), and was located in the district of Cannaregio near where the emigré silk weavers of Lucca had settled. In 1443 Saint Bernardino of Siena came to preach in Venice and was invited to stay at San Giobbe with his brethren of the Observant Franciscans. The Tuscan reformer became acquainted with Senator Christoforo Moro and predicted that one day this remarkable young man would be doge of Venice. Eventually with the new spirit of reform and renovation, the links with Tuscany both secular and religious, and the protection of a future doge, San Giobbe became one of the most significant monuments of the early Venetian Renaissance.

Only five years before Saint Bernardino arrived in Venice one of the greatest secular monuments commissioned by the state was begun in the highest Venetian Gothic style by the workshop of Bartolomeo and Giovanni Bon. This was the *Porta della Carta*, the precise significance of whose name, the Gate of the Paper, is lost to us. Later when the Giants' Staircase was built and the doges were crowned on its landing, the gate opposite, which led to the Piazzetta, assumed an obvious ceremonial function. But the Porta della Carta was not the principal entrance to the ducal palace; state processions entered and left the palace through the smaller doorway under the arcade of the Molo wing. In size and prominence the Porta della Carta might be compared with the oversized, ornate land gate of a Gothic palace like the Cà d'Oro, where the principal or waterfront entrance was much simpler by comparison. The Porta della Carta also served to join the Piazzetta wing of the ducal palace to the doge's chapel, as the presence of the large bust of Saint Mark might be taken to indicate. Indeed, the gate borrowed elements in its decoration from both these buildings. Lush Gothic foliage was taken from the delle Masegne crowning of the upper arches of San Marco while the tracery was borrowed from the Molo windows of the ducal palace. The door was surmounted by a statue of the doge, Francesco Foscari, kneeling before the lion of San Marco, just as a similar composition including the Doge Michele Steno was part of the delle Masegne balcony. The Porta like the balcony was crowned by a statue of Justice recalling that this gateway would be used by the people of Venice who came to present their petitions and recourses for judgement in the offices of the government magistrates – perhaps it was in allusion to a nearby room for the storage of these papers that the great gateway was named. In the same year that the Carta gate was begun Jacobello del Fiore painted a version of Guariento's immense fresco of the *Coronation of the Virgin* in the Great Council Chamber for Bishop Antonio Correr of Ceneda, and six years later in 1444 the fresco was the model for an altarpiece painted by the founders of the school of Murano, Antonio Vivarini and Giovanni d'Alemagna. Jacobello's version and the later San Pantaleone altarpiece were virtually the last restatements of the older iconography, just as state commissions for the figure of

Justice were no longer usual in Venetian sculpture save for purposes of replacement.

In 1443 the Florentine sculptor Donatello arrived in Padua to execute an equestrian statue in memory of the great Venetian *condottiere*, Erasmo da Narni called Gattamelata, who had died that year. Donatello's commission implied vast repercussions in the arts of Venice and the Veneto although in fact, his influence was assimilated only very conditionally within the workshops of the city and his work in the Veneto was for foreigners, not for Venetians. The Gattamelata statue was erected in Padua as were the bronze bas-reliefs depicting the *Miracles of Saint Anthony*; the extraordinary statue of Saint John the Baptist in the Frari, perhaps carved in Florence as early as 1438, was commissioned by Florentine merchants. Donatello's work stands in splendid isolation in the context of Venetian art, while the work of other Tuscan masters in Venice must be understood as subsidiary to whole architectural and decorative schemes. Tuscans worked virtually anonymously on allegorical bas-reliefs, statues and the carving of capitals for the ducal palace as well as on the mosaic decoration of the palatine chapel. With the passage of the years, however, the intervention of these Tuscan artistic personalities became more pronounced and individual. Castagno's frescoes in the vaults at San Zaccaria make a strong contrast with the delicate Gothic quality of the contemporary altarpieces there which were painted in the ornate artificial style of the International Gothic and set in frames as richly crowned as the arches of San Marco with pinnacles, kiosks and gilded statuary. The statues of Fortitude and Temperance carved by Pietro Lamberti for niches in the Porta della Carta illustrate the tendency towards a Tuscan realism distinct from the floriate elaboration of the Bon Gothic carving. An even more striking illustration of the individualism of Tuscan influence on sculpture is the large bas-relief that turns the corner of the Doge's Palace nearest San Marco. Like the San Zaccaria frescoes and the Murano School altarpieces, the *Judgement of Solomon* is often dated around 1443. It was signed *duo soti Florentini* and has been ascribed to various combinations of artists including Nanni di Bartolo or even Jacopo della Quercia, but the correct ascription is a problem for the art historian. The Venetians saw in the piece a forceful depiction of wisdom of good government that completed the allegorical programme on the immense Gothic building which was supposed to enshrine these virtues. Sin or evil represented by Adam and Eve was severely punished, but severity was tempered with the mercy illustrated by Noah's sons at the far corner, or with the wisdom of Solomon carved nearest the chapel. All these allegories of government were surmounted by the repeated personifications of Justice herself.

In the third and fourth decades of the fifteenth century the government pursued Foscari's policy of war on the mainland. Milanese aggrandizement on the Tuscan and Venetian borders was the principal concern of the Republic. The third Milanese war involved two great commanders. Both were *condottieri*

ABOVE *The Coronation of the Virgin* painted for the Bishop of Ceneda by Jacobello del Fiore was one of the many panels based on the composition of Guariento's vast fresco painted in 1365 for the Hall of the Great Council.

RIGHT The dark blue glass Wedding Cup blown and decorated by Angelo Barovier of Murano in the second half of the fifteenth century. It is one of the oldest documented surviving examples of Venetian glass.

who exemplified the sort of mercenary commander then making considerable impact not only on the military policies of the fifteenth-century Italian states, but also upon their culture. The first of these Venetian *condottieri* was Gattamelata, whose monument is one of the greatest pieces of European equestrian statuary. Just as Donatello's name was linked with the legacy of Gattamelata in Padua, so Castagno and Uccello had commemorated mounted *condottieri* in the Cathedral of Florence. The *condottiere* Carmagnola, who was tried and executed in Venice for treason in 1432, represented the other side of the coin. From 1434 until his death Cattamelata's enemy had been the Visconti general Francesco Sforza, whose career as a *condottiere* outstripped all others in Italy when he made himself duke of the whole Milanese state in 1450. In the meantime the advantage in the Milanese wars fell fairly consistently to the Venetians who won or regained lands near Verona, Trento and finally after the peace of 1441, from Mantua. In the same year Ravenna and Cervia also came under the sway of the Republic.

These wars did not seem to affect seriously the prosperity of the Republic. Sumptuary laws were enacted at just this time forbidding long trains to women's gowns and much is made in the chronicles of 1441 of the lavish private celebrations laid on for the wedding of the doge's son Jacopo Foscari to the heiress Lucrezia Contarini. In 1444 the wooden bridge at the Rialto collapsed under the crowds that had gathered on it to watch the entry into Venice of the Marquis of Ferrara's bride. Among the many native industries that flourished in this period, the glass blowers and sellers began to display talents and techniques that were not surpassed elsewhere for several centuries. The Barovier wedding cup, the earliest survival of the glass works of Murano, is usually dated 1437 and is the first example of enamel work on glass since antiquity; two years later over twelve glass factories were recorded in the Venetian lagoon. This activity coincided to a certain extent with the development of a school of painting native to Murano whose principal was Antonio Vivarini, at first under the northern influence of Giovanni d'Alemagna and later, from 1450, in partnership with his brother Bartolomeo Vivarini. The school of Murano carried on the lavish Gothic conventions of Jacobello and Gentile da Fabriano, as can be seen in the Santa Sabina altarpiece in San Zaccaria or in a *Madonna and Saints* of 1446. A splendid example of the transition from these late examples of the local Gothic style to painting containing distinct Renaissance motifs is the unique work of Antonio da Negroponte, the *Madonna Enthroned* at San Francesco della Vigna, supposedly painted in the middle of the century. Such a painting, despite the classical bas-relief allusions in the Madonna's throne, is still thoroughly Gothic in feeling.

But there is more than one example of this transitional phase which began to affect the workshops of the Venetian painters in the fifties. Certainly the most lasting influences were to be found developing in the family of Jacopo Bellini. The father, Jacopo, was clearly influenced by Gentile da Fabriano and the more delicate Pisanello. In one of his few surviving works, signed and dated 1448 and now in the Louvre, the Madonna and Child are depicted with a wistful grace and mystical delicacy that is as unmistakably Gothic as is the jewelled crown or the wrought gold halo of the Madonna. Jacopo also illustrates the over-elaboration of Gothic fantasies, as in the large monochrome *Scenes of the Passion*, perhaps painted in collaboration with Antonio Vivarini, where the background bristles with the extravagant pinnacled architecture of the Gothic imagination. This extraordinary painting has been often partly attributed to Jacopo for its similarity with his famous sketchbooks now divided between the British Museum and the Louvre: there is the same obsessive elaboration of fantastic architecture on an unreal scale. Several of the subjects depicted in the sketchbooks are from the Bible, but others illustrate classical themes. There is a certain similarity between Jacopo's rendering of sharply receding space and perspective, his use of the trimmings of antiquity, and of the fresco cycle that Jacopo's future son-in-law Andrea Mantegna was working on in Padua between 1448 and 1455. These scenes from the life of Saint James, extensively damaged in World War II, mark a turning point in the history of painting in the north of Italy. The commission to decorate the Ovetari chapel in the church of the Eremitani dedicated to Saints Philip and James was originally given to the Murano school of Antonio Vivarini and Giovanni d'Alemagna, assisted by Niccolò Pizzolo and Mantegna. At this time Mantegna was under the influence of his adoptive father, Francesco Squarcione, who had virtually founded a Paduan Renaissance by absorbing from Donatello and other early fifteenth-century Florentines their enthusiasm for antiquity. Mantegna's original use of classical decorative motifs in religious painting and his talent for rendering them in a strikingly realistic, *trompe-l'œil* manner, gained him wide popularity for his distinctive adaptations from antiquity. Not only did his treatment of decoration, perspective and architecture influence other artists, his modelling of anatomy, drapery and even desiccated landscape cast in a harsh light was likewise widely adopted by painters of the day. Even the mid-fifteenth-century mosaic of the *Death of the Virgin* in the Mascoli chapel in San Marco can be taken as an example of Tuscan influence expressed in a composition close in feeling to Mantegna's classicism.

But Mantegna's classicism was not the only new force working a radical change in the arts of Venice during the fifties: influences from farther afield than Padua were felt in the city's workshops. Precisely in this decade Leon Battista Alberti was commissioned to erect a new façade for the Church of San Francesco in Rimini henceforth to be known as the *Tempio Malatestiano*. The materials used there, easily-carved white stone from Istria and the coloured marbles quarried near Verona, were widely adopted in later Venetian façades. Several architects who later settled in Venice were said to have worked on the building. During this period the ruler of Rimini, Sigismundo Malatesta, was heavily involved in the complex politics of northern Italy, sometimes allied to Venice and at other times embroiled in the affairs of Florence, Milan, Brescia and Bergamo. Piero della Francesca, the most noteworthy Tuscan painter at his brilliant court, is supposed to have visited Venice in 1451 when he painted the panel of *Saint Jerome with a Donor* now in the Academy Gallery. However, his cold and extremely scientific approach to perspective influenced Venetian painters much less than did the Flemish and German colours, compositions and techniques that began to appear in Venice at this time. Humbler craftsmen from the Marches and Romagna also worked in Venice at the mid-century, and artisans from Faenza were probably responsible for the terracotta vault of the Martini chapel at San Giobbe. The blue, white and yellow glazed tiles and the high relief portrait medallions of the Evangelists in the spandrels recall the colours and techniques of the della Robbias who had introduced enamelled terracotta in Florence only a decade earlier. The chapel itself, built for the Martini, a family of silk workers originally from Lucca, was said to have been built by Alberti's disciple Bernado Rossellino; whatever the case, it is the most Tuscan artistic ensemble in Venice. In 1455 the circle of Alberti and his disciples designed and built for Pietro Barbo the Venetian Embassy in Rome, the Palazzo Venezia, which contained the prototype of many Italian Renaissance palace courtyards and monastic cloisters.

But for all these new influences indirectly linked with Venice in the fifties, the private patrons of the arts and the appropriate government officials were extremely cautious in their commissions and did not immediately accept the novelties imported from Florence, Rome, Rimini or even nearby Padua. Padua and to a lesser extent Florence did provide the model for some significant innovations in the cultural life of Venice during the mid-fifteenth century. In 1450 a school of Humanities was finally established in the heart of the city at San Marco. Classical letters and moral philosophy were taught and the curriculum included Platonist studies of the sort that were already accepted at Florence. A generation of scholars who were heirs to the teaching brought to the west by Greeks attending the Council of Florence now arrived in Venice. The most famous among them were Filelfo, George of Trebizond, Giorgio Merula and Giorgio Valla. Filelfo was a citizen of the Venetian colony in Constantinople and in the best itinerant traditions of Humanist teaching and scholarship he eventually left Venice for the more stimulating atmosphere of Florence. Despite the prestige of these teachers the Council of Ten ruled that the older school of the Republic, that of the Chancery at Rialto, should not be granted the charter of a university. A generation earlier the ancient university at Padua had come under the governance of Venice as a result of the submission of the da Carrara and the Venetians were prudently apprehensive of exposing their extremely conservative government to too much close scrutiny by men of the new learning. The council's decision reflected their determination to keep potential criticism and boisterous students at bay. The Venetians were being made aware at this very moment of the precious legacy of stable government

The façade of Palazzo Foscari, one of the two magnificent palaces constructed in the 1450s on the Grand Canal (the other belonged to the Giustinian family). Palazzo Foscari was built by the Bon workshop for the Foscari family of the doge.

they had to preserve. From Florence itself, and indeed from the pen of one of her leading humanists, Poggio Bracciolini, came praise of the Venetian Republic and of what began to be called the 'Ventian Constitution' in an essay published in 1450.

The humblest Venetian must have been aware of the considerable attention the riches and government of his city were attracting from every quarter; the Emperor Frederick III came to the city in 1451–2 and the celebrations for his reception were on a lavish scale. A regatta was staged and fifteen houses were requisitioned in the parish of San Giovanni Grisostomo to house his courtiers. The emperor himself lodged for a while with a rich merchant of the citizen class called Francesco Amadi whom he honoured with the rank of Count Palatine in the Empire. The 1450s also saw the construction of two of the most magnificent Gothic palaces on the Grand Canal: both were built at the bend or *volta del canal* and provided a splendid backdrop for the regattas staged on this stretch of the Grand Canal. The earlier of the two was the double house built for the ancient Giustinian family; this was followed by the neighbouring palace built by the Bon workshop for the Foscari family of the doge himself. In both houses the handsome tracery of the principal windows was copied from almost identical motifs introduced at the Doge's Palace almost one hundred years before. On the uppermost frieze of the Foscari palace their coat of arms appears supported by two bas-relief cupids that suggest the taste of a later age, although despite such hints at Renaissance classical motifs, Venice was at this time still pre-eminently a city of Gothic building. The palaces, the churches, the bell towers, the monasteries and public buildings all contributed to this impression. Many of the masterpieces of Gothic painting visible in the city, such as the frescoes of Guariento, Pisanello, Gentile da Fabriano and Jacobello are now lost to us, but the buildings remain. The Procuratie and the Library would not be built for another hundred years, the stone bridge at the Rialto even later; and that great landmark of the Venetian scene, the Salute Church, would not be completed for over two hundred years.

While to the average Venetian the mid-century embellishment of the city's Gothic fabric must have seemed impressive, the councils of the government were alternately concerned with the implication of events both on the far horizon and with events so close to home as to be almost entirely hidden in their true meaning from the city at large. The most distant, yet momentous and far-reaching of these events, was certainly the fall of Constantinople to the Turks in 1453. This event, which shocked and horrified the west, and indeed all of Christendom, provoked a rather typical reaction on the part of the Venetians. A trade agreement was signed with the conquering Sultan Mohammed II in May of the following year, and it was probably shortly after this that Venice introduced trade in Seljuk and other oriental or Turkey carpets to the west. By contrast to these distant developments the political power of certain high officials in Venice was deflected from the traditional service of the state to an abuse of office which permitted that most feared weakness of a closed government to flourish: faction. A small clique managed to seize virtual control over election to the powerful Council of Ten. With this power, these political rivals of the doge pursued a policy of persecution, striking at Foscari through his son Jacopo. Twice exiled, tortured and accused of murder in 1451, Jacopo was finally entrapped into a charge of treason. By deftly manipulating the doge's role in the subsequent trial and conviction of his own son, the Council of Ten succeeded in forcing Foscari's abdication in 1457. Broken-hearted after more than a third of a century of government, he retired to his magnificent palace on the Grand Canal, and is said to have died on hearing the bells pealing to announce his successor. The story of the persecution and pathetic death of Francesco Foscari became one of the legends of the Venetian people, but the government immediately realized the frightening implications of the doge's deposition. It was quickly proved that the abdication had been forced by a political clique on falsified grounds. Foscari's opponents were too powerful to be punished, but in the funeral orations pronounced in honour of the late doge he was completely exonerated, and the government saw to it that the unlimited powers of the Council of Ten from henceforth came under considerable scrutiny.

Foscari's tomb in the chancel of the Franciscan church is one of the most elaborate statements of the Venetian Gothic funerary movement. It consists of the traditional sarcophagus covered with a full-length effigy of the doge, all suspended beneath a heavily draped canopy in stone. The tomb was designed by Antonio Bregno and is full of High Gothic feeling, but the figures of Virtues, by now obligatory on a ducal tomb, were carved by Antonio Rizzo and represent an infiltration of Renaissance artistic taste in a flamboyant Gothic setting. Such a mixture of styles, where the dominant feeling is still Gothic, is carried on in two other building projects associated with Foscari's name. The Foscari Arch behind the Porta della Carta and the Foscari Loggia of the ducal palace were not completed until five years after the doge's death. The loggia was an open section in the middle of the first floor of the Piazzetta wing where a fair of local crafts was held on certain feast days and later in honour of the dogaressa's state entry. The Foscari arch opened from the vaulted passage behind the Carta Gate and was a full Roman arch surmounted by a forest of Istrian stone gables and pinnacles flanked by niches later filled with statuary in the early Renaissance style. The arch was completed at the same time as the loggia, although it had been begun as early as 1450 by Antonio Bregno, the architect of the great doge's tomb.

The 1460s represent another decade of transition in which foreign and local influences and innovations were accepted in varying degrees; much that was being made in the new Renaissance style, for example, was hardly known at all to the Venetians at large. Fra Mauro's map of the world of 1459, though essentially medieval in concept, became the charter of a highly important school of geographers and cartographers, although the Venetian who could read a map was still more concerned with the less learned maps or portolans that charted the trade routes to the east. The Chinese porcelain given to the Doge Pasquale Malipiero by Sultan Mohammed II in 1461 might have had tremendous repercussions on western art, trade and industry, but that influence lay dormant for the moment; an even more intriguing example of cultural exchange was the loan of Jacopo's son, Gentile Bellini, as a painter to the court of the sultan, though his influence on Muslim art proved negligible; Bellini was, like the Chinese porcelain, merely a gift for the sovereign's private pleasure.

A humbler art like the wood carving that was practised in the city was undoubtedly more widely known. Private houses and most public buildings still had beamed ceilings, while rooms designed to be impressive, like the Hall of the Great Council or the nave of a church, were covered with a distinctive compromise between light, strong beams and the impracticable stone vaults of buildings raised on firm foundations. The Venetian compromise was made in wood in the shape of an inverted ship's keel. In the 1450s, however, a remarkable flat ceiling was carved for the large meeting-room on the upper floor of the Scuola Grande della Carità, one of the oldest and richest of the *scuole* in the city. This ceiling is Gothic in feeling, decorated as it is with a motif of eight winged gilded cherubim. The stalls and intarsia work of 1468 in the choir of the Frari, illustrating the Renaissance fascination with perspective, derived from work done by the Lendinara brothers for the shrine of Saint Anthony of Padua. One craft, however, that seems completely indigenous was that of lacemaking. Dandola Malapiero is mentioned in 1462 as a patroness of a nascent industry, thus establishing the traditional encouragement given to lace makers by patrician ladies and later by the doge's wife, the dogaressa.

But as Gothic as the sixties may have appeared to the average contemporary Venetian, the student of Venetian culture is fascinated by the exceptions to the rule, by the appearances of novelty and innovation and the first assertions of individual genius over the workshop productivity of earlier periods. While the Venetians were struggling to defend their territories in the Peloponnese against the Turkish attack a remarkable ceremonial land entrance was built to the Arsenal. This gate, as significant a piece of secular architecture as the Porta della Carta, is widely recognized as the first appearance of Renaissance architecture in Venice. There is no doubt that its architect, Antonio Gambello, who had previously worked on Gothic building, had a Roman triumphal arch in mind and since it is dated 1460, it is indeed the first such construction in Venice. But Venetian eclecticism raises its head even here, and the capitals of Gambello's gate are not based on one of the classical orders as might be expected, but are instead a successful re-use of original eleventh-century capitals carved in an entirely Byzantine fashion. A year later a purely Tuscan kind of heavy stone rustication was laid for the ground floor of a great palace begun

The battlemented towers marked the water entrance to the fortified Arsenal shipyards. The land entrance was a triumphal arch built in 1460 by Antonio Gambello and was the first example of Renaissance classical architecture in Venice.

in the parish of San Samuele for Francesco Sforza, Duke of Milan. As though emblematic of contemporary shifting alliances and cynical treaties, the building was never completed. Remarkably the Palazzo Non Finito has been attributed to the Bon workshop and thus indicates, as does the example of Gambello, that the most highly developed workshop of Gothic stonecutters and sculptors was capable of a sudden stylistic volte-face in order to introduce in Venice a distinctively Florentine contribution to Renaissance architecture (and one intrinsically unsuited to a Venetian building site). Nonetheless, such innovation was still an exception to the rule of Venetian conservatism.

The emergence of the Renaissance often seems to assume the characteristics of a volte-face, or at least of a radical change, and even with a mass of agreed dates and known personalities it is extremely difficult to discover exactly how and why this new turn of taste and events came about. Powerful and important individuals may have played a decisive role, but it is also difficult to judge the degree of their influence. The election of the Venetian Pietro Barbo as Pope Paul II did not procure any particular advantage to his native city, though his reign (1464–71) corresponds with one of the most fertile periods in the development of the new local style. In 1462 the Doge Pasquale Malipiero died and that year is the *terminus a quo* for the work on his tomb in San Zanipolo where the ducal funerals began to be held. This monument marks the first appearance in Venice of the stonecutter-sculptor Pietro from Solaro near Lugano. Pietro's training was such that he and his family became known as the Lombardo family, although they did not come from Lombardy and their distinctive contribution to Venetian architecture, sculpture and taste in decoration is not known in Venice as Lombard, but rather as Lombardesque. Many of the elements of this style are present in the doge's tomb and will be repeated in the many other ducal tombs completed by Pietro, his family and their workshop. There is no doubt that certain details of the Malipiero tomb derive from Tuscan sources and particularly from Bernardo Rossellino, but other features of the monument depend on Venetian convention such as the Gothic canopy over the doge's effigy. The result is eclectic and yet distinctively Lombardesque and therefore typically Venetian. In 1464 Pietro Lombardo was commissioned to design a tomb for a Tuscan jurist who died in Padua. This monument is quite different in feeling and in Venice may be compared only to the Tuscan or Mantegnesque–Paduan architectural background of the Mascoli chapel mosaics. Broad fluted corinthian pilasters supporting a tall entablature with heavy swags and garlands of fruit are distinctive of the Paduan style whereas Lombardo's Venetian style was altogether lighter and less ponderously classical: the flat surfaces of both slender pilasters and frieze were carved with graceful, convoluted arabesques of vine and plant leaves, of stems and tendrils, delicate birds and occasionally fanciful faces and figures all interwoven in a harmonious pattern. The most constant architectural feature of the tombs and buildings designed and decorated by the Lombardo family was the lunette or semi-circular arch; the lunette above a doorway or surmounting a wall tomb was often filled with a sensitive bas-relief of half figures, such as the pietà in the Malipiero monument. Frequently the lunette was flanked by standing figures, usually the Virtues of funerary iconography, swathed rather than draped in the pencil-thin folds of a mantle or toga; the ends and apex of the lunette were often decorated by rosette-like acroteria. The overall harmony of finely carved surfaces, statuary and simple clean architecture appealed to the Venetian taste to such an extent as to influence all the visual arts of the early Venetian Renaissance until well into the beginning of the sixteenth century.

In 1467 the death of the commander Vettor Cappello, who had valiantly attempted the defence of the Peloponnese against Turkish aggression, resulted in the commissioning of a handsome funerary monument quite different in feeling from the Malipiero wall tomb, although the sculptor-architect Antonio Rizzo certainly felt the influence of the Lombardo workshop. The life-size figure of the commander, enframed in a lunette, is kneeling before the standing figure of Saint Helen with a bas-relief sarcophagus in the background. The monument was designed as an arch over the main door of the Gothic monastery dedicated to Sant'Elena. The figure is a moving portrait of an old man sheathed in a delicately rendered suit of engraved ceremonial armour; the pose recalls the kneeling doge above the Porta della Carta or depicted on the Venetian ducat rather than that of a funerary monument. Rizzo excelled in the carving of free-standing figures and probably in these years finished the famous statues of Adam and Eve for the Foscari arch. The Adam is one of the most powerful statues of the early Venetian Renaissance and much more expressive than Rizzo's free-standing figures for later tombs.

If the death of a doge and a Venetian commander introduced two artists whose work influenced Venetian taste in sculpture for the remainder of the fifteenth century, there were two other personalities at that time who also made signal contributions to Venetian culture and civilization. The first was the great scholar and former Greek Orthodox cleric, Cardinal Bessarion, who in 1468 donated his precious library to the Republic. In 1469 some of the first generation of German printers arrived in Venice and in that same year John of Speyer published, under a privilege granted him by the Senate, Pliny the Elder's *Historia Naturalis* and Cicero's *Ad Familiares*. Bessarion's gift made of the state a great repository of invaluable manuscripts, while the German printers and their followers helped to transform this wealth, not into a source of moral and philosophical speculation as would have been done in Florence, but into a much more Venetian enterprise – a local art and industry, the distribution of whose finished product would result in one of the most conspicuous Venetian contributions to the European cultural inheritance. The second person whose actions in 1468 were to have a lasting effect on Venice was Catherine Cornaro, the daughter of one of the wealthiest Venetian feudatories in Crete. In 1468 she married James of Lusignan, King of Cyprus, whose death five years later would result in Venice's acquisition of that rich Mediterranean property and the subsequent struggle against the Turk to keep it.

If the Venetian Renaissance in architecture began in 1460 with the construction of Gambello's gate at the Arsenal, by the end of the decade an architect had appeared in Venice who was to combine elements from the Lombardo vocabulary with his own probable training under Florence's Leon Battista Alberti to produce a style of building both unique and distinctively Venetian. Mauro Coducci began work on the façade of a church for the Camaldolese hermit friars at San Michele in Isola where the learned Fra Mauro had drawn his great map of the world only ten years earlier. This first Renaissance church façade grafted on to the Gothic building was extremely simple and very Albertian: the rusticated Istrian stone facing and a deep shell-fluted lunette recall, in shape and position Alberti's intended lunette for the Tempio Malatestiana. While Coducci was completing the work at San Michele, Pietro Lombardo was called to San Giobbe in 1470 to carry out a programme of enlargement and redecoration. In 1471 he sculpted a graceful Lombardesque doorway with a bas-relief lunette, three finial-like statues, and delicately carved supporting pilasters. He then began work on the extension of the chancel which he separated from the nave by a beautifully carved and decorated semi-circular archway.

In discussing the new developments in the arts of Venice during the sixties the most significant, and in many ways the most familiar one, has been left until last. This is of course the art of painting which in Venice evolved in a gradual way. There were not the abrupt innovations of architecture, such as the widespread use of the round versus the pointed arch, or the appearance of the classical orders to oust the clustered leaf capital of Venetian Gothic. Venetian sculpture, which could be said to have evolved from the traditions of Lombard Gothic stonecutters' workshops, was generally subsidiary to its architectural context in a large wall tomb, or was an integral part of a building, such as in the allegorical carving at the ducal palace. The distinctive characteristics of Venetian painting evolved very slowly, clinging to many conventions that would have been dismissed as anachronistic elsewhere. Thus the golden embossing, the richly coloured and patterned robes of the International Gothic were more easily assimilated by the Venetian school of Byzantine icon painting and mosaic making than were the more scientific innovations introduced in painting by Giotto. Colour was always more important to the Venetian painter than were learned theories of perspective; even Piero della Francesca's supposed visit to Venice in 1451 did not alter that fact.

The forceful realism and lapidary classicism of Mantegna might have had as little influence as had Castagno or the master of the Mascoli mosaics, were it not for the strong link Mantegna forged with a Venetian workshop through marriage. Mantegna's initial influence on Venetian painting reduces itself to the banal factor of his marriage to Jacopo Bellini's daughter Nicolosia in 1453, while he was still working on the Ovetari chapel frescoes begun by the Murano school under Antonio Vivarini and his brother-in-law Giovanni d'Alemagna. A few years after his marriage, and just before he began to be extensively engaged on commissions at various courts, Mantegna painted a picture that helps define his place in the evolution of Venetian painting. The subject was *The Agony in the Garden* and the composition can be related to a study made in his father-in-law's sketchbooks. His brother-in-law Giovanni, who was to embody the whole development of Venetian painting for over a generation, made his own version of the painting about four years later in 1460. Much has been written about the comparison of these two paintings and the relationship between the brothers-in-law. Bellini's version is the more Venetian, the more lyrical and richly coloured of the two. At this early stage in his career, however, Bellini's landscapes were frequently influenced by Mantegna as, for example, in the background of the Correr *Transfiguration*.

Giovanni Bellini's early painting was also influenced by other currents. The so-called *Madonna Greca* in the Brera, which was commissioned by one of the magistracies of the state, was originally painted with a Byzantine golden ground. The triptychs he painted for the church of the Carità between 1460 and 1464 were composed of single figures, some of which are extremely close to the Murano school and especially to the delicate figures of Antonio Vivarini. In his treatment of anatomy, too, Bellini takes a certain softness of outline from the few undraped figures Antonio painted, but the most influential of his anatomy instructors was again his brother-in-law Mantegna. The lineature and sculptural handling of sinewy muscles emphasized by an intensely contrasting light and shadow appeared in many of Giovanni's pietà, and most strikingly in the figure of Saint Sebastian from the altarpiece painted for the Dominicans probably in the second half of the sixties. Saint Sebastian and the pietà were favourite subjects of this period and were quite in keeping with the almost Tuscan severity and asceticism of Mantegna's tortured version of Sebastian's martyrdom, now in Vienna. Mantegna's influence was assimilated by more than one Venetian painter. Another brother-in-law who became well known for his large narrative canvases, Gentile Bellini, continued to imitate Mantegna's desiccated landscapes of stratified rock while Antonio Vivarini's brother, Bartolomeo, adapted Mantegna's heavy linear treatment of hair and drapery to his own vivid Venetian palette.

Venetian painters of this generation might easily have continued under the influence of Mantegna and perhaps developed like Carlo Crivelli, who left Venice in 1457. He took with him a Mantegnesque repertoire of harshly delineated figures and garlands of heavy fruits as well as the embossed haloes and gilded stucco-work derived from the metallic motifs of Jacobello and Giambono's International Gothic. Instead a lyrical note prevailed in Venice and the most typical Bellini subject became the two-thirds-length Madonna and Child, partly derived from the *madonnieri* and their icon-like work. In 1475 there appeared in Venice a single figure who was to supplant Mantegna's influence completely. Antonello da Messina was so significant for the development of painting, not only in Venice but in all of Italy, that he was credited with introducing Giovanni Bellini and the Venetians to the technique of painting in oils. Whatever the truth of this debatable claim, the year 1475 may be taken as the moment in the history of European art when the Venetians, especially their prime representative for the next thirty years, Giovanni Bellini, became heirs to the rich northern traditions of Flemish painting. Just before the appearance of Antonello, Bellini painted his own interpretation of a traditional Venetian subject, the *Coronation of the Virgin*, for the church of Saint Francis at Pesaro in the Marches near Urbino. This great painting, still in its original frame, illustrates Bellini's mastery of perspective, his splendid sense of composition in the flanking four saints and a typically delightful landscape framed by the back of the throne which Christ and his mother share. The frame-like throne and the frame surrounding the painting itself demonstrate the inextricable relationship that existed between the shallow picture space depicted in Venetian painting and the space defined by architecture. The details and taste of this architecture are unmistakably Lombardesque. The picture's frame is composed of delicately carved pilasters and entablature, while within the painting the Lombardesque throne is inlaid with precious marble plaques and roundels of the sort that distinguish Pietro Lombardo's work at Santa Maria dei Miracoli and at the Palazzo Dario, both built within the following decade. Bellini does not otherwise use much architecture, nor sharply receding perspective depth in his compositions. When architectural elements do appear or where the contemporary frame survives, the Lombardesque motifs are obvious. For example there is a Madonna seated on a Lombardesque throne adoring a sleeping Child painted in 1475, now in the Accademia Gallery; and much later there were the organ doors painted for Lombardo's church of Santa Maria dei Miracoli, where the *Annunciation* is set in a room entirely panelled in slabs of veined marble exactly like that employed to face the interior walls of the church itself.

Otherwise Bellini's use of architectural backgrounds in his painting followed another innovation traditionally ascribed to Antonello, the *sacra conversazione*. This, like the introduction of oil painting, was supposedly due to Antonello's training under Flemish masters and particularly in the Van Eyck school. Antonello first introduced this new concept of composition in the altarpiece he painted for San Cassiano in 1476. Partly ruined fragments of it exist in Vienna. The idea, which so influenced Venetian painting, had already been partly anticipated by Bellini in the Pesaro altar. It consisted of a gathering of saints standing near the enthroned Virgin; these holy figures appear to be linked by a mystical bond beyond the comprehension of the spectator, a sort of sacred conversation group. Bellini particularly knew how to capture the mystical atmosphere of Antonello's concept and many of his most important later paintings are based on this composition. Where the mystical atmosphere and remote attitudes of the saints seemed to exclude the worshipper entirely, Bellini and the Venetians sometimes introduced a single or small group of cherubim or angel musicians, partly derived from Gothic convention, happily strumming, plucking and playing away, undisturbed by the high import of the rest of the scene.

The period when all this superior artistic activity was evolving was not exclusively a period of high culture and spiritual growth. It was also a time of considerable struggle for the Venetians, as the Turks attempted to conquer the last territories remaining loyal to the fugitive emperor of Constantinople. The Turk concentrated his attacks on the emperor's stronghold in the Peloponnese, where the Venetians had ruled since the establishment of the Latin empire of the east two hundred and fifty years earlier. Despite the valiant efforts of commanders like Vettor Cappello, one bastion after another, such as Negroponte and Scutari, fell to the Turks in the 1470s. In 1477 Turkish forces crossed the Balkans and invaded the Friuli. In the next year the Senate, having paid for part of this warfare with a legacy from one of her most successful *condottiere* finally determined on a monument to him. However, more than a decade was to pass before the great equestrian statue to the memory of Bartolomeo Colleoni was completed. The Colleoni monument marked an isolated appearance in Venice of 'High Renaissance' sculpture, an anticipation partly accounted for by the fact that the original commission was given to a foreigner, the Florentine Andrea del Verrocchio; the modelling of the horse itself has even been attributed to sketches by Verrocchio's pupil Leonardo da Vinci. In 1479, the year this Renaissance statue was commissioned, the richest Venetian merchants were still building Gothic palaces for themslves. The finest of that year was certainly the Palazzo Soranzo-Van Axel, built on an intersection of canals leading from the heart of the city directly to Rialto. Like many other Gothic palaces it incorporated carved friezes, capitals and a colonnade from an older house of the Byzantine period. Such a late date for an important Gothic palace underlines the conservatism of the Venetian merchant class.

It was the government and its highest servants who in the last quarter of the fifteenth century anticipated the full acceptance of a Renaissance taste. Yet the government could not concern itself exclusively with the city's adornment. In 1476 a *Sala d'Armi* or armoury for the storage of arms was built within the precincts of the Arsenal, and was considered of such crucial importance to the Republic that it could not be shown on the great woodcut map that was made of the city at the end of the century. Part of the collection of arms housed there is now preserved in the ducal palace, a unique example in Europe of a state armoury preserved intact. Three years before, in 1473, the state had public ovens built near the Arsenal to supply provisions for the merchant and defence fleets. These utilitarian buildings were not built in the new style but on Gothic lines, just as the ancient Byzantine church of San Giovanni in Bragora in one of the city's poorer quarters was rebuilt in 1475 to the simple Gothic taste of an earlier generation. A much more ambitious Gothic project had been begun by the architect Antonio Gambello at the convent of San Zaccaria. The traditionally conservative plan of nave and side aisles ending in three polygonal apse chapels, where the architect could display tall lancet windows with tracery, were here elaborated into a full ambulatory behind the high altar with four radiating polygonal chapels. The ambulatory was not covered by a wooden ceiling as was the nave of the humbler San Giovanni, but was vaulted. The lower order of the façade of San Zaccaria was begun with plinths and a rich facing of coloured inlaid marble. That part of the building finished in Gothic taste proceeded slowly for more than thirty years, until 1480, when the project was undertaken in an entirely different spirit by Mauro Conducci.

Until then the principal Renaissance structures in Venice were the wall tombs of her doges. Antonio Rizzo designed a huge monument to the Doge Niccolo Tron that stood opposite Francesco Foscari's Gothic tomb in the chancel of the Frari. Rizzo's design rose from the floor as a magnificent five-storey setting for the display of free-standing figures such as Virtues, shield-bearing knights and the doge himself. The figures stand in tight niches set in the pilasters and frieze of the tall composition. This same arrangement was adopted with a greater feeling for space and harmonious balance by Pietro Lombardo in his monument to the Doge Pietro Mocenigo begun in 1476. In Lombardo's version the figures that stood in the lower frieze became twin caryatids or supporters of the ducal sarcophagus, on which a magnificently draped armour-clad oversize figure of the doge now stands. This central part of the composition is framed in a three-storey arch which gives unity to the various niches and figures which divide the sides of the monument. At the same time that Pietro Lombardo was displaying his mastery of free-standing statuary he, or more probably his workshop, executed two commissions illustrating the Lombardo taste in bas-relief. The first, of 1476, was to complete the upper order of bas-relief busts of saints on each side of the entrance to the monks' choir in the nave of the Frari, and the second, recorded in 1478, was the charming and naïve decoration of the Giustinian chapel in the old church of San Francesco della Vigna.

It was in the last two decades of the century, however, that the Lombardo and their workshops were to change the face of the city. A period of peace undoubtedly benefits any extensive rebuilding, and providentially, the government came to terms with their determined antagonist the Sultan Mohammed II in 1479. The treaty, which was negotiated by a secretary of the Republic in the absence of the *bailo*, or resident ambassador, involved the cession of

Scutari, Albania and the island of Lemnos, and the payment of a tribute of one hundred thousand ducats for the retention of commercial privileges in the Ottoman Levant. The secretary responsible for the treaty was one Giovanni Dario, who was richly rewarded by both the sultan and the Republic for his successful negotiation of an end to hostilities. The Republic rewarded Dario with the munificent gift of a plot of land. After peace with the Sublime Porte seemed secure Venice's principal concern was once again with her mainland territories. In the meantime Dario's achievements as a successful servant of the state in the most important of her resident embassies was enshrined in the much admired Palazzo Dario, built for him on the Grand Canal by the Lombardo workshop. On the lower part of the façade Dario had inscribed in Latin the dedication of both his life and his house: 'Giovanni Dario to the spirit of the city'. The sultan's gifts to Giovanni Dario included lengths of cloth of gold, for material of any kind had great value. In the 1480s the Venetians introduced the pomegranate and pointed arch pattern into the velvets often worn as a single stole by the highest officers of the state and in the silks that were woven and sold throughout Europe. In the decade after the discovery of America the pineapple became a popular motif in Venetian cut velvets and damask.

The Lombardo taste in decoration was seen everywhere in Venice in the eighties. A splendid screen of veined marble surmounted by a handsome lunette was built as a gateway to link the *scuola* and church both dedicated to San Giovanni Evangelista. Within the lunette the eagle of the evangelist stands with wings displayed atop the books of Revelation on a representation of Patmos. Eagles were a popular Lombardesque motif and appear within the curves of the bas-relief garlands on the *piano nobile* frieze of Palazzo Contarini Polignac which was built later in the century by a collaborator of Pietro Lombardo. In 1480 another collaborator of his, Mauro Coducci, started work on the tall Istrian stone façade of San Zaccaria; the ranges of columns remind one of San Marco, while the division into five horizontal zones is something like Rizzi's Tron monument. As at San Michele in Isola Coducci crowned the whole with a deep semi-circular lunette. In the following year Coducci built a bell tower for the cathedral of San Pietro in Castello; its lines are Gothic, but as it is entirely faced in Istrian stone its appearance is strikingly original.

The year the cathedral bell tower was begun was a critical one for Venice and for her relations with the Church. In 1481 Venice had turned her attention to her traditional sphere of influence over the Po Valley and especially Ferrara. The Duke of Ferrara was challenging the staple rights of the Venetians by establishing his own salt-pans in defiance of the Venetian monopoly. Attempts to enforce their traditionally respected hegemony resulted in a league against Venice headed by Pope Sixtus IV, who reasserted his claims as feudal suzerain of Ferrara. Venetian refusal to accede to this shift in alliance resulted in excommunication of the Republic in 1483. But centuries of isolation from the major currents of peninsular and European politics, save in the periods of their own straightforward imperial expansion, left the Venetians fairly indifferent to the papal fulminations, and virtually unaware of the hostility they were beginning to provoke in Italy and throughout Europe. The Venetians of the day were probably more concerned with the fires that broke out in the city at this time. After the fire in 1479 which gutted the doge's apartments, a second conflagration in 1483 destroyed an even larger section of the ducal palace and the ancient Scuola di San Marco was practically burnt to the ground.

Both of these fires resulted in spectacular commissions for the closely allied, though often competing, workshops of Pietro Lombardo and Antonio Rizzo. Rizzo became *protomagister* or chief architect of the ducal palace and was therefore responsible for the long four-storey Istrian stone façade on the small canal. On the courtyard side he repeated the two floors of Gothic arcading of the Molo and Piazzetta wings while making of the upper two storeys a vast screen for an endless proliferation of the finely carved bas-relief motifs – trophies, arabesques and sinuous plant life – that were the ubiquitous hallmarks of the taste of the period. His sombre and stately marble ceremonial staircase, each tread inlaid with arabesque patterns in lead, led to a landing where the doges would henceforth take their coronation oath and receive the ducal bonnet or *corno*. The whole of Rizzi's creation, completed by Pietro Lombardo, was the most splendid backdrop for the great ceremonies staged in the courtyard of the palace. Self-conscious glorification of the city and the state was also a large part of the first official history of Venice commissioned from the pompous Latinist Marcus Antonius Sabellicus in 1484.

The following year the Lombardo workshops were given the commission to rebuild the Scuola di San Marco. In time they were to provide it with a façade that is easily the most astonishing theatrical confection in Venice and a splendid complement to the Colleoni monument, which had finally been begun in the studio of Verrocchio only three years earlier. In this period too Pietro Lombardo built the jewel casket of a church, Santa Maria dei Miracoli, and the richly encrusted palace for Giovanni Dario. Both emphasize the Lombardo love of precious marbles: porphyry or verde antico inlaid in roundels or white cipolin marble cut in slabs of matching grey-green veins. The delicate carving of arabesques remained the Lombardesque hallmark on door frames and pilasters, just as it appeared in the elaborate marble altar frames built for the paintings of Bellini and his contemporaries. The collaboration between a painter and the frame maker was so much a part of a commission for an altarpiece that the painting frequently repeated details of a capital from the frame, or else the sculptor sought consciously to imitate the painter's rendering of such an architectural detail in his carving. This was the case of the great altarpiece painted during the eighties by Giovanni Bellini for Lombardo's handsome church dedicated to San Giobbe. These great commissions are among the treasures of Venice and are best seen in the context of the frames and altars

The young Giovanni Bellini's *Agony in the Garden* was painted in about 1460 when the artist was still under the strong influence of his brother-in-law, Andrea Mantegna.

The Piazza San Marco in 1496 by Gentile Bellini. In the foreground, members of the Scuola Grande di San Giovanni Evangelista carry their relic of the Holy Cross in the Corpus Domini procession.

designed for them, such as Bellini's glowing *Sacra Conversazione* painted for
the Pesaro family chapel in the Frari in 1488 or Cima da Conegliano's *Baptism*
painted for the high altar of San Giovanni in Bragora five years later. Unfortunately this is possible only in a few cases, just as only a few of the *scuole* in Venice
still house the cycles of narrative painting executed for them late in the fifteenth
century.

The cycle of *teleri* or narrative canvases commissioned in 1490 from Vettor
Carpaccio to decorate the meeting-room of the Scuola di Sant'Ursula is one
of the most complete pictorial records of late fifteenth-century taste as
well as a splendid example of the rich patronage of the city's *scuole*. The
intention of these narrative cycles was not only to recount the life and legends
of the patron saint of the confraternity, but to portray for posterity the members
of the *scuola*; the myriad Venetian faces that crowd the margins of Carpaccio's
canvases are markedly individual in spite of the uniformity of the robes and
costumes of the older members. The young noblemen of the day, often
excluded from membership of a *scuola*, were included here as a colourful part
of the scene, strutting about Venice in the varicoloured doublets and hose
that proclaimed their membership of the young men's clubs known as the
Companies of the Hose. These clubs were high spirited affairs staging festivities
in the city's palaces and squares and making their own contribution to Venice's
cultural life with music-making, dancing and improvised comedy. After his
twenty-fifth birthday the Venetian patrician was obliged to enter the Great
Council and wear the long sombre robes of his rank in the service of the state.
The paintings of Carpaccio document the opulent materials worn in his day,
the varieties of velvet, brocades and silks woven in Venice, and the gowns
trimmed with fur imported from the Russian ports on the Black Sea. The backgrounds and details of these lively narratives further reflect the contemporary
taste. The imaginary buildings of legendary or exotic cities are sometimes pas-
tiches of local architecture while Carpaccio's skill in depicting transparent
stretches of water bespeak his Venetian origins. These canvases are surprisingly
accurate in many details, from the square-rigged merchant carracks being built
at that time in the Arsenal to the oriental carpets whose patterns and colours
are first documented in these very paintings. Carpaccio received many commissions for his vast canvases. There were paintings for the Scuola di Santo Stefano, for the Albanians who ordered scenes from the *Life of the Virgin* and
for the Slav merchants who commissioned an especially famous series still to be
found *in situ* at their *scuola* narrating the legends of three of their patron saints.
The *Saint Augustine in his Study* belongs to the first years of the next century,
but along with the *Dream of Saint Ursula* showing the vision of the maiden
asleep in her bed, it represents a wonderfully detailed rendering of a late fifteenth-century Venetian interior. Of an even more certifiable and fascinating
accuracy is Gentile Bellini's great painting of the *Corpus Domini* procession
of the relic of the Scuola di San Giovanni Evangelista in the Piazza San Marco.

This shows the brick-paved Piazza as it was in 1496, just before the surrounding buildings began to be transformed by the taste of the Renaissance. The old Procuratie stands on the left of the picture while the Byzantine hospice of the Orseolo appears on the right attached to the base of the bell tower. The façade of San Marco, richer in gilding than now, was still embellished by the original Byzantine mosaics set in all its archways.

Another painting in the series for San Giovanni Evangelista shows the old wooden Rialto bridge as it appeared towards the end of the century. In the corner of yet another of the scenes there is the recognizable portrait of Catherine Cornaro, who had returned to the city in 1489 having surrendered the government of her husband's kingdom of Cyprus to Venice in exchange for a tiny feudal realm in the foothills of the Dolomites. Individual portraiture was just beginning to be popular in the Venice of this period. Private patrons still commissioned devotional pictures in the *madonnieri* tradition like Bellini's *Madonna of the Alboretti* which was painted in 1487. Portraits were usually within the context of the large devotional or allegorical pictures popular in commissions from the state or in the *teleri* of the *scuole*. In a large votive painting Bellini depicted the Doge Agostino Barbarigo in his robes and crown of state kneeling before the enthroned Virgin with Saint Mark and Saint Augustine. This painting and many similarly composed in the following centuries were not state commissions but were meant to be hung in the apartments of the family palace. Just as the figure of the kneeling donor or devotee might be traced to northern conventions of an earlier period, so too the vogue for individual portraiture seems to have come from the north and specifically from Flemish models. Again Antonello can be credited with the introduction to Venice of a Flemish type of portraiture where a bust of the subject facing the viewer is set in a closed space with a small landscape in the background. It is perhaps significant that one of Bellini's first essays in the style was a portrait not of a Venetian but of the German banker Jacob Fugger.

In about 1488 Bellini painted a splendidly forceful portrait which is supposed to represent the naval commander Jacopo Marcello who had died in action against the Turks and who was buried in the Frari church in another fine tomb designed by the Lombardo workshop. The commemoration of great commanders seemed again central to the patrician family's artistic and political conscience. In 1495 Venice joined an alliance of Alfonso of Naples, Lodovico il Moro, Duke of Milan, the Emperor Maximilian and Pope Alexander VI in order to defend the peninsula from the invading forces of Charles VIII of France. In the same year the battle of Fornovo was fought and the French expelled from Italy. In the following year the equestrian statue of Bartolomeo Colleoni was finally set up in front of the Scuola Grande di San Marco, whose façade had been recently completed by Mauro Coducci. The square in front of the great Gothic pantheon of the city thus contained a spectacular example of a local type of early Renaissance architecture and decoration as well as a masterpiece of sculpture reflecting the traditions of Florence and the Rome of classical antiquity as well as Venetian skill in bronze casting. The last year of the century saw the continuation of Lombardesque building projects. Coducci built a palace at Sant'Angelo, later to be known as Palazzo Corner-Spinelli, and a unique spiral staircase with loggias, the Scala del Bovolo, was added behind the Gothic Contarini palace at San Paternian. This picturesque treatment of a Venetian Gothic external staircase remained unique because contemporary architects like Coducci popularized a staircase built inside the house. Lombardesque taste at the end of the fifteenth century was widespread in all the arts. The hand-illuminated *promissione ducale* or the *commissione* of a procurator like Bertuccio Contarini of 1485 display the same Lombardesque taste for elaborate arabesque embellishment. The printing that was done in Venice at this period adopted Lombardesque decorative carving for woodcut and engraved ornamental illustration. The *Hypnerotomachia Poliphili*, for example, written by a Dominican from San Zanipolo and printed by Aldus Manutius, is often called the most beautiful printed book of the Renaissance, and is thought to have been illustrated by an artist of the first rank influenced by Lombardesque motifs. It was also in these years that Ottavio Petrucci obtained the privilege from the Republic for the first printing, or rather engraving, of musical scores, thus early contributing to Venetian pre-eminence in the world of European music.

By the end of the century the original Lombardo workshop was led by Pietro's son Tullio who carved his masterpiece, one of the subsidiary figures for the large tomb, now partly dispersed, of the Doge Andrea Vendramin. These years also saw an increase in the activity of the Lombardos' collaborator Mauro Coducci. Not only was he building the palace at Sant'Angelo with its distinctive window tracery, perhaps derived from Alberti, but he was also commissioned by the Scuola di San Giovanni Evangelista to build them a double-ramp ceremonial staircase to lead to their upper hall, which had been recently decorated with the great cycle of painting by Carpaccio and Gentile Bellini. In 1496 the state asked Coducci to build a clock tower to stand at the end of the vista that led from the water down the length of the Piazzetta and which would also be a gateway to the mercers' street leading to the Rialto. In the following year he undertook the building of a church near the Rialto dedicated to Saint John Chrysostomos in which he reinterpreted a Byzantine martyrion plan (derived from the central cube elevation of San Marco) in the vocabulary of Renaissance architecture.

In 1499 the Republic drew up a treaty with Charles VIII's successor, Louis XII, by which the duchy of Milan was ceded to the French. As part of his revenge against this betrayal by the Venetians, the deposed Duke of Milan, Lodovico il Moro, conspired to stir up the Turks against the Republic. Venetian entanglement in the political intrigues of Europe, the infidel harassment of her trade in the Levant and the Portuguese discovery of a route to the East which by-passed the Mediterranean, all contributed directly to crises in the next one hundred years that threatened the very existence of the Republic. Yet those hundred years encompassed the golden age of Venetian culture, a strong and confident statement of a rich and splendid civilization in all the arts.

7

The Golden Century

1500–1599

The sixteenth century was unquestionably the golden century of Venetian culture and civilization. Counting from the date of the city's legendary foundation in AD 421 the Most Serene Republic had lasted over one thousand years and yet it was in the sixteenth century that Venice came closer to extinction and complete annihilation than at any other time in its history. The Portuguese circumnavigation of Africa temporarily crippled her trade in spices, and the reawakened aggression of the Turks not only threatened her imperial possessions, but their war fleet challenged Venetian supremacy at sea throughout the eastern Mediterranean. Yet the Venetians won the greatest naval victory over the Turks in just this century. Within the splendid city itself, by the middle of the century considered the wonder of Europe, disastrous fires twice ravaged the great ducal palace, destroying the best part of the artistic legacy of the two preceding centuries. But the impetus of the last decades of the quattrocento lasted through the entire hundred years of the cinquecento, producing in successive waves schools of painting and architecture. One master after another emerged to dominate not only Venetian art, but to a large extent the art of all Italy, thus assuming a pre-eminent position in European culture. The greatest sovereigns of the west sought the work of Venetian masters, although in the first years of the century the fathers and grandfathers of these powerful patrons of the arts had sought to dismember the Venetian state and to destroy the millennial republic.

The infamous league that attacked Venice in the first decade of the sixteenth century accepted the moral leadership of Pope Julius II of the della Rovere family, that great warrior figure of the Renaissance Church who had inherited the twin traditions of his family as *condottiere* and of his uncle Sixtus IV as patron of the arts (the della Rovere inheritance from Urbino became the nucleus of the Uffizi collections). It was in his temporal role as suzerain of the north Italian papal vicars that the pope came into conflict with the Venetians, for the lands of the Church shared more than one border and disputed more than one territorial claim with the Venetian mainland empire. Despite the service of Venetian *condottieri* in papal armies, the recent election of two Venetian popes, and the fact that the Republic represented the only effective Christian opposition to the infidel Turk, the papacy distrusted this republican state. Venice had earlier overthrown the great wealth and power of the Patriarch of Aquileia, and had consistently claimed extensive prerogatives over the ecclesiastical authorities of her capital and territories. Their local bishop, styled the Patriarch of Venice, had to be by law a Venetian nobleman. He was treated with elaborate courtesy by the Republic, but almost as if he were a foreign ambassador from the Vatican he was kept in isolation as far from the heart of the government as possible. His small cathedral was remote from the city's centre on the island of Castello, and when matters concerning the Church arose in the deliberations of the Great Council the patrician relations and kinsmen of any ecclesiastical dignitary were required to retire during the ensuing debates.

The mutual suspicion between the papacy and the Republic was aggravated by the Venetian policy of expansion on the mainland. In keeping with their determination to secure land for cultivation and the natural resources necessary for their industries the Venetians sought to acquire more of the extensive salt-pans that stretched along the coast of the Adriatic. To the south lay the duchy of Ferrara with its strategic dominance of the Po and its long history of treaties and alliances with the Venetians. Further south were the cities of the border province called the Romagna; Ravenna had in more than one sense bequeathed its immense cultural heritage to Venice and the minor feudal lords of cities like Rimini, Pesaro and even Urbino had frequently sought their fortunes with the armies of the Republic. But in the fifteenth century, with the return of the popes from Avignon and with rich and cultivated Italian cardinals coming to Rome from the great quattrocento republics and principalities, the papal capital had grown rich and powerful herself, and the lords of the borderlands gravitated to Rome to seek their fortunes at the court and with the armies of the pope.

Typical of the fifteenth-century papacy's growing hostility to Venice were the verbal attacks of Pius II. He did not see the Venetian expansion as the logical policy of a government determined to secure food from the mainland when supplies from overseas were being constantly threatened by poor harvests, local rebellions and the increasing vulnerability of her merchant convoys. Rather the pope watched with alarm as the Venetian army conquered or forced the submission of one powerful feudal lord after another. The Venetians defeated the Patriarch of Aquileia, the da Carrara, and the della Scala; they even forced an alliance with the Gonzaga of Mantua reducing the powerful Visconti-Sforza dynasty of Milan to stalemate and thus opening the whole of Italy to invasion by the French. The most frequently repeated accusation of Pius was that Venice represented a crushing tyranny over weaker states and cities, a charge that was given the lie in 1509 when her subject cities rose in defence of the Dominante and then volunteered to return to dependent status within the reconstituted empire. Such voluntary subjection was not unknown to the Venetians, for it had happened when they had undertaken to protect Salonica from the Turks almost a century earlier.

In any case papal propaganda helped create an immensely powerful league against the Republic and very nearly reduced Venice to complete military defeat and destruction. Yet in this very decade some of the greatest works of Venetian culture and civilization, some of the finest products of her arts were created and the foundations laid for a golden century. The reasons behind this extraordinary paradox are too complex to examine in detail. The most significant factor in the survival of Venice has always been her physical situation; an island protected from invasion by an impregnable system of natural defences. But Venetian civilization was also preserved by its own impetus and momentum, and by the fact that artists who wished to enjoy the most important commissions in the Republic's territories in the late fifteenth century had to go to Venice. In the Veneto the great moment of Padua had just passed and the time of Vicenza was yet to come. The Venetian government, the Senate, and especially the office of her procurators, offered commissions to painters and architects on a scale unequalled in Italy save at the court of the most cultured Renaissance popes. In Venice the death of a prince – the doge or single procurator – in no way affected the terms or the continuity of a state commission. This was a factor which many artists found remarkably attractive in a time of aged popes, temperamental princes and hotly contested dynastic succession. An artist working for the Venetian state was most frequently rewarded in terms of honours, appointments or pensions. Although the artistic quality of official hagiography may be debatable, value judgements are particularly dangerous here as the state commissions in painting awarded to the generation of Giovanni Bellini's predecessors and contemporaries have almost all disappeared.

The evidence of architecture has proved more durable. The practical requirements of certain state officials at this time, together with the native conservatism and eclecticism in building, may account for the remarkably sober harmony of the most extensive project of the first year of the century, the then two-storey building, fifty arches in length, built as apartments for the nine procurators on the northern side of the Piazza. Just as its architect, Mauro Coducci, had reinterpreted Byzantine forms for the church of Saint John Chrysostomum at the end of the last century, so now his design for the long, arcaded *Procuratie Vecchie* was undoubtedly influenced by the Byzantine arcading of the Orseolo hospice standing opposite. Coducci built other more apparently original buildings in this year for private clients. Admittedly the Palazzo Zorzi on the Rio San Severo also has an exceptionally long, low façade overlooking its small canal, with a series of relatively narrow tall windows suggesting again a reinterpretation of the Veneto-Byzantine arcaded façade. But the palace he built for the Loredan family at San Marcuola owes more to the rectangular, three-storey dimensions of fifteenth-century Gothic palaces and in its details to his work under the Florentine, Leon Battista Alberti. Coducci's treatment of this façade, with its distinctive but seldom-copied windows, was to have a tremendous effect on Venetian taste in palace architecture. Through a clever use of columns to disguise the tripartite divisions of a traditional Venetian palace façade Coducci succeeded in creating the illusion of a regular classical arcade.

It is not surprising that in a century that was marked by the Venetian consciousness of her own greatness one of the most impressive works of art should be a splendid representation of the entire city in woodcut. So fine in detail as to be unsurpassed in accuracy for the rest of the Republic's life, this gigantic aerial view of Venice, printed on six folio sheets, was long attributed to Albrecht Dürer, whose familiarity with the city dated from his first visit in 1494. Scholars rightly questioned the attribution, just as they have drawn more pedantic attention to inconsistencies of perspective. This undisputed *tour de force* of woodcutting is now assigned to an otherwise lesser-known artist, Jacopo de' Barbari. Nonetheless it is relevant to see Venice as a link between the northern skill in woodcutting and engraving and her own growing reputation as a centre of printing. In the last five years of the preceding century one quarter of all the books printed in the world were printed in Venice. Although such a statistic suggests a massive production and distribution this was not the case. The editions produced in Venice were works of art, influenced in some of their details, and indeed often in the taste of their woodcut illustrations, by the decorative style of the Lombardo workshop. Other early Venetian books concerned travel with woodcut views of the world's cities. Woodcuts also began to be printed and sold as works of art in themselves. Many reflected German techniques and style such as the young Titian's impressive *Triumph of the Faith* executed in about 1509. Northern woodcuts of this period frequently provided the designs for Venetian majolica ware decorated with narrative subjects; otherwise arabesque patterns on the Lombardesque model were used for Venetian pottery. As for the preparation of books, such were the high standards of Venetian printing that the foremost among the city's printers, Aldus Manutius, founded the Neacademia for the discussion and determination of accurate classical texts by his scholarly friends, fellow collectors and commentators. While one of Aldus's aims was to prepare accurate classical texts in both Greek and Latin, and to print them beautifully, at least one of his editors sought to establish a canon of purity and correctness for contemporary written Italian. In 1501–2 Pietro Bembo prepared critical editions for Aldus of both Dante and Petrarch. In his *Prose della Volgar Lingua*, set in Venice in 1502, he advocated that Tuscan should be adopted as the national tongue, and that Boccaccio's pastoral *Ameto* and Petrarch's verse should be the models of all contemporary Italian prose and poetry.

It was the figure of a great scholar that Carpaccio chose to depict, according to tradition, when he portrayed Cardinal Bessarion as Saint Augustine in his study for the Slavonian Scuola di San Giorgio. In addition to the bound books and manuscripts that Carpaccio shows lining the shelves of the collector Bessarion-Augustine's study, there are the small chased hand-bells and other cast and modelled objects of the master founder's art, side by side with the bronze objects and statuettes that were being produced in imitation of antiquity. This virtual counterfeiting of small classical bronzes evolved partly from the vogue for collecting antique bronzes fostered by Mantegna's Paduan master Squarcione. The finest of the local imitators, following Donatello's lead, were Paduan, pre-eminent among them being Andrea Briosco il Riccio and the sculptor known as L'Antico. In addition to small-scale male and female nudes in the poses of classical antiquity these artists imitated the Hellenistic fancy for realistic bronzes of animals such as crabs and toads, and small oil lamps made in the form of grotesque and contorted satyrs. The taste for *bronzetti* eventually became so very widespread among Venetian connoisseurs that later in the century major sculptors were to produce some of their most sensitive and charming work on this small scale.

Carpaccio's Augustine-Bessarion conflation provides a useful representation of certain other tendencies in Venetian culture. Bessarion was a collector and scholar in the mould of Petrarch, and it is significant that both donated their important collections to the state during their lifetime. The collector Carpaccio depicted had died thirty years before and during his lifetime had gathered or commissioned objects for his own private delectation. Later private collections were based on widespread competitiveness allied with great riches, until later in the century only sovereigns and powerful princes could afford the rarest treasures. In the early sixteenth century the most discerning as well as the richest of these omnivorous collectors were often cardinals, the princes of the Church. When Cardinal Zeno died in 1501 his wealth endowed several churches as well as a magnificent funerary chapel in a section of the porch of San Marco. He was the first person to be buried in the palatine chapel since the learned Doge Andrea Dandolo over a century and a half earlier. Cardinal Zeno's legacy to Venetian culture in the bronze decoration of his mausoleum by Briosco and Antonio Lombardo, and the building of San Fantin by Abbondio, was matched in less than a generation by the great bequest of the Cardinal Patriarch of Aquileia, Domenico Grimani.

About to begin a letter, St Augustine learns in a vision of St Jerome's death. St Augustine's study is cluttered with objects of theological significance and symbolic of Renaissance culture, and the artist, Vettor Carpaccio, is thought to have taken the figure of the learned Cardinal Bessarion (1403–72), collector and benefactor of the Marcian Library, for his portrait of Augustine.

By the time of Cardinal Grimani's bequest in 1523 Venetian taste and patronage of the arts had undergone many significant modifications. The most important were perhaps those in painting. By 1502 Carpaccio's clear, shadowless narrative painting was somewhat old-fashioned, but obviously still suited to the requirements of the numerous rich *scuole* of the city and still attracting practitioners like Cima da Conegliano. But Venetian painting on a smaller scale was developing differently. Leonardo da Vinci had visited Venice in 1500, and his treatment of shadow, or *sfumatura*, the blurred and smoky outlines of figures and landscapes, was adopted by the newer generation of Venetian painters studying under the venerable Giovanni Bellini. In 1504 the Neapolitan poet Jacopo Sannazzaro's *Arcadia* was published by the city's printers. The *Arcadia* provided certain other details in the Leonardesque landscape and became an extremely important influence on the taste of the times. It was the first literary composition using the pastoral conventions of classical antiquity since Boccaccio's *Ameto*, and it was written in Italian by a Latinist whose literary output enjoyed a great vogue. The Arcadia he described was a poetic country of lush and sometimes melancholy landscape, well suited to the subtle shadows of Leonardo. The arcadian idyll was given an even more Venetian context with the publication in 1505 of Pietro Bembo's Platonist *Asolani*, a dialogue on the nature of love set in the foothills of Catherine Cornaro's miniature kingdom at Asolo.

An arcadian landscape, distant hills, and nearer figures modelled in a Leonardesque *sfumatura*, the whole composed in terms of an Antonello sacred conversation with a Madonna enthroned before a rich Venetian brocade curtain painted in the Flemish manner: these are some of the visual elements and currents of influence to be found in one of the greatest masterpieces of Venetian cinquecento painting, the so-called *Madonna of Castelfranco*, painted in about 1504 by the young Giorgione. Giorgione was probably the most brilliant of Bellini's pupils, although his early death six years later and the current reattribution of almost all his pictures, save this and one other, make it difficult to assess accurately the tremendous effect his genius had on his contemporaries and on an entire generation of slavish imitators and more inspired disciples. The backgrounds of Venetian painting had undergone a transformation, from the harsh desiccated landscape of Mantegna to the softer contours of the more mature Bellini. Both these older painters, like Carpaccio, had often included distant walled cities either full of tiny domes and spires copied from familiar buildings or else elaborate architectural fantasies based on antiquity. Giorgione's gentler wooded landscapes were the settings for more picturesque rustic buildings such as partly ruined towers, rickety wooden bridges, old mill houses and the thatched huts of the mountain peasantry. In these details Giorgione and later the young Titian in his drawings, alluded to the influence of Albrecht Dürer. Dürer arrived for his second and most significant visit to Venice in 1505, making his widely appreciated sketches of the rustic mountain villages he passed through on his way to this great capital of Italian culture.

The acceptance of Dürer's influence on Venetian art through his water-colour landscapes, his woodcuts and engravings, his drawing and even his painting was facilitated by the fundamental role his countrymen played in the commercial life of the city. The great German banking families, the Fuggers and the Wechslers, along with other merchant families from Nuremberg and Augsburg, had long since assumed an active role in Venetian commerce with the east. It was they who provided the precious metallic ores along with other raw materials for carriage and exchange in the Levant. In 1505 the German merchants commissioned the architect Spavento to enlarge and rebuild their emporium or Fondaco that had been damaged by an extensive fire at the Rialto only four years earlier. In the same year Dürer was commissioned to paint an altarpiece for the German church in the style of the Venetian *sacra conversazione*. The *Rosenkranzfest*, now in Cracow, is still very German in feeling and indeed included a portrait of the Emperor Maximilian kneeling before the enthroned Virgin. This work for the German merchants was one of the most important of Dürer's Venetian commissions, just as the young Giorgione accepted the honour of a commission to fresco the landward walls of the Fondaco in 1509, or as Bellini himself had accepted a profitable *sansaria* or brokerage from the German merchants exactly thirty years earlier.

Giovanni Bellini was still the leader of the Venetian school of painting in the early sixteenth century. Dürer not only referred to his pre-eminence in his letters but borrowed a number of characteristically Bellinian compositions for his own work. In Munich there is a very Venetian half-length Madonna and standing Child placed before a vividly coloured curtain; in another painting, also in Munich, Dürer enlarged the group of saints in the two wings of Bellini's Pesaro altarpiece to nearly life-size representations of the four evangelists. Bellini himself borrowed the compositions of others as when he copied almost exactly Cima da Conegliano's splendid *Baptism* in his own mellow version for Santa Corona in Vicenza. Cima's crystalline colours are softened by Bellini's warmer flesh tones cast in a crepuscular light. This distinctive golden glow of the work Bellini did after Leonardo's visit to Venice reaches an apogee in a masterpiece that Bellini painted some time after 1501. In that year Leonardo Loredan was elected seventy-fifth doge of the Most Serene Republic, and Bellini's richly Flemish portrait of this great doge could almost be taken as symbolic of the Republic's glory in a golden century.

Loredan's reign, however, was from the very outset neither as serene nor as resolute as the famous image of him might lead us to believe. War against the Turks, stirred up by the vengeful Sforza, resulted in Venice's loss of the important Peloponnesian ports of Modon, Lepanto and Coron in the first year of the century, and peace was made with Bajazet II only three years later. The struggle to contain Turkish aggression in these years was commemorated by

Tiziano Vecellio, a young follower of Bellini who painted a devotional picture of the *condottiere* Bishop of Paphos, Jacopo Pesaro, kneeling with the banner of the Borgia pope he served, and being presented to Saint Peter by his patron Alexander VI. The colours and execution of the painting owe much to Bellini, as does the composition, although Pesaro on his knees with a banner before the enthroned saint also reproduces the standard recto composition stamped on the Venetian ducat.

In 1503 Pope Alexander VI died and Julius II (another member of the della Rovere family) was elected his successor. In the same year the ruler of Rimini, Pandolfo Malatesta, made a testamentary disposition bequeathing his city and its surrounding territories to the Republic of Venice. In 1506 Maximilian I, the Holy Roman Emperor, entered Italy to drive the French from the duchy of Milan. Venice opposed this invasion by imperial troops, who crossed the border separating the empire from the Republic and entered the former territories of the Patriarch of Aquileia, now a mere puppet appointee of the Venetians. The early victories in the Friuli went to Venice, but by the end of 1508 the powers gathered in Italy to expel the French discovered more in common than had at first seemed possible – especially when they managed to agree on apportioning the potential spoils to be gained by attacking the Venetians. On 10 December a league was made between Louis XII of France, the Emperor Maximilian I, Henry VIII of England, Ferdinand of Aragon, the Duke of Ferrara and the Medici Republic of Florence. Pope Julius II, as moral instigator of the league, was guaranteed the possession of the Romagna principalities which had been seized by the Venetians on the death of Cesare Borgia. For his part in the attack the pope excommunicated the Venetian State.

In May of 1509 the League of Cambrai, as this first great wartime alliance of European sovereign powers was known, defeated the Venetian forces at the battle of Agnadello and immediately the entire mainland empire of the Dominante fell into enemy hands. The defeat was total and the collapse complete. The capital, in a state of alarm, expected an invasion and the most sober-minded realized that the defences of the surrounding lagoon might not withstand the onslaught that could be mounted by such a powerful and numerous coalition. Some contemporary accounts have described the Doge Leonardo Loredan as having been tongue-tied and ineffective when addressing the Great Council on this grave crisis while others describe his appearance of determination and resolve, an image of Venetian greatness in adversity and defeat. He insisted that Venice was being punished by God for sins of luxury and indolence, for her lack of moral fibre and for the Venetians' greatest sin, that of pride. On the point of defeat their resolve to fight against such overwhelming odds was paralysed. But suddenly the situation changed. The natives of the mainland towns rose in rebellion against the occupying armies – armies that must have believed, according to their commanders' propaganda, that they were liberating these very peoples from an oppressive tyranny. On 19 July

IOANNES BELLINVS

The Doge (1501–21) Leonardo Loredan dressed in gold brocade robes woven with the pomegranate pattern fashionable in the late fifteenth century, by Giovanni Bellini.

Venice herself produced a commander in the field who made up for any former lack of decisive action; on that day Andrea Gritti captured Padua. Seizing what little advantage was to be had, the Venetians managed to establish a tenuous hold on Vicenza, Monselice and the Polesine as well.

In the event Venetian survival in 1509 was due not to the force of counter-attack, but to a secret weapon developed by the inner councils of Venetian government to a subtler and more effective degree than was known to any other government in Europe. The weapon was diplomacy, and it was deployed by the most trusted servants of the Venetian State, her patrician ambassadors. Venetian diplomacy succeeded in destroying completely this first great European alliance known as the League of Cambrai. While treating and suing for armistice and peace, and hoping desperately to hold on to the few regained fragments of their broken empire the Venetian ambassadors also sought to divide the conquerors among themselves and defeat the victors on the very eve of their conquest. They succeeded within the year. Pope Julius II quarrelled with the French in 1510 and revoked the ban of excommunication; and in the following year the Venetians joined with the pope in forming the so-called Holy League against France.

Close to disaster though Venice had been, the critical period had lasted a very brief time indeed. For this reason the effect of such a near defeat on Venetian culture is difficult to determine. Giorgione had continued his work for the Germans at their emporium during the year before the great attack was made on the Venetian empire. Scholars also attribute the serenely contemplative atmosphere of the *Three Philosophers*, now in Vienna, to 1508 as well; and Giorgione's famous *Tempesta*, recorded in the collections of Gabriele Vendramin as early as 1530, was part of the arcadian idyll popular in Venice just before the storm broke. The dates of Giorgione's paintings, however, are questioned as frequently as his very authorship is put in doubt. This latter difficulty is often complicated by Giorgione's collaboration with his young contemporary Tiziano Vecellio of Cadore, known as Titian, another pupil of Giovanni Bellini, who came into his own soon after the threat of the league had vanished from the Venetian horizon. Another factor that contributes to the difficulty of making any useful generalization about the chronology of Giorgione's painting is that he died in 1510, apparently in his early thirties. One of the paintings he was working on at the time for a member of the patrician Marcello family may have had the details of its landscape background finished by Titian. The hand of Titian has been recognized in the group of rustic buildings in Giorgione's famous *Dresden Venus*. The buildings are identical to a background Titian painted in his youthful masterpiece, the *Noli me Tangere*. Whatever may have been the true extent of Titian's work on Giorgione's sleeping Venus, the mature Titian returned to the beautiful composition for the famous female nudes he painted almost forty years later. Another painter of their generation, Sebastiano, later to be called del Piombo from the leaden seal of his office at the papal court, left Venice for Rome in 1511 taking with him much that he had learned as a pupil in the school of new Venetian painting and therefore much that would contribute to the final phase of High Renaissance painting elsewhere in Italy.

In the meantime, while Giorgione and Titian represented the future of the Venetian school of painting, their master Giovanni Bellini was halfway through the last decade of his life, surrounded by painters who assimilated more or less successfully the lessons of the newer generation. Sebastiano had made organ doors for the church of the Germans where he depicted four glowing Giorgionesque saints enlarged to a scale that prefigured the monumental character of much later work. In about 1509 Gianbattista Cima from Conegliano painted a rich *Adoration of the Shepherds* set in a very Giorgionesque landscape, while Carpaccio continued instead to follow the older conventions with a *Presentation in the Temple*, meant for the church of San Giobbe, and world famous because of the delightful angel musician who strums away beneath the dais of the scene. Carpaccio's full-length portrait of the *condottiere* Francesco Maria della Rovere, dated 1510, is in its myriad detailed plants and careful, clear draughtsmanship also a survivor of an earlier style, just as was the anonymous canvas depicting the reception of the ambassador Domenico Trevisan at Cario in 1512. Bellini, however, assimilated many of the newest influences in these last decades of his life. His masterpiece of 1505, the San Zaccaria *Maddona and Saints*, is perhaps the transition piece. Dürer later wrote to his friend Pirkheimer in Nuremberg saying how the aged master was still in the vanguard of all that was being done in Venetian painting. The result is obvious in his last altarpiece for Mauro Coducci's neo-Byzantine church dedicated to Saint John Crysostomum which Bellini signed and dated 1513. The range of Venetian painting under Giovanni Bellini can be illustrated by comparing the figure of Saint Christopher with the same saint painted under Mantegna's influence forty-five years before. In 1514 Bellini painted an extraordinarily animated scene known as the *Banquet of the Gods*, which influenced Titian's *Bacchanal* painted for Alfonso d'Este in 1519 as well as a whole series Titian painted decades later in his fullest maturity.

On the whole, however, Bellini's painting even in this last period retained a certain solemnity which was a part of the refinement of his earliest period. The typical Bellinian Madonna in small devotional pictures was a frontal two-third-length figure – a traditional composition derived from the *madonnieri* that almost completely disappeared from the vocabulary of later Venetian artists. The accessories of his painting often served a limiting function: a curtain behind the Madonna contributed to the colour composition, but like the Byzantine gold ground, it also cut off the background space, focusing the worshipper's attention on the central figure. In Bellini's *sacra conversazione* paintings, the architectural backgrounds are symmetrical, shallow in depth and peopled with motionless saints in rapturous silence. In later Venetian painting, as in much other Italian painting, architecture is asymmetrical, incomplete, or a mere prop for some theatrical effect that makes little logical sense: a great billowing curtain, or a massive classical column supporting nothing; often anything as definitely limiting as an architectural background disappears altogether. The surrounding saints, or indeed the Madonna herself, gesticulate or are posed in a way to emphasize the artist's skill at depicting foreshortened anatomy or the folds, shadows and textures of rich clothing and drapery. Landscape background often obtrudes in the form of giant trees dwarfing the principal figures, or else an indefinite landscape casts much of the foreground into heavy shadow.

Much more than the near defeat of Venice by the forces of the League of Cambrai, the death of Bellini in 1515 marks the close of a specific period in Venetian cultural history. Taste in architecture had already begun to change, but much more gradually. In the period before Giovanni Bellini's death building in the city was continued along the lines established at the end of the preceding century. The Procuratie in the Piazza had a second storey added matching Coducci's lower floors, but this addition was carried out by the team of Bartolomeo Bon, the Gothic stonecutter, and Guglielmo de' Grigi from Bergamo. These same two men working in the Lombardo style began a new building for the Scuola di San Rocco in 1515, although in a few years time this commission was taken over by the newer generation of architects. In 1524 Grigi was awarded the commission for the polygonal Chamberlain's Palace on the Rialto, faced on all five sides with a sober restatement of Lombardesque motifs executed in Istrian stone and inlays. In the meantime Coducci's great palace for the Loredan at San Marcuola was finished by the Lombardo workshop, the handsome frieze decorated with the finely carved heraldic eagles that frequently appear in Lombardo secular decorative carving. The newer tastes in decoration were represented by the Loredan's hiring Giorgione to fresco the water entrance of their magnificent palace, although the theme chosen, according to contemporary documents, was traditional enough: a *trompe-l'œil* display of trophies of banners and arms. The *andron* or water-gate of a Venetian palace was where the souvenirs of military service were housed: arms, enemy prizes, galley lanterns and suits of Milanese or German armour.

In other buildings, Venetian architects essayed a style different from that of the ubiquitous Lombardos and their workshop. The churches of San Sebastiano, San Fantin and San Salvador represent the new architecture. The first two follow a plan well suited to the cramped building sites of Venice: a squarish nave, small chapels built inside the walls and with three openings for chapels across the east end. It was an arrangement that clearly owed a good deal to the simple plan of the conservative fifteenth-century Gothic church. San Salvador has a similar plan, although here the nave is lengthened and covered by a Byzantine progression of domes. The three churches are linked by a simplicity of style: the fancy Lombardesque carving and elaboration have disappeared and the former lightness and intricate grace are replaced by a more correctly classical sobriety and stateliness. The original façades of the first two churches are very plain, entirely of Istrian stone, and the principal doorways are not embellished with either lunettes, bas-reliefs or Lombardesque pilasters alive with arabesque decoration. The entrance doors are small and contained within a classical aedicule composed of half columns supporting a triangular pediment. One common characteristic determined by the building sites is the lack of projecting side chapels. In the case of San Salvador the church is enveloped by humble housing so that the later façade is an imposing classical set piece in the midst of a heterogeneous crowd of minor buildings; the spacious nave behind the entrance wall has an impact lacking in churches less hidden by the surrounding city.

Although after 1509 Venice avoided involvement in the fluctuating European balance of power, certain other developments taxed her resources. In 1516 when the Treaty of Noyon was signed between France and the Holy Roman Empire guaranteeing Venice the restoration of her mainland empire, the Sultan Selim moved to reconquer Syria and Egypt, and Alexandria was lost to the Venetians. By 1524 the Venetians sought to organize and develop another aspect of their commercial prosperity that might obviate dependence on the Levantine trade. The private banks at the Rialto were amalgamated in the Bank of the Piazza under the surveillance of *provveditori sopra i banchi*, whose institution represented a far-sighted investment in future wealth and another subsequent cultural renaissance. In the meantime the shipbuilders of the Arsenal and the merchants of the Rialto still demanded the protection of their investments in the Levantine trade. During the next two hundred years the Republic was involved in costly efforts to defend this source of state revenue. In 1520 Corfu was fortified and eventually armed with seven hundred cannon. The island provided the Republic with a secure base for her overseas fleet and a flank for the defence of Crete and Cyprus.

In 1517 Martin Luther nailed his ninety-five theses to the door of the university at Wittenberg and only three years later a disciple of Luther's was a guest at Venice's principal Augustinian monastery and preached in Santo Stefano. But Venice's traditional suspicion of the Church was little inflamed by the extremist Lutheran approach to reform. The strict observant orders were already well established in the city and in 1510 two laymen of the most prominent patrician families had forsaken the world to become hermits at Camaldoli. The example of Vincenzo Querini and Tommasso Giustinian, and that of other Venetian patricians like Gasparo Contarini, established a conservative reform movement within the city's religious houses that helped prepare the way for the counter-reformation of the Church and the Council of Trent. None of the richest and most powerful Venetian prelates was guilty of the excessive abuses of Rome. Their harmless nepotism merely assured a succession of loyal Venetian patricians in certain benefices and their simony, if it was that at all, occasionally benefited the Republic directly as in the case of the Patriarch of

Aquileia, Domenico Grimani (who was to be succeeded in his office by three nephews), who was allowed by the Vatican to make a testament in 1523 leaving many of his treasures to the Venetian state. His magnificent collection of classical statuary, both Pergamene works and Roman copies, long provided models for the study of antiquity by Venetian sculptors. Cardinal Grimani's interest also extended to northern painting and included panels he owned by Memling, Patenir, Dürer and Hieronymus Bosch. The famous Grimani breviary, now one of the treasures of the Marciana, was a particularly splendid example of Franco-Flemish illumination.

Private patronage of the arts in this period was not restricted solely to the princes of the Church. The Franciscan friars commissioned the *Assumption of the Virgin* from Titian which was completed and placed over the high altar in the Frari in 1518. This tall panel is one of the landmarks of Titian's long career. The base of its pyramid composition is a dense, shadowy mass of gesticulating disciples above whom the statuesque, red-robed Virgin ascends to heaven on a golden ground. The thrust of the Virgin's Ascension is counterbalanced by the horizontal divisions of the painting which are emphasized in the architecture of the contemporary frame. The golden ground, the use of a large panel instead of canvas, and even the relationship between the composition and its frame were all traditional elements elsewhere considered archaic by 1518. The following year the Pesaro family commissioned a painting from Titian for their family altar in the Frari. Once again, figures in the panel alluded to the naval victory of Bishop Jacopo Pesaro at Santa Maura in 1502, just as they had in the votive painting Titian completed fifteen years earlier for the Pesaro palace. The earlier work was heavily influenced by Bellini whereas the later commission took Titian almost seven years to complete and its innovations created a scandal. The enthroned Madonna was not at the centre of the painting, but placed to one side at the apex of a compositional triangle of other figures; striking portraits of the Pesaro family and even the billowing papal banner seemed unduly prominent; the painting was considered too profane for an altarpiece, too obviously devoted to the glories of the Pesaro. The Pesaro family were, like the Grimani, great patrons of every branch of the arts: Plautus's comedy *Miles Gloriosus* was first performed in Venice in the fifteenth-century Gothic palace of the San Beneto branch of the family. Few other private patrons of this period have been satisfactorily identified with the works they commissioned although Titian's many striking portraits of Venetian patricians became world famous. Even a splendid painting like the so-called *Sacred and Profane Love* of 1515 has only recently been deciphered as the kind of didactic allegory often commissioned by patrician patrons on the occasion of a marriage.

Titian's work in these years was not only limited to Venice and the interlocking families of the Venetian patriciate; the shifting political alliances of the mainland opened far grander possibilities within the endless ramifications of the staggeringly rich Renaissance principalities. The great patroness of

The Assumption of the Virgin was painted in oils on wood by Titian in 1518 for the high altar of the Frari church. The Franciscans complained that prominence was given to the group of gesticulating apostles.

Mantegna and Bellini, Isabella d'Este, Marchioness of Mantua, owned Titian's
Fête Champêtre, now in the Louvre. Alfonso d'Este, Duke of Ferrara and
son-in-law of the Borgia pope, Alexander VI, commissioned many paintings
from Titian, including the famous *Bacchus and Ariadne* of 1523, while Isabella's son Frederico Gonzaga brought Titian to his court at Mantua in 1524.
Later it was he who presented Titian to Charles V in the year of his coronation
as Holy Roman Emperor at Bologna. This encounter in 1530 came to represent a cultural rapprochement between Venice and the Holy Roman Empire,
and thus could be construed as a token expiation for the Venetian part in the
Holy League against Charles which she had joined in 1526 with the pope,
their former common enemy France, the rival republic of Florence, and the
rightly mistrusted border duchy of Milan.

These years of shifting alliance were only a prelude to an event which would
have implications not only for Venice but for the whole of civilized Europe.
The struggle for a balance of power within the Italian peninsula in these decades
led to an invasion more inevitable than that of the allies of Cambrai. Under
Charles V, the greatest emperor of the west since Charlemagne, the imperial
troops swept into Italy, reached and besieged Rome itself, and in 1527, the
Medici Pope Clement VII their prisoner, put the great capital to the sack. The
sack of Rome, largely at the hands of the emperor's Lutheran *Landeskneckten*,
was the *coup de grâce* for the already debilitated civilization of High Renaissance
papal Rome. The disciples and followers of the world-famous artists who had
worked for three great papal patrons, Sixtus IV, Julius II and Leo X, fled from
the onslaught of these new northern barbarians.

Three artists in particular sought refuge in Venice under the misapprehen-
sion that the fate of the papal capital might be analogous to the sack by the
Vandals and that under Charles, who had imprisoned a Medici pope, ecclc-
siastical patronage of the arts would be impoverished if not completely destroyed. Pietro Aretino came to the city where printing and literature were
highly considered among the arts and where Pietro Bembo's *Prose della Volgar
Lingua* had been published two years before in 1525. Danese Catteneo came
to a city where the most prominent sculptors still worked in the Gothic traditions of stonecutters, but also where antique sculpture was appreciated and
studied; and he came in the excellent company of another sculptor from Rome,
Jacopo Tatti, called after his Florentine master, Sansovino. Sansovino soon
found his career in Venice as an architect. He came to a city of enlightened
state patronage, to a city where many of the ancient churches were being remodelled; where the extraordinary palatine chapel itself was in need of constant
repair and redecoration; where both the chapel's administrators and the chief
of state did not balk at public commissions on a vast scale and where, because
of recent fires, there was much work to be done in the very commercial heart
of the city as well. Besides the attractive and remunerative commissions from
the state there were the rich lay confraternities known as *scuole* where the

commissions for rebuilding were passing to the newer architects. Various national groups in the city presented a picture of equal prosperity to the refugee artists. The Greeks bought land for their own church in 1526 and the Jews who had been allowed to return to the island from the mainland in 1516 began building a synagogue in Cannaregio for their German-speaking congregations in 1527. This building stood near the site of old bronze foundries and the Venetian word for casting gave its name to their quarter, *il ghetto*. In addition the Theatine order also arrived in Venice in 1527 bringing with them the reformed monastic and militant spirit that only ten years later would make Venice the place chosen by Ignatius Loyola for his own ordination as well as the gathering place for the exceptional prelates who made the last significant attempts to reform the Roman curia and effect a reconciliation with the protestants before the Council of Trent. This religious ferment went hand in hand with ecclesiastical building programmes and a cultural vitality that was obviously attractive to men fleeing from the destruction of a jaded, decadent and now defeated papal Rome.

The cultural vitality of Venice just at the time of and shortly after the sack of Rome can be illustrated in many ways. Gasparo Contarini had described the impressive structure and workings of the millennial government in his *de Magistrati Venetorum* published in 1524, while among the recently multiplied magistracies of the Republic was that of the Waters, instituted in 1530, which granted extensive power to ensure the preservation of Venice's natural setting. Also at this time the learned cleric Pietro Bembo wrote his Latin *History of the Republic* covering the years 1487 to 1513, while the patrician Marin Sanudo, writing a curious hybrid of Italian and Venetian, was adding to his immense chronicle of daily life which would eventually fill sixty monumental volumes of diaries. The Franciscan mathematician and philosopher Francesco de' Giorgi published a learned volume on the harmony of the universe in 1525, a treatise that would influence the proportions of Sansovino's largest church building, San Francesco della Vigna. In 1529 Michelangelo came to Venice and admired the frescoes Pordenone had executed for the cloister of the Augustinians at Santo Stefano with which he decorated the façade of the nearby palace of Titian's friend, the Flemish merchant Martin d'Anna. Also in 1529 architects of Venetian power proposed a huge super-galley for the fleet, the *Quinquireme Faustina*, powered by two hundred oars and carrying three hundred pieces of artillery, but considerations of cost defeated the project. The consent of the government or one of its committees was required for any major expenditure, but the doge or the individual procurator still enjoyed tremendous influence in many areas affecting Venetian culture.

In 1527, on the personal intervention of the Doge Andrea Gritti, Adriaan Willaert, a Flemish follower of Josquin des Pres, was appointed *maestro di cappella* at San Marco. This appointment completely altered the geographical orientation of European music. From the period of Willaert's appointment onwards, Venice was the seat of western music. Previously Venetian church music had partly derived from Byzantine tradition. The organ, a Byzantine instrument, was considered so important in the Venetian church that the most important post in the ducal chapel after the maestro was that of organist of San Marco. Medieval choral conventions had been added to Venetian music from papal Rome, but it was in the years following the Sack that the Venetian reform of ecclesiastical and secular music was introduced from the Flemish lands of the Holy Roman Emperor. Added to Flemish contrapuntal technique was the local development of the madrigal which carried the evolution of polyphonic composition even farther. Willaert's chief pupil and successor, Ciprian van Rore, another Fleming, brought Venetian music closer to a harmonic conception of music with his experiments in chromatism. The finest composers of the next two hundred years would work in the traditions of Venetian music even when some of the most prominent were again found in the emperor's German realms.

The presentation of Titian to the Emperor Charles v by the Marquess of Mantua in 1530 represented a shift in Italian and European culture: the crown, symbolic not only of the empire but of sovereignty in the patronage of European art, passed out of the hands of the Medicis and their pope. The period following the coronation of Charles v was a particularly splendid one for Venetian culture and civilization. The rest of the sixteenth century can be divided arbitrarily into periods marked by historical events, but it is difficult to know how significant the average Venetian may have thought them. Certainly the man in the street was aware of the threat to the Republic's existence in 1509, and the news of the atrocities perpetrated during the sack of Rome eighteen years later would have shocked him profoundly, even if he were completely unaware of the arrival in Venice of the famous refugees Aretino, Catanese or Sansovino. Around 1545–8 another epoch could be described when the Farnese pope, Paul III, summoned the council that met at Trento to reform the Holy Roman Church. At the same time Titian painted his equestrian portrait of Charles v, and also in that year, 1548, the young Tintoretto gave a new direction to Venetian painting with his *Miracle of Saint Mark* for the Scuola Grande di San Marco. However, various buildings under construction in the city probably interested the average Venetian much more than these special incidents in Venetian art history. Talk of scandal was widespread in 1545 when the ceiling of the new library collapsed and its architect, Jacopo Sansovino, was thrown into prison; and undoubtedly the election of the Doge Francesco Dona in the same year was of even greater general interest. The ducal elections provided the city with frequent excuses for celebration; although the doge was elected for life most were old men when they reached their high rank. With the exception of a few long reigns such as those of Andrea Gritti or Leonardo Loredan the sixteenth-century Doge of Venice ruled for an average of six years, several in that period enjoying office for little more than twelve months.

The period from 1530 until the middle of the century saw a great deal of artistic activity supported by the public patronage that continued to attract artists to Venice, where the death of the prince did not interrupt or interfere with the commission. In 1531 the most famous architectural theoretician of the day, Sebastiano Serlio, settled in Venice. In the older guide books many buildings in the city, especially palaces, were attributed to his hand although there is no documentary evidence that he built anything in Venice. He did, however, invent and publish an architectural device which was almost as widely used in the city's palaces as the ubiquitous quatrefoil tracery of the Gothic period. The Serlian window is basically a three light opening, the central window of which is topped with a curved arch rising above the flat lintels of its flanking side windows. In the Venetian version the two side windows often had rectangular openings above them as well, making the whole pattern appear inscribed within a square. The first Serlian window appeared in a woodcut plate in the first book of Serlio's *Regole Generali di Architettura* published in Venice in 1537. However, only two decades later did a Venetian palace façade incorporate Serlio's design. The major architectural commissions of the thirties were those given to Sansovino. In 1532 he began work on the large new building to house the Scuola Grande della Misericordia and two years later his plans for rebuilding San Francesco della Vigna were accepted by the Franciscan community there. The former building was never completed and San Francesco involved so much modification and collaboration that its interior is primarily of interest as the most extensive application of Renaissance harmonics and numerology to architecture, though with little to identify it as Sansovino's work.

In 1537 Sansovino was given the commission for the library building in the Piazzetta. From the outset it is clear that he intended a building exceptionally rich in sculptural detail, a building that corresponded to the most recent theories and speculations about classical decorum, and yet a building that would fit into the peculiar Venetian context. Otherwise there were no particularly practical requisites or considerations for a library building in the early sixteenth century. Earlier libraries had generally been part of monastic establishments and were in design rather like their other conventual rooms. Whereas the refectory or chapterhouse were located on the ground floor, the earliest libraries avoided the threat of damp by being situated on the first floor. Sansovino's design though incorporating these conventions was more determined by the library's position on the Piazzetta than by its function. Like the relationship between the first Procuratie built opposite the Orseolo hospice on the Piazza, Sansovino's library repeated the pronounced arcading of the ducal palace, thus making of the Piazzetta a ceremonial corridor. The ground floor arcade of the library was plainer than the richly decorated floor above, thus restating in an entirely different idiom the basic relationship between the two orders of arcading at the Doge's Palace. The library's upper bays were based on a motif from the Roman Teatro di Marcello where tall half columns frame an arch sprung on smaller columns. It is the richness of the building's decoration that makes it a unique contribution to European architectural history and a particularly forceful statement of Venetian wealth, grandeur and self-confidence. There is carving on every surface of the *piano nobile* of the building, in the spandrels, in the attic frieze and in the tight interstices of the fluted columns, pilasters and columnettes. The spandrel sculpture executed by Danese Cattaneo is particularly classical with heavily muscled lounging deities reminiscent of the Roman river gods in the lower bays, and the graceful winged victories of antiquity in the upper order. In the same year that he began work on the white Istrian stone building intended to house the bibliographical treasures of the Republic, Sansovino also started a much smaller building project in a position of similar prominence. This was the *Loggetta*, a small three-bay construction built at the base of the bell tower. It was to be a colourful and highly decorated building with pairs of richly veined precious marble columns, bas-reliefs, small bronze statues in niches, and the whole framed and outlined in rich red Verona marble. The Loggetta stands opposite the Porta della Carta. Its architecture of classical bays and sculptural decoration makes it a continuation of the richly carved library, but the use of multicoloured marbles is a reference to the façade of the ducal chapel. Its function as a building has varied; during part of its history it served as a guard house for the captain of the Arsenalotti when the Great Council was in session every Sunday.

The Loggetta and especially the Marciana were typical of the Republic's use of the arts and sciences for a proud self-glorification. In this spirit one of the finest geographers of the day, G. B. Ramusio, a worthy heir of Fra Mauro, was commissioned in 1540 to prepare a large cycle of maps in the ducal apartments to illustrate Venetian trade routes in eastern Europe, Africa and Asia as well as tracing Marco Polo's voyages. While these maps were a commission of the government, both Sansovino's buildings in the Piazzetta were commissioned by the procurators, the administrators of the patrimony of San Marco. These officials were also responsible for the continuing excellence of the doge's music under the Gabrielli, and for the repairs to the chapel fabric represented by the replacing of deteriorated mosaics with new designs by Lotto, Titian and later by Tintoretto and his workshop. The procurators had hired Coducci to rebuild their office residences along the northern edge of the Piazza forty years earlier and then added the clock tower at the end of the prospect of the Piazzetta from the Molo. By allowing Cardinal Zeno's funerary chapel in the porch of San Marco to block the Piazzetta doorway of the ducal chapel, the procurators had made of the west front opening to the Piazza the only viable ceremonial entrance to San Marco, incidentally rendering the progression of the mosaics in the narthex meaningless. But the closure of the south door of San Marco did not affect Sansovino's transformation of the Piazzetta into a grand ceremonial corridor, flanked by impressive arcades, with a brief inter-

Canaletto's view of the Molo and a corner of the Doge's Palace looking towards Jacopo Sansovino's Marcian Library (begun 1532–7). To the left are the domes of the two votive churches built to commemorate the plagues which ravaged Venice in the sixteenth and seventeenth centuries: Palladio's Redentore (1576) on the Giudecca and the double domes of Longhena's Santa Maria della Salute (1630) dominating the mouth of the Grand Canal.

section made by the Porta della Carta and the Loggetta and with Coducci's clock tower providing a backdrop to this vista of Venice from the waterfront. The great Piazza was not yet so rationally ordered: the Byzantine structure of the Orseolo hospice was allowed to stand for another fifty years and the only attempt made to create an architectural unit of the Piazza was carried out by Sansovino late in his career with the remodelling of San Geminiano.

Another important state architectural commission was less purposefully decorative and reflected the rising alarm over the recently threatened defensive role of the Venetian fleet. Saracen pirates appeared in the Adriatic in 1533 and one especially, known as Il Moro of Alexandria, preyed on lone Venetian ships in their home waters. A peace treaty with Sulieman II in 1540 resolved some of the menace though Nauplion and Malvasia had to be surrendered and the tribute to the sultan for Venetian Cyprus was increased. A fortress was planned to guard the principal San Nicolo entrance to the lagoon. Michele Sanmicheli, a Veronese master of the art of military defences, undertook in 1542 to create an impressive low bastion of huge blocks of Istrian stone facing the narrow channel through which all Venetian shipping passed; behind these solid defences he virtually transformed the entire mud-flat island into a model of modern fortification. Two years later when the first general ministry of war, the *collegio della milizia*, was established, Sansovino completed his own exercise in fortification, the heavy and forbiddingly rusticated *Zecca* or State Treasury and Mint on the Molo. The impregnability of the building was, however, merely an architectural conceit as the ground floor was open to provide small shops for the merchants whose stalls had been displaced by the new buildings; the same sort of provision would eventually be made on the ground floor of the library. Sansovino's designs were not merely an embellishment of the city's ceremonial centre, but also an attempt to organize the chaotic cluster of small merchant enterprises that by tradition had established themselves in the heart of Venice.

However, decoration was not to be neglected and militaristic conceits did not preclude other themes: the beautiful small bronze statues cast in 1545 to be placed in the niches of the Loggetta included one personifying Peace. For all his success in introducing these fine examples of High Renaissance Roman taste to Venetian sculpture, an attempt at innovation in architecture resulted in disaster for Sansovino. The vaulted ceiling he designed to cover the Marciana's principal *piano nobile* room collapsed that same year and the architect was thrown in jail. The Venetians were properly annoyed that such an expensive novelty should prove a failure, especially as they well understood the impracticability of broad and shallow stone vaulting in a building that would shift and settle as much as any built in Venice.

However, the imprisonment of Sansovino was brief. His friends petitioned successfully to have him released so that he might return to work and correct his error of judgement. The petition for his release was organized by Aretino who was a widely acknowledged arbiter of Renaissance taste after the publication of his *Dialogues* in 1532, and by Titian who enjoyed some of his most important commissions in this period. Charles V ennobled Titian in 1533 and in the following years he worked at the court of Urbino where he painted the first of the famous Venuses based on Giorgione's Dresden masterpiece, and at Mantua where he came in contact with the Mannerism of Giulio Romano which influenced almost all his later painting. In 1536 he painted his largest canvas, the *Presentation of the Virgin in the Temple*, for the *sala del albergo* of the Scuola Grande della Carità. Here Titian reinterpreted a number of conventions common to the Venetian *teleri*. The long narrative painting designed for a specific wall in the *scuola* included portraits of members of the confraternity as well as other familiar motifs such as the foreground figure of the old egg seller borrowed from Carpaccio's Saint Ursula cycle. The architecture of the background includes a mixture of elements from local and more cosmopolitan conventions. The landscape is of Titian's native Cadore, the brick wall is patterned like those of the ducal palace, while the loggia in the middle distance is purely classical, just as the heavily rusticated temple steps or the classical torso fragment in the foreground are distinctly Roman. The whole seems almost a conscious reinterpretation in High Renaissance terms of one of the finest of the Bellinian school paintings, Cima da Conegliano's *Presentation* of 1500, now in Dresden. By 1542 the mannerist style that Titian had encountered earlier in Mantua was brought to Venice by Giorgio Vasari who had been invited by Aretino to prepare scenery for a lavish dramatic production by one of the Company of the Hose. Through Sanmicheli, Vasari painted a fully Mannerist ceiling for the palace of Giorgio Cornaro, one of the most important patrons of the day.

In the year Titian and his friends supported Sansovino's reinstatement as protomagister of San Marco, 1545, Titian left Venice for a visit to Rome. His susceptibility to Roman models was already evident in a portrait of the Doge Andrea Gritti where the pose and modelling of the old man's hands were copied from the widely known *Moses* of Michelangelo. The year after his triumphant arrival in Rome Titian produced a psychologically profound group portrait of the pope who had just convoked the Tridentine Council, Paul III, and his Farnese nephews; in about 1547 he painted the powerful *Mocking of Christ* which helped transform concepts of brushwork, impasto and the depiction of light and outline in a way which later inspired Rembrandt; and·in 1548 he painted his masterpiece of *condottiere* portraiture, *Charles V at the Battle of Mühlberg*, that repeatedly served Velazquez as a model of royal portraiture. If Titian's style became more introspective and distinctively personal in these years, contemporary opinion also reflected a change in the general attitude towards the art of painting. Paolo Pini's *Dialogo della Pittura* appeared in 1548, establishing the distinction between *invenzione*, *disegno* and *colore*. In the same year there appeared on the Venetian scene a young artist who regarded himself as a disciple of the mature Titian, but who also readily accepted style and techniques from outside the native Venetian tradition: Tintoretto is supposed to have written on the walls of his studio: 'The colour of Titian, the drawing (*disegno*) of Michelangelo.' Tintoretto also illustrated the third of Pini's useful categories, *invenzione*, in the canvas that heralds his sensational effect on Venetian painting, *The Miracle of Saint Mark and the Slave*, painted in 1548 for the Great Hall of the Scuola di San Marco. The flying figure of the interceding saint swooping head first into the scene is startling even today.

While the mid-century signalled new directions in the arts of Venice, the fifties and sixties were decades in which the political strategies of the Republic were concerned with programmes of fortification abroad, reorganization of the military for service in the colonies and on the mainland and defending the merchant convoys from attack by pirates. Such defensive measures were essential because in these two decades Venice enjoyed a renewed prosperity from a vigorous trade in Levantine spices. In this period the government also encouraged its patriciate to continue the extensive programmes of land reclamation on the mainland that had been begun in the forties. This reclamation and cultivation of agricultural land in the Veneto and the consequent building of farm villas engaged both Venetian patricians and the landowners of subject cities like Padua, Treviso, Vicenza and Verona. The architects of their villas, of whom Andrea Palladio was the most famous, came from an artistic tradition whose relationship with Venetian civilization was not unlike the cultural cross-fertilization that had existed between Padua and Venice a century earlier.

At first these architects worked in the cities of the mainland under the patronage of the local nobility; Sanmicheli built palaces in Verona as did Palladio in Vicenza. The Dominante usually provided commissions in Venice for specific kinds of building suited to local requirements; Sanmicheli was asked to build fortifications, and much later Palladio built churches and a theatre. In 1555 a competition was held for a new Rialto bridge to be built in Istrian stone and Palladio was asked to submit designs along with the greatest architects of the day: Michelangelo, Vignola and Sansovino. His three-arch design was not chosen, partly because his ideas were too aggressively classical for the Venetian taste in architecture which had been conditioned by considerations of convention, tradition and eclecticism. Possibly for similar reasons Palladio's several projects for palaces in Venice never found patrons. Although Sansovino had introduced in the library building motifs from High Renaissance Rome, in his private commissions he followed the much more conservative taste of his patrician patrons. His Palazzo Corner della Cà Grande, built for a scion of one of the richest Venetian families, borrowed the rhythms of its façade from the Loredan palace built by Coducci nearly fifty years before. The most novel architecture of the mid-century was the great palace built for the Grimani family

Titian's largest oil
painting, *The Presentation
of the Virgin in the
Temple*, was painted
between 1534 and 1538
for a room of the Scuola
Grande next to the
convent of the Carità.

A Saracen rescued by St
Mark and lowered to
safety in a boat of
Venetian merchants. One
of the Venetians is a
portrait of Tommaso
Rangone, the
philosopher-doctor from
Ravenna, who
commissioned the work
from Tintoretto in 1562
for the Scuola Grande di
San Marco.

near the Rialto. The architect was Michele Sanmicheli, but the result is so unlike anything he had already built in Verona that the heavy classical feeling of the building is in this case perhaps more accurately attributed to the individual taste and requirements of the owner. The traditional water-gate entrance was treated as a barrel-vaulted Serlian atrium probably derived from Sangallo's carriage entrance to the Palazzo Farnese in Rome. The deep window units of the upper floors are a heavy version of the Marciana bays with the central *portego* formula based on the eponymous design of Sebastiano Serlio. To whomsoever the central Serlian window composition is ascribed, it makes its most impressive appearance in Palazzo Grimani.

When the Grimani Palace was nearing completion in the early sixties, the architect who had added the upper floor adapted this motif for another palace he was building across the Canal. At the Palazzo Coccina-Papadopoli the distinctive Serlian composition of the three light *portego* windows assumed the characteristic appearance used in many palaces built in Venice over the next two hundred years; Grigi's Palazzo Papadopoli is a conservative, almost two-dimensional treatment of a Venetian façade. Even Sansovino, after his work at the Marciana had been completed to the sixteenth bay in 1554, appeared to adopt a similar restraint. The public building he undertook at the Rialto in the following year was severe in comparison with his work on the Molo and in the Piazzetta. Sanmicheli's Palazzo Corner Mocenigo at San Polo is also restrained in comparison with his project for the Grimani; the flat Serlian composition of the principal floors' central windows is outlined in strips of Istrian stone and the *rio* façade stands on a base of rough-style Roman rustication unusually heavy for Venice.

The interiors of Venetian palaces, however, were not handled with such *gravitas*. Beamed ceilings were picked out with gilded designs in gold, the walls were lined with stamped and gilded leather to a height of five feet, above which hung the portraits and votive paintings of the Bellini, Titian or later Veronese. The *terrazzo* floors of crushed coloured marble were often worked in intricate heraldic designs and the large fireplace hoods were frequently supported by caryatids that in the richest houses were not only carved by the best sculptors, but gilded as well. The massive furniture was usually of oak or walnut and in some cases it was carved by master sculptors like Sansovino, who repeated the popular caryatids on the front of tall cabinets, or as the legs of immense tables. Where human heads and torsos were not used, architectural motifs were with an abundance of miniature columns, capitals and pediments carved from more exotic wood. The second cinquecento Grimani Patriarch of Aquileia brought Raphael's assistant, Giovanni of Udine, to Venice to decorate the rooms of his family palace at Santa Maria Formosa. The elaborate stucco work decoration applied to the barrel-vaulted staircase, which still exists today, may have provided the model for Sansovino's Scala d'Oro or golden staircase for the Doge's Palace begun in 1557. In the same spirit of the elaborate embellishment of a palace was the well-head Sansovino carved, as the Bon had done at the Cà d'Oro, for the Cornaro of San Maurizio or the even more extravagant twin wells richly executed in bronze between 1554 and 1559 by master casters from the Arsenal foundries and placed in the courtyard of the ducal palace. The great riches of the private houses impressed even the Venetians and it is significant that in the mid-forties a list of private collections appeared in Venice compiled by Michiel, the so-called Anonimo Morelliano. It is an extremely valuable testimony of a patrimony now almost entirely dispersed, if not lost or destroyed.

In contrast to these rich interiors the new sobriety and *gravitas* in architecture continued to be widespread in the sixties. In some instances there were conscious echoes of earlier conservative cinquecento buildings like San Fantin or San Sebastiano; in fact Sansovino was working on an extension of the chancel of the former at the same time as he was designing the simple flat Istrian façade of San Geminiano at the west end of the Piazza. The façade of this church which was pulled down is now known only from contemporary paintings and engravings. It was commissioned from Sansovino by Tommaso Rangone, an extraordinary individual who in 1553 also hired Sansovino to design a new façade for the principal church of the Merceria, San Zulian. At San Zulian the central door of an otherwise extremely plain façade is surmounted by a portrait statute of the self-styled philosopher-physician Rangone himself, flanked by Greek and Hebrew inscriptions praising his own doctrines and generosity. Were it not that he were seated in the long robes of his profession rather than standing clad in armour, the statue would belong to the convention of memorials to *condottieri* such as the one erected only a decade earlier depicting Vincenzo Cappello standing above the door at Santa Maria Formosa. Whereas the appearance of Rangone represents a unique memorial to a man of his profession, statues of Venetian military commanders on the façade of a church would make an even more extraordinary appearance a hundred years later at Santa Maria del Giglio.

In 1556 Andrea Palladio of Vicenza came to Venice to accept a commission from the convent attached to the church of the Carità. His work there and two years later on the refectory for the Benedictines of San Giorgio Maggiore represents a different interpretation of the current sober taste in building. Palladio's was a fully Roman classicism based not only on his own observations and sketches in Rome (the bays of the single completed wall of brick arcades at the Carità were virtually copied from the Colosseum), but also from studies under his Vicentine patrons and their circle of academicians. The *Accademia Veneziana*, often called *della Fama*, was founded in the year of Palladio's arrival in Venice and included Sansovino's son among its founding members. These early academies were primarily concerned with literature and especially with theatre, in the latter case giving a formal organization to private performances and the festive representations of the Companies of the Hose.

In 1565 the patrons of one of these, the Dolfin, commissioned Palladio to build the first theatre in Venice at their house; it was a wooden affair erected in Sansovino's sober courtyard of Palazzo Dolfin. Among the members of the Academy who wrote sonnets on the Petrarchan model, verse in the new *canzonetta* form, or prose and dialogues on the models of Bembo, there were those like Daniele Barbaro who were devoted to the study of classical architecture. His annotated edition of the ten books of the *de Architectura* by the Augustan theoretician Vitruvius was published in Venice in 1556. Barbaro's Vitruvius included not only general discussion of classical building as such but also minute instruction for the correct proportions of a door frame or cornice. This kind of teaching backed by the authority of the monuments of imperial Rome was combined with popular or learned theories of harmonics and numerology often loosely based on a classical author like Pythagoras.

Palladio's refectory at San Giorgio illustrates several of these cross currents; the monumental doorway is a copy of a Roman door in Spoleto, the classical ordered window frames are Vitruvian, while the numerology and proportions which make the interior one of the great monuments of Renaissance classicism are the devising of the architect. For all its stark grandeur Palladio envisaged his refectory finished with the appropriate decoration: a supper scene of gigantic proportions filling the entire end wall with its mass of figures and a theatrical background composed of a *capriccio* of classical architecture. The great painting, now in the Louvre, had as its subject the *Marriage at Cana* and it took Paolo Callari from Verona eighteen months to complete it.

The year before Veronese had collaborated with Palladio on the decoration of the villa he built for the Barbaro brothers, the Patriarch of Aquileia, Daniele, and the senator, Marc'Antonio, at Maser near Belluno. The cycle of Veronese's frescoes at Maser has a country freshness and is executed on an intimate scale with landscapes, *trompes-l'œil* of dogs, children, charming jokes and humorous allusions. But there are also densely allegorical subjects based on astrological and mythological programmes devised by Daniele Barbaro. Even earlier there existed an important link between this particular patron and the painter. Barbaro, as one of the most learned and talented men of his generation (his *relazioni* of 1550 as ambassador to England are still considered to be among the most important historical documents of the Republic), was asked to devise an allegorical programme for the principal meeting-rooms of the government in the wing of the ducal palace that was undergoing redecoration after a series of disastrous fires. At first a little known painter was assigned to carry out Barbaro's project. He chose two assistants who later executed many of the frescoes in villas built for Venetians on the mainland: Veronese, who thus first came into contact with Barbaro, and G. B. Zelotti, who later collaborated with Palladio in villas for the Foscari at Malcontenta and for Leonardo Emo at Fanzolo. Through this commission Veronese brought a new vitality and rich primary colours to the Bellini-Titian school of Venetian painting.

In the same year Titian had returned to settle in Venice after his second visit to the court of Charles V at Augsburg. This period in his long life was primarily devoted to the grand international commissions such as the *Danae* of 1553 and the cycle of mythologies for Philip II of Spain of 1556–8, as well as to highly Mannerist work like the firelit night vision of the *Martyrdom of Saint Lawrence*; or intensely personal paintings like the moving *Entombment of Christ* painted in 1559, in which he appears as Joseph of Arimethea; or the profound self-portrait he painted in the following year. Although Titian no longer left Venice, his compositions became increasingly well known abroad through the engravings made of his subjects by Cornelius Gort. While Titian's completed work was either sent abroad or became the increasingly introspective vision of an old man, the younger Tintoretto's best work, full of the dynamism of his tremendous physical energy, was done almost exclusively for the *scuole* or merchant confraternities in Venice. Tintoretto's Michelangelesque vision found its greatest expression during the sixties and seventies in a powerful cycle of decoration executed for the great Scuola di San Rocco which had been completed in 1560 by Lo Scarpagnino, the classical heir of the Lombardos' building traditions.

Veronese's career in Venice began in 1553 with Barbaro's allegorical decoration for the hall of the Council of Ten. The tremendous foreshortenings of these paintings recall Titian's early Mannerist ceiling panels painted in 1542 for Sansovino's island church of the Spirito Santo. However, Veronese soon abandoned these powerful distortions of perspective and anatomy derived from Vasari and Giulio Romano to concentrate on composition in the rich colours that had been typical of the best Venetian painting earlier in the century and to which he added the clear colours partly based on the palette of Correggio. Veronese did return to ceiling panels that required foreshortening, such as for the frescoed ceiling at Maser or the ceiling canvases in San Sebastiano, where in 1556 he depicted sharply receding static scenes seen from a position immediately below, in contrast to the Mannerist tumbling torsos that defy the viewer's attempts to associate himself with a single viewpoint. Veronese's perspectives thus owe more to Mantegna's cupola in the Camera degli Sposi, the first foreshortened perspective ceiling *di sotto in su*, than they do to Giulio Romano's all embracing *Gigantomachia* which had so influenced Tintoretto and Titian.

Veronese could be taken to represent a number of distinctive elements in the history of Venetian artistic patronage. Like many of the greatest Venetian painters he came to Venice from the mainland, bringing with him the artistic traditions of Parma and Mantua. Again like many others he was first introduced as an assistant in a workshop executing a commission for the state. At the same time he received a minor commission to paint ceiling panels for the sacristy of a monastery church, San Sebastiano. His talent was recognized by Daniele Barbaro, man of learning and eminent ecclesiast and servant of the state, who employed Veronese in the decoration of his own pleasure villa. It is just at this time that individual Venetians, collectors and men of learning, began to be patrons of the arts on a truly important scale, and Titian's innumerable portraits of Venetian patricians date from the 1550s onwards. Curiously enough extensive private patronage had previously fallen to rich and ambitious *condottieri*, Gattamelata or Colleoni being outstanding examples, and later to the *condottieri*-princes who provided armies for the Republic, such as marquesses of Mantua or the dukes of Urbino; one of Veronese's earliest commissions was a portrait of the *condottiere* Pese Guariento of Verona. The artistic patronage of families or individual Venetians was most often associated with prominence in the government, the office of doge or procurator, or else patronage of a religious establishment in the building or decorating a private chapel. Tommaso Rangone's commissions for Sansovino or Daniele and Marc'Antonio Barbaro's commissions were among the first made by men of learning, humanists as such, even though the Barbaro brothers were also a Patriarch of Aquileia and a senator.

Through his employment with Palladio at Maser, Veronese received the commission for the great *Miracle at Cana* at San Giorgio and then returned to San Sebastiano. This church eventually became a shrine to the artist himself, with virtually all the pictorial decoration being the product of some period of the artist's active life. Tintoretto made of the Scuola di San Rocco an equally personal shrine, and within the Venetian system of painters' workshops his was perhaps more immediate and his work found more followers. Paradoxically his painting now seems more individual and less a product of local traditions than Veronese's work. In both cases, and this is the really distinctive feature of Venetian patronage and the arts, it was the state that commanded their services again when they were old men, full of honours, riches and prestige. Titian had earlier gone outside Venice for his work and for his commissions. By the time Cornelius Gort began to engrave Titian's subjects in 1556 Titian was the acknowledged leader of painting throughout Europe; his commissions from the emperor, the pope, the king of Spain and the discerning Renaissance princes of northern Italy had assured this pre-eminence. He chose to settle in Venice, and he did undertake certain commissions for civic projects such as a ceiling panel for his friend Sansovino's library and a state votive picture finished by his workshop, but not on the scale of Veronese's or Tintoretto's work in the ducal palace. One of Veronese's last paintings was the *Apotheosis of Venice*, the centrepiece of the Great Council Hall ceiling, while Tintoretto and his workshop covered the entire end wall above the doge's throne in the same room with a vast *Paradise* that was, for its size alone, long considered one of the wonders of Venetian painting. However, lest it be thought that Titian was supplanted by either of these artists, it is sufficient to recall that in 1576 he bequeathed one of his greatest canvases, the *Crowning of Thorns* painted in 1570 and now in Munich, as a priceless legacy to Tintoretto.

The two decades following the mid-century were a period of intense activity at every level of Venetian society. In the great Scuola di San Rocco Tintoretto continued his gigantic labour symbolized by the immense *Crucifixion* which depicted in suitably sombre tones the rich variety of Venetian life and costume. By the late sixties the number of glass factories producing delicate confections of Murano had grown to thirty-seven. The mastery of this craft and the secret of the pure transparent *cristallo* glass was passed on from generation to generation in the same restricted families, while the demand grew greater for shallow crystal *tazze* with lacy ornate handles or intricate lyre-like stems edged in a distinctive aquamarine-coloured glass. In the same way the lace of Burano was considered the finest that could be bought. In 1566 Philip II of Spain ordered from Burano the bridal trousseau in lace for his fiancée Mary Tudor. At the same time a number of events seemed to work against the fullest development of Venetian culture. The publication of the Tridentine Index two years after the close of the Council in 1563 produced a heavy-handed censorship that curtailed the printing of books. This was a blow to one of Venice's most important industries and one from which the city's presses did not recover until well into the following century. As a by-product of this apparent impoverishment, however, there was the growth of an oral tradition bringing with it a refinement of the Venetian dialect, especially in improvised comedies performed in theatres like the wooden one Palladio built in 1565 at Palazzo Dolfin. This new scope for comedy was particularly developed by itinerant actors from the mainland, who brought with them a repertoire of comic types from Padua and Bergama that eventually became the cast of characters in the seventeenth-century's *Commedia dell'Arte*.

The Council of Trent affected the arts in Venice in subtler ways as well, and over such a long period of time as to be hardly recognizable as the result of that epochal ecumenical council. In the early years of the Council the effect may have been minimal, but by the end large numbers of Venetian clerics, including the patriarchs of Venice and of Aquileia, attended the sessions. The year the twenty-year-long Council ended, the collaboration of Palladio and Veronese at the Refectory of San Giorgio came to a close. Two years later Palladio was appointed protomagister of the rebuilding that had been planned for San Giorgio since the preceding century. Palladio's church was built on lines predetermined by the earlier plan, but some of the Tridentine recommendations for church building clearly influenced the final result. The clear divisions of the space allotted in the interior to the laity, to the celebration of the sacraments and to the devotions of the regular clergy, the starkness of the interior and its axial orientation towards a dominant high altar, were part of the Tridentine reform promoted by clerics like San Carlo Borromeo. In other aspects of his ecclesiastical projects, Palladio seemed more concerned with the modern solution to problems posed, not by the Church but by pagan antiquity. In his writings on the subject Palladio called his churches 'temples' and when he took over the rebuilding of San Francesco della Vigna from Sansovino he set out to solve the problem of how a basilican Christian church, that is to say a building with a tall nave and two lower side aisles, could be given the appearance of that *nec plus ultra* of classical architecture, the temple. Palladio's solution at San Francesco became an integral part of the two other churches he built in Venice, San Giorgio and the Redentore. The solution was an Istrian stone façade composed of two superimposed classical pediments, a higher one to cover the roof line of the nave and a lower, broader one whose outer angles would mask the side aisles. In the central section of the façade this lower, wide pediment disappeared behind the giant orders that rose either from plinths or from the ground to complete the illusion of a classical temple front.

In 1567, only three years before his death, Jacopo Sansovino carved in a workshop at the Arsenal his two largest marble statues in Venice, the giant figures of the Venetian tutelary gods of war, Mars and Neptune. Placed on the landing of Rizzo's staircase built seventy-five years earlier, their size has given it the name of the Giants' Staircase. These two enormous figures are a landmark in the curiously spasmodic evolution of Venetian sculpture. Rizzo and the Lombardo family of the late quattrocento and early cinquecento had worked in the Gothic stonecutters' tradition of free-standing or bas-relief sculpture as part of an architectural whole. Apart from buildings, this convention applied to numerous funerary monuments and later, but with diminishing frequency, to the decoration of chapels such as those at San Giobbe, and more rarely to an entire façade like that of the Scuola di San Marco. Quite foreign to this tradition was the introduction from Padua of small bronzes imitating antique models, or from Renaissance Rome the bronze sarcophagus of Cardinal Zen executed after a lost design by Rizzo. The most important freestanding statuary in the city was a foreign importation as well: the Colleoni monument was planned by the Florentine Verrocchio in terms of Donatello's *Gattamelata* and Rome's Marcus Aurelius, although it was cast by a Venetian, Alessandro Leopardi. Leopardi was an important figure in early cinquecento bronze sculpture, not so much for completing the Colleoni, which remained an isolated monument in Venice, but for the casting of the three flag standard bases in the Piazza. These were executed in 1505 in the tradition of highly decorated bronze work common in the cannon foundries of the Arsenal, where the Alberghetti family and Niccolò de' Conti had cast the elaborate bronze wellheads placed in the courtyard of the ducal palace in 1556.

To a large extent it can be claimed that the foreign sculptors who came to Venice after the sack of Rome in 1527 easily fell in with the traditions and conventions of Venetian sculpture prevalent until then. Of these refugee artists the main one, Jacopo Sansovino, worked as an architect as well as a sculptor. The Republic could easily have limited his commissions to sculpture; they did not, and Sansovino became the protomagister of San Marco primarily in his capacity as architect, with the disastrous result that the library vaulting collapsed.

However, some of his earliest work in the ducal chapel was as a sculptor in bronze. The panels made for the procurators' tribunes in the chancel, executed between 1537 and 1544, were based on a use of bas-relief decoration that echoed Donatello's bronze reliefs in Padua and earlier panels Sansovino knew in Florence. The extraordinary curved bronze door for the sacristy commissioned in 1546 recalls the work of Sansovino's Florentine compatriot Ghiberti, not only in the two beautifully executed bas-relief scenes, but also in the small portrait heads that jut out of the borders. These two works, the great marble giants and the fine bronze statues integrated into the architecture of the Loggetta, are good examples of Sansovino's range as a sculptor. Danese Cattaneo, who was responsible for most of the statuary and carved decoration on the façade of the library, entered into the stonecutter-sculptor traditions of Venetian sculpture. At San Giovanni e Paolo he continued another of the earlier traditions by carving the sculptural decoration for Grapiglia's funerary monument to the Doge Leonardo Loredan. However, the history of this particular tomb also indicates the extent to which the conventions inherited from the Lombardesque masters were disappearing. The original concession for a tomb in the chancel of the great Dominican church was granted during the doge's lifetime after the Republic had emerged triumphant under Loredan's leadership from the threat of the League of Cambrai. The generation of Loredan's heirs wanted an immense structure that would somehow incorporate the high altar. Not long after, however, the whole was replanned as a traditional wall monument although almost half a century passed before the tomb was completed in 1572. The idea for the Loredan monument incorporated in a high altar with three statues surmounting the whole suggests, in fact, the kind of altar that sculptors like Girolamo Campagna would produce in bronze in the next generation.

In the meantime Alessandro Vittoria from Trento was engaged on many of the most significant commissions for sculpture of the mid-century, thus providing the transitional link between the work of Sansovino and the more mannerist or baroque work of the end of the century. On his arrival in Venice in 1543 he joined Sansovino's workshop and executed four of the river god figures in the spandrels of the Marciana façade. By the middle of the century he was active as a medallist and then, at about the same time that Sansovino executed his twin giants, Vittoria worked on two oversize figures to decorate the principal entrance to the library. These large-scale caryatids were eventually to suggest a motif for the baroque work of Longhena, but until then they were not widely copied in Venice; on a much smaller scale, however, caryatids were very much a part of Venetian interiors, and some surviving fireplaces thus supported are attributed to or signed by Alessandro Vittoria. Vittoria also worked with Sansovino on the Doge Francesco Venier's stately wall tomb in San Salvador and was responsible for the elaborate stucco decoration of the golden staircase in the ducal palace. Stucco was never regarded as an inferior material for sculpture in Venice. In fact its light weight gave it much to recommend it, and before the vast workshops of baroque sculptors appeared in the following century a building could obviously be more quickly completed with stucco statuary than with large pieces of marble work. This was the case at San Giorgio where Vittoria was employed under Palladio's guidance to fill the immense niches of the interior with a panoply of the appropriate saints. Also ascribed to the sixties, is Vittoria's famous bronze doorknocker of a trident-bearing Neptune, modelled with a feeling for masculine anatomy and musculature as fine as the small bronzes of antiquity. In marble Vittoria carved a small *John the Baptist* for San Zaccaria more appropriately ascetic in physique and more a product of the Renaissance in feeling. The doorknocker belongs to a Mannerist phase of Vittoria's work, whereas the Saint John is closer to a similar though larger marble statue carved by Sansovino for the baptistry of the Frari. Sansovino's is a very moving rendering of the Baptist, and the sculptor was obviously pleased with it because he left instructions that he should be buried in that particular chapel.

Sansovino died in 1570 in one of the apartments lent to him in the Procuratie Vecchie; in that same year Palladio came to live in Venice, and the aged Titian painted the tortured *Mocking of Christ*, which in its handling of light and shadow and in its subdued palette could be said to have been influenced by Tintoretto who acquired it on his death. The school of Tintoretto developed in a sombre spirit. Tintoretto's great achievement in these years was the continuation of his Herculean undertaking for the Scuola di San Rocco, where San Rocco's principal attributes as patron of those stricken by plague governed the whole iconographic scheme as literally as in ancient Byzantine hagiography. San Rocco's healing, feeding and giving drink find their equivalent in the miracles of Moses on the ceiling of the chapter hall and in the corresponding miracles from the life of Christ on the walls. For his later work in the Doge's Palace Tintoretto attracted a whole school of followers whose acres of derivative canvas monopolized taste in painting in the following century. A more original disciple had passed briefly through Tintoretto's studio at this time; a young Greek from Crete called Domenicos Theotocopulos left Venice in about 1570 for Spain where he became widely known as El Greco.

At this same time Veronese was working on the rich and colourful canvases for the chancel of San Sebastiano. The next two decades of Venetian painting belonged to him as he successfully captured the exuberant spirit of a triumphant Republic. In 1570 Venetians rejoiced in the election of their eighty-fifth doge, Alvise Mocenigo, the first of the four last doges of the century whose reigns encompassed a burst of true glory for the arts of Venice. Yet the enthusiasm of the average Venetian could not but be tempered by the tremendous threat posed by the renewed hostility of the Turks. In this very year Cyprus had been lost, and the brave captain of Famagusta, Marc'Antonio Bragadin, taken prisoner after the surrender of the city, flayed alive and his stuffed skin sent to Istanbul to be displayed as a trophy in the arsenal of the powerful Turkish fleet. The alarm felt by the Venetians over their defeat and the loss of such a bulwark in the Levant spread quickly. Europe's attention had been drawn to the eastern Mediterranean only five years earlier when the Turks launched their furious attack on the island stronghold of the Knights of Malta where the great siege ended in stalemate victory for the Christians. Despite heavy losses at Malta the Turks were soon able to renew their attacks both on land and sea. After the fall of Cyprus an international league was formed along the lines of a Crusade. Pius v assumed its spiritual leadership and was represented by Marcantonio Colonna. Papal Rome was joined by the most powerful Christian nation in Europe, Philip II's Spain, under Don John of Austria, the Republic of Genoa under their great admiral Andrea Doria, while the war fleet of the Venetian Republic was made ready under the command of Sebastiano Venier. The great battle was joined on 7 October in the waters off Lepanto in the Peloponnese. The allied victory that day seemed decisive, and indeed Christian forces never again won such a great naval victory over the Turks. In large part their triumph was due to the unusual degree of co-operation between talented but otherwise temperamental commanders. A large measure of the success was also due to the highly developed skills of the Venetians in the kind of naval engagements still fought in the Mediterranean. With this skill went the refinement and development in the sixties of the *galleass*, the principal armed galley of the Venetian fleet. These ships were some fifty metres in length; they were propelled by a new system of rowing with all the oarsmen on a bench pulling the same oar, which meant a great increase of speed. At Lepanto this particular advantage was none too obvious as these great galleys, weighted down by their heavy armament, had to be towed to the front of the Christian line where their artillery bombarded the Turkish fleet into a state of disarray and confusion. The galleass could carry seventy cannon, eight large pieces in the prow, ten on the poop and the rest smaller pieces shooting through ports near the oars. Sailing ships had been tried for battle manœuvres, but failure of a wind could mean disaster for a fleet's strategy, and so the Battle of Lepanto was won in ships not unlike those that had dominated naval warfare in the Mediterranean since the long ships of ancient times.

Once the Turkish battle fleet was broken and scattered, thousands of prisoners were taken and sent back to Venice where they were housed in a quarter called the *Catecumeni*, from the catechism schools that were set up for their conversion. In Venice the victory resulted in an inscription and appropriate statuary added to the gate of the Arsenal to commemorate the event; the Dominicans at San Giovanni e Paolo established a chapel dedicated to the Madonna of the Rosary, on whose feast the victory had been won. The altar of this chapel became one of the principal sculptural commissions of the day, with statuary by Alessandro Vittoria and Girolamo Campagna, while the ceiling was decorated by Paolo Veronese. The government commissioned a vast representation of the battle for the Doge's Palace from Tintoretto, a painting that was destroyed in the fires that swept through the building only a few years later.

Venice was exuberant over her crucial role in the victory, and Sebastiano Venier was acclaimed everywhere as a great hero and as the saviour of Christendom. But the ranking commander of the enterprise was in fact Don Juan, who early in the battle season of 1572 obstinately refused to pursue the advantage of victory and sailed away from the eastern Mediterranean, leaving Venice with only Corfu as an isolated base from which to continue her lonely naval struggle against the Turks. During subsequent negotiations the sultan cleverly managed to capitalize on the squabbles of the allies and to rebuild his decimated fleet within a year. By 1573, therefore, Venice was forced to treat alone with Selim II and to renounce her rights to Cyprus.

This armistice held good for the better part of the rest of the century and allowed the Venetians to resume their momentarily abandoned role as the proud saviours of Christendom and repository of a rich and flourishing culture. A deeply artistic heritage and the strong Christian sentiments that lay beneath it could be typified by the commission in 1571 of four paintings by Veronese for the Coccina family, prominent merchants whose new palace had just been completed near the Rialto. Three of the large panels painted for the palace represented religious subjects, such as *The Road to Calvary* and *The Marriage at Cana*, while the fourth was a votive picture in the tradition of that of Doge Agostino Barbarigo painted by Bellini. In it members of the Coccina family are presented to the Virgin by their patron saints with a company of personified Virtues standing by. With obvious pride in their artistic taste the façade of their new house is included in the background. Also typical of Venetian splendour was a painting like the vast banquet scene Veronese painted in 1573 for the refectory of the Dominican monastery of San Zanipolo. This is a display of richly dressed figures and the lavish appointments of spectacular banquet, with the glitter of a gold service displayed between the columns of vast theatrical loggias and porticos. Dwarfs, monkeys, parrots, cats, dogs and a whole cast of extras attend this lavish extravaganza, which Veronese intended to represent the Last Supper. The Dominican monks of San Zanipolo might have accepted the undeniable incongruity, but the local office of the Roman Inquisition did not. Veronese was summoned before them and subjected to an interrogation, the transcript of which still makes fascinating reading. In his cross-examination Veronese defended artistic licence while the officials of the Holy Office held out for orthodoxy. It is indicative of the brief period of co-operation and good relations that existed between the Church and Venice after the Council of Trent that the Holy Office's view was upheld. But the Church's victory was pyrrhic: Veronese simply changed the name of his splendid picture from *The Last Supper* to *The Feast in the House of Levi*.

The year of Paolo's trial, 1574, was again a heady one for Venice. In July

The Feast in the House of Levi, alive with the extravagance of sixteenth-century Venetian riches and framed by the currently fashionable Palladian arches, was painted by Paolo Veronese for the refectory of the Dominicans at San Giovanni and Paolo.

the new Valois King of France, Henry III, passed through Venice after escaping from his role as elected King of Poland. Venice already had a reputation for the magnificence of its state entertainments and even though the very seat of the government was almost destroyed only two months before Henry's arrival, his reception was so spectacular that it quickly assumed the proportions of legend. The disaster was a fire that broke out in the centre of the city in May 1574. On the upper floor of the newest wing of the ducal palace the large halls of the Senate and the Collegio were gutted. The *Signoria* or the Privy Council met in the Collegio and foreign ambassadors were received there; its loss was obviously particularly unfortunate at the time of a visit of a king of France. The rooms beneath these two halls were also partly destroyed, an even more awkward loss as it was there that the doge had his private apartments. A programme of restoration was begun almost immediately and taken in hand by a relatively little-known architect, Antonio da Ponte. At the same time the Senate appointed a Mocenigo relation of the doge and a Contarini neighbour of his to take in hand the celebrations in honour of Henry III.

The doge and senators met the king at the Lido and the king's symbolic entry into the city took place when he passed under a triumphal arch designed by Contarini's friend Andrea Palladio. After the various ceremonies of protocol and welcome were held in the ducal palace the king was escorted to the palace of the Foscari where he was to stay. There a suite of rooms was put at his disposal and the artistic riches of Venice laid at his feet. Quite literally at his feet as the mosaic pavement of his bedroom is said to have been designed by Veronese, while a portrait of the king hung on the richly draped walls in a frame carved by Alessandro Vittoria. Vittoria also carved the caryatids of the giant hooded fireplace, and the government had them gilded. The festivities for the king were full of an extravagance and frivolity that obviously appealed to his taste. He is said to have never recovered from the incredible banquet where all the plates, glasses, cloths and elaborate centrepieces were sculptured in sugar. He was shown some of the innumerable treasures of the Republic, including the illuminated charter of an ancient Crusader order of chivalry which evidently impressed him and on which he later based his foundation of the *Ordre de Saint Esprit*. He took away with him too the Italian fashion for quadrille dancing, the *balletti* that at the French court became known as *le ballet*. One morning during his four days in Venice he visited the great docks and sheds in the Arsenal where an immense keel was pointed out to him. He and his suite then repaired to the Doge's Palace for the great banquet and that same evening he returned to the Arsenal to see the same keel, now finished in every detail as a ship, sail fully rigged, manned and armed from the dockyard. The French king was amazed and returned to France and the court of his Florentine mother with a taste for Venetian luxury and extravagance that earned his reign a reputation for unrelieved frivolity and decadence.

The impetus of Henry's visit and the victory of Lepanto carried the city through two great crises in the following years. In 1575 Veronese began his marvellous ceiling for the Collegio under the then *Provveditore alla Fabrica* Marc'Antonio Barbaro, and, as part of the redecoration of the fire-ravaged ducal palace, Giovanni Campi produced the wonderful plasterwork decoration for the Hall of the Four Doors. This same year a great plague broke out in Venice. It raged for two years killing fifty thousand of the islands' population. Titian in his nineties died from the epidemic and in 1576 a special dispensation was granted so that the great painter might be buried in the Frari church near two of his Venetian masterpieces. Titian's grave was thus not far from the Scuola di San Rocco where in the year of the master's death Tintoretto was completing the vast cycle of paintings in the upper hall. In that same year the relics of San Rocco, the patron of the plague-stricken, were exposed in the city and the pestilent epidemic lifted and was gone. The city was jubilant with relief, the Senate declared the feast of San Rocco one of the many occasions for a solemn ducal visitation and in the following year it was determined to erect a great votive church in thanksgiving for the city's preservation.

In a sense the votive church dedicated to the Redeemer was a monument to the great patrons of the cinquecento. Marc'Antonio Barbaro entered fully into the debate as to what form the church should take; he favoured a round temple, perhaps like the chapel Palladio later built for his villa at Maser. The site for the Redentore was donated by a Contarini of the San Sanuele branch that had amassed one of the most impressive private collections in the city, that had supervised the arrangements for the visit of Henry III and that were now hosts to Palladio himself. The Doge Alvise Mocenigo laid the cornerstone to the great church which came to be considered as the apogee of Palladio's career as an architect in Venice. The Redentore was nearly completed when he died in 1580 and in a sense its position on the Giudecca is symbolic of Palladio's role in the history of Venetian architecture: an essential part of the backdrop, but not belonging to the heart of the city. Both the interior and the façade of the Redentore are sober and conservative in comparison with some of the architect's more Mannerist exercises. The raised entrance may have been a consideration of function as well as of architecture. The church stands on a tall crypt and thus rises above the votive processions that crossed the broad Giudecca Canal on a bridge of boats. The recommendations of the Council of Trent are even more successfully interpreted and striking at the Redentore than they were at San Giorgio.

The Counter-Reformation was in full flower at this time and some of the most impressive and influential clergy in the Church's history assumed considerable power over governments and individuals. Despite her traditional suspicion of the Vatican the Venetian government fell briefly under the sway of the more extreme demands of the Jesuits, and in 1577 the Senate expelled all actors from the city. The papacy indicated its approval of Venetian religious fervour when Gregory XIII sent the Republic the Golden Rose of the year. In many ways Tintoretto was a product of the spiritual fervour of Counter-Reformation catholicism, not only in the dark, incense-laden atmosphere of interiors lit by the effulgence of celestial intervention, but also in his devotion to the great Christian cycle at San Rocco which he pledged to complete with three paintings a year for the rest of his life.

The government of Venice sorely needed the confidence her victory at Lepanto and the visit of Henry III gave it; it also needed the respite afforded in the treaty negotiated with the Sublime Porte and she was grateful for San Rocco's intervention on her behalf in the great plague. Symbolic, perhaps, of this need for confidence was the election of the hero of Lepanto, Sebastiano Venier, as doge in 1577. Venice also required the dedication to the state of her artists, especially after 20 December of that year when the second great fire in three years swept through the Doge's Palace. The oldest remaining wings of the palace were gutted; the decoration of the Hall of the Scrutiny where Tintoretto's *Battle of Lepanto* had hung, and the Great Council Chamber which enshrined an even greater legacy of Venetian culture and civilization, were lost for ever. The cycles depicting the history and legends of the millennial Republic, painted by Pisanello, Gentile da Fabriano and other masters of International Gothic crowned by Guariento's vast *Coronation of the Virgin* were destroyed in the holocaust along with famous works by Giovanni Bellini and his contemporaries. The loss was tremendous and the building itself was in grave danger of collapse. Palladio was consulted and recommended tearing down the two most damaged wings or at least rebuilding their external walls in his modern classical idiom. Fortunately the wise conservatism of the Republic prevailed and an accurate reconstruction and reinforcement of the fourteenth-century building was undertaken instead. The government was prompt in commissioning a team of artists to decorate the two great halls that had been devastated. Paolo Veronese and Jacopo Tintoretto, both elderly men, were given important commissions and a younger generation of painters assisted them. This younger group owed more to Tintoretto than to Veronese and painting in Venice in the following generations would be dominated by Tintoretto's son, by Palma Giovane, by the family of painters known as the Bassano and by Andrea Vicentino, all working in the style and technique of the older Tintoretto.

The last two decades of the sixteenth century were carried to their close by the same momentum of artistic achievement that had earlier preserved Venetian civilization through the dark days of the League of Cambrai, and had renewed her confidence after the disasters of defeat abroad and fire and plague at home. Praise of the Republic's remarkable political continuity was a theme of Paolo Paruta's *Della Perfezione della Vita Politica* published in 1579, and consciousness of her unique cultural heritage appeared in the first comprehensive guide book to the city written by Sansovino's son, Francesco, and published in 1581 as *Venetia Città Nobilissima et Singolare*. Francesco Sansovino's praise of Venetian Renaissance architecture was evidently widely shared, for in the following year the ancient Orseolo hospice, which had stood on the southern side of the Piazza for over five hundred years, was torn down to make way for a new building to house the nine procurators of the Republic. If Palladio's classical plans for the Doge's Palace had failed to convince the government, the procurators led by Marc'Antonio Barbaro were freer to commission as they pleased. They chose the project of a disciple of Palladio, Vincenzo Scamozzi. Scamozzi was a conservative architect of purist and academic tendencies whose buildings often foreshadowed the sombre restraint of the later neo-classical movement in architecture. His designs for the Procuratie Nuove were based on the bays of Sansovino's library which in 1583 he completed as far as the Molo. Other official projects proceeded apace and by 1585 the major redecoration of the Hall of the Great Council was finished, with Veronese's masterpiece the *Apotheosis of Venice* in the place of honour as the central panel of a vast carved and gilded ceiling. The structural work supervised by Antonio da Ponte was also completed during this period, and even the handsome cary-atid fireplaces carved by Tiziano Aspetti for the ducal and state apartments were in place. With such extensive building and decorating projects completed and others confidently begun Venice seemed once again capable of turning her prosperity to the account of her culture. Despite the virtual loss of Levantine wealth and commerce, Venice nurtured and developed other of her assets, just as an earlier defeat at arms had been converted into a victory for her diplomacy. In 1583 the *Bancogiro* was instituted at the Rialto; the government saw that its successful operation was given top priority. It was presided over by a sena-tor and was opened every day at noon; in fact it was closed only four days in the entire year. When the money collected from the bank's transactions was to be deposited in the State Mint an impressive procession was staged, not by water, but on foot straight through the heart of the city amid the proud merchants of the Republic.

The last fifteen years of the century saw the completion of a great many undertakings begun in the period of the High Renaissance, while other projects prefigured the baroque taste that was developing from a contrived or Mannerist exaggeration increasingly popular in the visual arts. At first baroque elaboration and virtuosity were most evident in the applied arts and crafts, and also in Vene-tian music. In 1585 Giovanni Gabrieli was made First Organist of San Marco, succeeding his influential uncle Andrea. Both men were impressive teachers of their art and Andrea, a pupil in his turn of Willaert, had helped to develop the art of organ composition with the creation of the *canzone* form in 1571 and later with the *toccata*, the earliest form of virtuoso composition for that instrument. The work of both uncle and nephew was not limited to the organ, and Giovanni became especially known for his bold experimentation with new combinations of instruments. In fact the first example of a *sonata* (a piece played) as distinct from a *cantata* (a piece sung) was published by Gabrieli in 1597; he called it *Pian e Forte*, a title that would lend itself to a much later and even more widespread development in the world of music. But the instruments for which Gabrieli and his uncle composed were not those familiar to us today. The sixteenth-century forerunner of an orchestra consisted of a viol, a flute, a cittern and a bandore (the English names of two types of sixteenth-century guitars played with a plectrum – the latter provided a base accompaniment), a lute and a viol de gamba. Excepting this last the string instruments were plucked and not bowed. Brass instruments became more common in the early part of the seventeenth century, although they were already popular in Venice. Such an arbitrary and hypothetical reconstruction of a sixteenth-century orchestra illustrates only the groupings for which music was then composed; Venetian painting throughout the sixteenth century indicates combinations that reflected the popularity of solo virtuosity and improvisation. There were the angel musicians of Bellini, the brass and drums Carpaccio depicted, the flautists and lutenists in the Arcadian settings of a later generation, the full orchestras entertaining the guests at Veronese's spectacular banquets, and the chamber organs played with special feeling by musicians seated at the feet of Titian's voluptuous Venuses. Titian and Carpaccio even included sheets of music in two of their most famous canvases. The architects of the day studied theories of musical harmony: proportion was based on musical intervals, and the brass instruments of martial fanfare were a part of the bas-relief trophies carved on buildings like the library, or on the façades of palaces like the Palazzo Corner della Cà Grande. Music was not therefore the exclusive prerogative of the *maestro di cappello* or the titular organist of San Marco, but very much a part of life in Venice in the sixteenth century as it continued to be for the next two hundred years.

Towards the end of the eighties the Venetian High Renaissance began to draw to a close. Veronese died in 1588, a year after Tintoretto completed a quarter of a century's work at San Rocco with the great masterpieces he painted for the ground floor hall. The ceiling decoration of the Senate chamber was already in the hands of Tintoretto's pupils, as was the final execution of an undertaking worthy of the master's most youthful energy and genius: the vast *Paradise* which covered the entire eastern wall of the Great Council Chamber above the daïs of the Signoria.

There remained in these final years of the cinquecento a few major building projects to be completed. Scamozzi's continuation of the library was finished in the year of Veronese's death and Antonio da Ponte began to build on his competition-winning designs the first stone bridge across the Grand Canal, the world-famous Rialto. The shops on the bridge are faced with a roman-style rustication similar to that da Ponte used for the handsome two-storey façade of the new prisons he built across the Ponte della Paglia from the Doge's Palace. On the Piazza the first ten bays of the new Procuratie were well under way. The church of the Redentore was completed by 1592 and two years earlier Palladio's collaborator in sculpture, Alessandro Vittoria, finished his handsome palace for the Balbi family. In several of its details, such as the broken pediments and the magnificently carved arms on the façade, the Palazzo Balbi influenced the early work of later baroque architects. Otherwise Palazzo Balbi is a conscious and conservative piece of Venetian scenography, fitting perfectly into the city as a pendant to the neighbouring Foscari palace, and built in record time for a patron who lived aboard a barge moored opposite in order to judge better the effect of the façade when seen from the water. Vittoria's other architectural commission at this time was for the Scuola della Giustizia e della Buona Morte at San Fantin; the member of this *scuola* comforted those about to be executed, saw to their burial and looked after their families – a typical example of the charitable function of these confraternities and their valuable role in the Venetian welfare state.

By 1593 the church of San Giorgio was complete enough for the abbot of the day to commission an important programme of decoration. Tintoretto, now approaching eighty, painted two large canvases for the chancel, one of which is a moving and mystical interpretation of the Last Supper as the Institution of the Mass. Equally Tridentine in feeling is Girolamo Campagna's splendid bronze group for the high altar: a golden globe supported by the four evangelists and surmounted by God the Father. Niccolò Roccatagliata's two magnificent bronze candle-stands in the chancel are of a Mannerist complexity and elaboration, matched by the exquisite if slightly efféte miniature statuettes of the patron saints George and Stephen on the rail of the monks' choir. The following year a young Flemish woodcarver decorated the choir stalls with beautiful bas-reliefs from engravings of the life of Saint Benedict. Van der Brulle's work reflected the increasing popularity of bas-relief wood carving as decoration, as well as indicating the large numbers of non-Italian artists, often Flemish, attracted to Venice in the following century.

Until the advent of Baldassare Longhena and a fully developed Venetian baroque architecture, church building in Venice was often merely derivative, such as in the case of Francesco Smeraldi's Palladian façade for the cathedral church of San Pietro in Castello, or the cold and rather academic interpretation of a Palladian interior that Scamozzi designed for San Niccolò da Tolentino in 1591. In 1593 Cardinal Giovanni, the last Grimani Patriarch of Aquileia, died and in the following year Marino Grimani of San Luca was elected eighty-ninth doge of the Republic. A contrast can be drawn between the two branches of this great patrician family in a way emblematic of much that had passed in the Venetian cinquecento and of what was to come in the baroque period of the seventeenth century. Cardinal Giovanni was the third Patriarch of the Santa Maria Formosa branch and part of the great collection made by his uncle had been entailed on him. It was a hoard of invaluable treasures that had inspired sculptors and painters throughout the cinquecento; on his death Giovanni left everything to the state as his uncle, the first Grimani cardinal patriarch, had intended. In 1597 Alessandro Vittoria saw to the removal of the great Grimani collection of classical statuary from the palace at Santa Maria Formosa to rooms in the Marciana where it still attests to the grandeur of cinquecento patrician patronage. The reign of Doge Marino Grimani is usually remembered for an event in the same year, when on 4 May his wife Morosina Grimani was crowned Dogaressa of the Venetian Republic amid extravagant celebration and spectacular festivities mounted with a truly baroque lavishness and complete disregard for the current sumptuary laws. The dogaressa, a worthy patroness of the lace industry, was sent the Golden Rose by Clement VIII, a last gesture of the friendly relations between Venice and the Church that, only a few years later in the new century, were given the lie as Venice lay under a ban of excommunication fulminated by Paul V, the patron of Bernini and the pontiff of baroque Rome.

If the three Grimani Patriarchs of Aquileia recall the patrician taste for assembling impressive collections and the life and career of another cinquecento Patriarch, Daniele Barbaro, suggest the extensive patronage of painting, architecture and humanist studies practised by a patrician ecclesiastic, these men also represent the compromises that were the foundation of the amicable relationship that existed between the Counter-Reformation papacy and the Venetian state following the reconciliation with Julius II and during the period of the Tridentine council. Towards the very end of the sixteenth century this easy relationship began to change in a way that would provoke a fundamental suspicion and hostility between Venice and the Vatican. The climate of tolerance that existed in the city, a residuary legacy from the university city of Padua, attracted a number of unconventional thinkers, self-styled philosophers and men of letters. On the invitation of the noble Giovanni Mocenigo the renegade Dominican philosopher Giordano Bruno of Nola arrived in Venice in 1591. Bruno was to live as an honoured guest with Mocenigo and instruct him in the arts of memory: all apparently innocent enough. But Bruno, besides being an extraordinarily intelligent and learned man, was also wanted by the authorities of the Church. Early in his career he had been implicated in a murder; later his scathing invective had made him unpopular in England where he had debated at Oxford and consorted with the circle of Philip Sidney; then he had sought the protection of Henry III and in turn fled from France, eventually embracing the cause of Calvinism and all the while writing obscure Latin and Italian treatises which reveal him today as one of the most individual and 'modern' thinkers in the history of Italian philosophy and science. The official version of what happened to Bruno in Venice is somewhat at variance with a widely accepted tale that the monk began having an affair with Giovanni Mocenigo's wife. But whether that was the truth or whether Mocenigo was simply exasperated that the monk was not fulfilling his promise as an instructor in arcane matters, the patrician denounced Bruno's presence in Venice to the Venetian Inquisition and the monk was promptly arrested.

Bruno was placed in the hands of the infamous Venetian department of the

Holy Office. The Congregation of the Inquisition had been established in Rome in 1542 to stamp out heresy or heterodoxy among the clergy. The Venetian distrusted it not on principle, but simply because it represented a foreign power claiming legal jurisdiction within the Republic's territories. This offended the agreement whereby rich and powerful benefices like the Patriarchate of Aquileia were given only to Venetian patricians and never to foreign nominees, and whereby the tacit allegiance of Venetian prelates was first to the Republic and then to the pope. After much temporizing the Holy Office was finally allowed to function in Venice, but on condition that one member of the tribunal be a Venetian noble – not even a cleric. It was this relatively harmless Inquisition that had examined Veronese in 1573. Such an extraordinary compromise was sorely tried by the case of Bruno who cleverly abjured all that he was accused of before the Inquisitors. Then pressure was brought to bear and the Venetians were finally forced to surrender the monk to Rome. In Rome Bruno defended his innocence with complicated philosophical paradox and as a result was declared a heretic and burned on the Campo dei Fiori in 1600. His ghost is said to haunt the house of Giovanni Mocenigo. For Venice the guilt or innocence of a renegade monk was not the issue, but rather the right to try him, which was based not only on a concept of legal jurisdiction but in Venetian eyes on the very sanctity of the sovereignty of their state. It was this issue that was to come to a head in five years' time and to destroy forever the tolerance and compromise that had been reached between the Church and the State during the sixteenth century and which had, through the great prelates of the day, so enriched the culture and civilization of cinquecento Venice.

8

The Baroque
Façade
1600-1699

The seventeenth century in Venice was from the outset the age of the baroque, though the first thirty years could be regarded as a prelude to the appearance of its single most significant exponent. Apart from the distinctively Venetian work of Baldassare Longhena, the seventeenth century was a period of relatively little important activity in the major arts. Foreign artists, probably attracted to Venice to study in the great workshops of the cinquecento, remained to become the only noteworthy masters of the Venetian school, and by then the tremendous energy, inventiveness and confident mastery of that period had been dissipated. In Venice baroque vitality was more evident in the crafts and minor arts, in the making of lace and glass, the carving of furniture, in printing and engraving, and in the theatre and in the music accompanying dramatic performance. It was a theatrical age, an age of melodrama and histrionic gesture, and although Venice may have provided an appropriately splendid stage-set the great actors of the age were elsewhere. At the beginning of the century they were at Rome, where a succession of rich and magnificent prelates seemed to revive the splendours of the High Renaissance papacy. Then suddenly the silver trumpets of papal ceremonial blared a call to a war that lasted for thirty years and left Europe torn and exhausted. After the appalling carnage and futile destruction a new and smaller theatre was needed to ennoble the hollow gestures and empty words of a vainglorious age. The spotlight fell on the extraordinary acting and magnificent productions at Versailles, where it remained fixed until a lighter and less pompous spirit drew the world's attention once again to the magic and enchantment of the lagoon city. The eighteenth century in Europe could not have had the character and appearance it did without Venice; the legend of Venetian decadence became part of the script of the *ancien régime*, although few of the actors realized that the charming and seductive backdrop to their comedy would survive them as an invaluable legacy to European culture as well as their most eloquent advocate and justification. Many of the arts of the Venetian seventeenth century were devoted to providing the finishing touches to the extraordinary stage-set that Venice was to become.

If Venice played no major role in the history of European art in the seventeenth century, her politics were equally tangential to the principal developments of those hundred years. Her association with the Vatican of the baroque period was one of mutual suspicion and distrust, aggravated by conflicting claims of legal jurisdiction until the Venetian state was for the third time in her long history put under papal ban of excommunication. Political hostility precluded her from adopting seventeenth-century Roman taste or custom at a time when the papacy was heavily under the influence of Most Catholic Spain. The Spanish ruled most of Italy in the seventeenth century, either through powerful viceroys or through matrimonial alliances. These introduced Spanish customs and fashions to Italian courts, along with the Spanish confessors and clergy who became a by-word for subversion and intrigue. The duchy of Savoy and the Most Serene Republic remained virtually the only independent powers in Italy, until the Spaniards, by continually attacking the border-straddling Savoyards and their vacillating alliances, finally drew them into the Thirty Years War. Spain tried to overthrow Venice from within. After the infamous Spanish plot of 1618 was uncovered and thwarted, Venice withdrew from European entanglements and maintained a neutrality so convincing that certain foreign ambassadors thought Venice might even be enticed into apostasy and join the protestant camp during the great religious war. But the real concern of Venetian foreign policy was once again with the renewed hostility of the Turks and their threat to Crete and to the Venetian possessions in the Morea.

For the first decade of the seventeenth century several of the more extensive building and decorating projects of the preceding century were continued on an equally magnificent scale. In almost every case, however, the results were second-rate in comparison with the original undertaking. The last of the Gothic external staircases in the courtyard of the ducal palace was torn down in 1602 to make way for a rather confused and cramped piece of architecture in Istrian stone, masking the transept rose window of San Marco: and, in the midst of it, a large clock face was mounted. In 1610 the final noteworthy modifications to the Doge's Palace were made when the ground floor of the western wing was remodelled. A round-arch arcade like that of the Molo wing was opened on the western side of the courtyard, where the ducal stables had been housed, and the upper windows of both the Molo and Piazzetta wings were fitted with handsome neo-classical frames. This slight evidence of the Venetian taste for neo-classical sobriety was more pronounced in the addition Scamozzi built in 1609 for the Contarini Palace at San Trovaso. The enlargement was an adjoining building of dimensions similar to the original gothic palace, a conventional practice in Venice since at least the fifteenth century. The Istrian stone façade of Scamozzi's Palazzo Contarini degli Scrigni is a cold exercise in neo-classical symmetry, virtually ignoring rather than disguising the traditional tripartite plan and façade division of the Venetian palace. Scamozzi's regularly disposed pilasters were later copied by conservative Venetians in reaction to the sculptural excesses of Longhena's façades. The great *campo* façade of the Palazzo Pisani at Santo Stefano begun only four years later by the proto of San Marco, Bartolomeo Manopola, is an example of this conservatism, as was Longhena's own first palace built for the Giustiniani Lolin in the early 1620s. Typical of the tentative and somewhat unsatisfactory architecture of these first decades was the celebrated Bridge of Sighs built in 1606 to connect the prisons of the Republic with the tribunals located in the ducal palace. The plain Istrian stone facing is enlivened only with slightly raised rectangle patterns, a two-dimensional treatment of surface that the mature Longhena successfully supplanted. The conservatism of Venetian church building can be seen in the interiors designed by Scamozzi for the Theatine order at San Nicolo da Tolentino and for the church-hospice known as San Lazzaro dei Mendicanti. The former was eventually to be decorated with the most severely neo-classical façade in Venice, while the latter came to represent the theatricality and richness of the high Venetian baroque. In plan, however, both were extremely sober. The former was on Palladian lines of a Latin cross covered by a dome and the latter was similar to Sansovino's almost square plan for San Zulian, with no projecting side chapels but with a chancel flanked by two smaller chapels built out from the east wall. San Lazzaro dei Mendicanti was a slightly elongated version of Sansovino's plan, the basis for which could be traced even further back in Venetian tradition to the extremely simple Gothic churches of the quattrocento.

The militant spirit and prosperity of the stricter monastic orders which was reflected in extensive building projects, undoubtedly contributed to the government's determination to maintain control over ecclesiastical establishments and check the increasing pretensions of the Holy Office and the papal legates. A test case arose in the first years of the century, and reached a climax in 1606 with the bitter conflict between the newly elected doge, Leonardo Donà, soon to be regarded as one of the Republic's heroes, and the Borghese pope, Paul v, one of the most forceful pontiffs of the Roman church. These two men had met years before during one of Donà's embassies to Rome and in a bantering way the conflicting claims of secular and ecclesiastical jurisdiction in Venice had been broached in conversation. The two men were true to the words of their earlier disagreement: when the Republic refused to yield its legal jurisdiction in the case of a criminal priest, the exasperated pope fulminated a ban of excommunication. The Republic reacted by ignoring the ban, by outlawing its publication in Venetian territory and by arresting any priest within the city who denied the sacraments to Venetian subjects. It is significant that with very few and minor exceptions all the religious orders complied. A friar of the Servite order was appointed theological adviser to the Republic, and it was on his advice that Donà acted during the crisis of the Interdict. The Republic did not concern itself with the dangers of defying the powerful papacy of the Counter-Reformation; the government immediately expelled the Jesuits, the most militant supporters of the papacy. But where negotiation broke down there was retribution. Fra Paolo Sarpi, the theological consultant of the Republic and arguably the greatest thinker Venice ever produced, was attacked by a band of assassins obviously in the pay of Rome, stabbed and left for dead. Fortunately he recovered and Venice's resolve was stiffened. Her ambassadors' position abroad was considerably strengthened by this underhand attack, that shocked all Christian Europe, and the Vatican was humiliated by the discovery of its complicity in the attempt on Sarpi's life.

In 1607, through the mediation of Henry IV of France, the ban of excommunication was lifted and the Vatican withdrew her larger claims to interference in the affairs of the Most Serene Republic. Henry IV seems to have regarded Venice with special affection, a small token of which was the gift to the Republic's armoury of his own magnificent suit of white armour still on display in the ducal palace.

Another tangential benefit of the crisis of the Interdict was the increase in the number of theatres in the city after the expulsion of the Jesuits. This revival combined with the appointment of Claudio Monteverdi as *maestro di cappella* of San Marco on the death of Giovanni Gabrieli in 1613, opened the way for one of Venice's most lasting contributions to seventeenth-century European culture. Monteverdi had come to Venice from Mantua, where he had published his *Vesperi della Beata Vergine* only the year before. He composed much ecclesiastical music for San Marco which is now lost; bearing in mind Gabrieli's use of a combination of instruments in his works for the ducal chapel, it is likely that many of Monteverdi's orchestral innovations were heard there for the first time. For example it was Monteverdi who first marked the violinist's part for pizzicato playing, a novelty which coincided neatly with the development of the modern violin by the Amati family in Cremona. Monteverdi's refinement of lyric drama six years earlier in Mantua, where his opera *Orfeo* was first produced for the duke, concurred with the renascence of theatre in Venice. By the time he died thirty years after his appointment at San Marco Monteverdi had written four more operas. Monteverdi's contribution to music, especially in his realization of the dramatic and expressive qualities of discord, made of the opera a serious art form with an eventual impact on European music far beyond the restricted circles in which it was first introduced.

The Republic's defiance of the Holy Office and the expulsion of the Jesuits during the crisis of the Interdict also meant a freer atmosphere in Venetian intellectual circles and at the University of Padua. This resulted in another happy coincidence for Venice's role in European civilization. In 1608 the professor of Mathematics at Padua, one Galileo Galilei, purchased an intriguing new sort of spyglass sold by Flemish merchants in Venice. Making some simple alterations he increased the magnification first eight and then thirty fold. Turning his telescope on the heavens, Galileo made remarkable discoveries which he published in his *Siderius Nuncius* in 1610. He was the first to see the mountains of the moon, to discover that the Milky Way and the nebulae were made of thousands of stellar bodies, to see the rings of Saturn and four of the satellites of Jupiter as well as to discover the nature of sunspots. Although the profounder implications of Galileo's discoveries were slow to be appreciated, the Signoria was anxious to encourage him in his work and they paid him the signal honour of mounting the Campanile in state to see the telescope demonstrated. The Signoria was particularly interested in its potential use aboard the Republic's ships, and indeed it was in these terms that Galileo presented his discoveries to them.

In 1615 Paolo Sarpi, the monk who had advised the Doge Donà in his stand against Pope Paul V, published his *History of the Council of Trent*, which is still considered to be an indispensable if controversial work on the subject. Vicenzo Scamozzi's *Idea dell' Architettura* also appeared in Venice in 1615. Scamozzi died the following year leaving the Procuratie Nuove completed to the first ten arches nearest the Campanile. Scamozzi's building gave a trapezoidal shape to the Piazza and left the bell tower standing isolated at the wider end near San Marco. On the ground and first floors his design was based on Sansovino's bays of the Libreria, while on the upper floor he adopted Palladio's simple aedicular windows with alternating segmented and triangular pediments surmounted by statuary. After Scamozzi's death, work on this last great secular project of the Republic was not resumed for almost a quarter of a century.

Galileo left Venice and Padua to return to his native Tuscany, where through Spanish influence the church held sway in Florence. In 1616 it condemned as heretical the idea that the earth moved and the Tuscan mathematician turned astronomer suffered the censure of the Inquisition. In these same years the Republic was beginning to show an increasing indifference to the currents of European politics that eddied about her. Her primary concerns were closer at hand. Her merchant convoys and even her northern Adriatic fleet were repeatedly attacked by pirate raiders based on the Dalmatian island of Segna. In 1613 these pirates, known as the Uskoks, took the Venetian captain Cristoforo Venier captive and flayed him alive. Uskok ferocity was encouraged by the Austrian archdukes with whom there was a dispute over the fortified town of Gradisca on the Austrian border of the Republic. When the Austrians and Venetians succeeded in negotiating an armistice in 1617 the archdukes found their erstwhile allies more of a nuisance than they had anticipated and finally they engaged in a massive deportation of the entire corsair population to Carniola.

A territorial dispute with the archdukes of Austria was neither unexpected nor a grave threat to the Republic; even the presence of pirates in the Adriatic was very much a part of Venetian history. But in 1618 a threat to the very existence of the Republic was uncovered that represented a danger comparable only with the insidious conspiracy of Marin Falier three hundred years earlier. This was an attempt by the Spanish states in Italy to bring Venice to her knees before the great might of the Hapsburgs. The Spanish viceroy of Milan played an auxiliary role by closing the passes over the Grisons Alps to Venetian commerce and military supplies, while the principal plot was engineered by the Spanish viceroy of Naples, the Duke of Ossuna. Through his ambassador Bedmar and the servants of the papal legate the duke succeeded in subverting a number of Venetians to strike at key positions within the city to create the maximum confusion and distraction until his own fleet could arrive in the lagoon to launch a direct attack on the city. Luckily his infiltration was neither as secret nor as well organized as he believed, and although Ossuna's fleet did appear in the Adriatic the *coup de main* in the city was a fiasco. Bedmar's spies were hanged in the Piazzetta, to the consternation of the Venetians and the foreign ambassadors who learned of the extent of the plot by hearsay and rumour, the most effective way the government had of encouraging vigilance and suspicion.

Unfortunately the strategy of rumour and denunciation later claimed at least one innocent victim. The patrician Antonio Foscarini, sometime ambassador to England and distinguished servant of the state, was denounced to the Council of Ten for conversations he had held in the house that the Countess of Arundel had hired from the Mocenigo at San Samuele. The precise nature of these supposed conversations might not have mattered to the Ten; any encounter between a patrician Venetian and a foreigner was by law regarded as grounds for the suspicion of treason. In Foscarini's case, however, the Ten were extremely negligent in examining their informer and Foscarini was arrested, secretly tried, and then executed between the columns of the Piazza. When it was discovered afterwards, partly due to the outraged intervention of Lady Arundel, that a disgruntled secretary had invented the entire episode, the Ten publicly admitted their error before the Great Council, who ordered Foscarini's body disinterred and re-buried with fullest honours at the expense of the state. Another scandal touched the reputation of the Ten in 1626 when the son of the Doge Giovanni Correr was brought to trial for murder. Two years later the government enacted what was known as the Correction of the Ten, in which it was stipulated that whilst the Council of Ten would have jurisdiction over the criminal prosecution of patricians and over crimes against the state, they would otherwise have no judicial power without the express warrant of the Great Council.

Apart from the Correction of the Ten the first decades of the seventeenth century saw a considerable amount of regulatory legislation introduced to control excesses of the patrician class. For example, the nobles had in the previous century taken to building pavilions set in gardens in the city. These were known as *casinò* (small houses) and were used for informal entertaining. They were the legacy of an even earlier period when the Venetian patriciate maintained villas on some of the outer islands of the lagoon: the Giudecca, Murano and Torcello had once been particularly fashionable. When in the sixteenth century the government encouraged investment and reclamation on the mainland the patricians built farm-villas throughout the Veneto. In the city *casinò* soon became very popular and a number were built in the large gardens on the less populous northern edge of Venice; a survival of this fashion in building is the sixteenth-century Casinò degli Spiriti once overlooking the garden parterres of the Palazzo Contarini dal Zaffo. The seclusion and informality of these small houses made them an ideal venue for gambling; this association has left the legacy of their Venetian name to every European language in the gambling casino.

In 1609 the government tried to suppress the *casinò*, but they were never completely successful even after the government opened the famous Ridotto in 1638 where gambling came under state control. The original Ridotto was part of the private theatre belonging to the Dandolo family in the parish of San Moise. Patricians built or owned a number of private theatres in the city; the Vendramin established the *Teatro di San Luca* in 1622 while other patricians mounted performances of classical tragedy, *commedia dell'arte* and even opera in their palazzi. Monteverdi's *Combattimento di Tancredo e Clorinda* was first performed in Venice in 1624 in the palace of the Mocenigo at San Samuele. Venetian interest in music, both in practice and theory, was also represented in the publication of Ludovico Zacconi's *Practica della Musica* in 1619 which was a compendium of the methods employed by composers of the polyphonic school of music. Monteverdi professed himself uninterested in the canon of usage established by Zacconi because he wished to define a *seconda practica* based on monodic development which he would call '*la perfettione della musica moderna*'.

Monteverdi was not the only foreign artist of note to settle in Venice; there were others from Mantua where the death of the last Gonzaga duke in 1628 resulted in a European war that was settled in favour of a French claimant only in 1631. Venice remained studiously neutral though her sympathies were pro-French as she was opposed to more extensive Spanish power in northern Italy; the Venetians had already been openly on the side of France against the Spanish Hapsburgs for the restitution of the Valtellina to the Swiss Grisons in 1623.

A detail of the woodwork of the *trompe-l'œil* bookcase at the Scuola Grande di San Rocco.
This type of illusion was often a feature of the art and architecture of seventeenth-century
Venice.

All these quarrels as well as those that broke out over the duchy of Parma were offshoots of the dreadful religious wars that spread throughout Europe in the second decade of the century and are known to history as the Thirty Years War. This war was in fact a struggle for a balance of power in Europe. Every question of dynastic succession in Europe was an excuse for further and more complicated alliances to correct any imbalance that might have been caused by victory or defeat on the battlefield. The war was self-perpetuating and the carnage and destruction were immense. Venice remained neutral and even managed to avoid the quarrels of her near neighbours. She may have seemed a haven for the arts although it can be argued that the greatest of seventeenth-century painters, sculptors and architects flourished where political aggression and martial enterprise were the order of the day: the Rome of Bernini, Velazquez' Spain or the war-torn Flemish and Dutch provinces from which Rubens and Rembrandt emerged. In the early twenties Jan Liss of Oldenburg and Bernardo Strozzi of Genoa came to paint in Venice; Domenico Fetti, the court painter to the Duke of Mantua, settled in the city and brought his study of the ducal collections to the local workshops which were producing acres of canvas inspired by Tintoretto. Palma il Giovane executed cycles for the scuola Alessandro Vittoria built at San Fantin as well as for the sacristy of San Giovanni e Paolo. These long, dark Tintoresque paintings were installed above polished walnut wainscoting punctuated by caryatids, ornamental brackets or allegorical figures carved by Flemish master woodcarvers.

It was in architecture, however, that Venice achieved the finest baroque expression of her native genius. However, Baldassare Longhena's first palace built in 1623 for the Giustiniani at San Vidal was somewhat similar to Scamozzi's restrained Palazzo Contarini degli Scrigni which stood opposite on the Grand Canal. Low relief rustication and pilasters break up the Giustiniani façade, though unlike Scamozzi Longhena respected the conventional tripartite division of a Venetian palace. The only hint of his later baroque extravagance are the tall round-arched windows with a carved mask to decorate the keystone and a bit of cloth executed in bas-relief Istrian stone, both motifs borrowed from Grapiglia's façade of the nearby Loredan Palace. Keystone heads and masks were some of the most popular and ubiquitous contributions of the seventeenth century to the city's decoration. Sansovino had used the motif for his library, but it seems to have been Longhena who popularized them as palace decoration. These masks soon became part of other arches as well, and appeared on the numerous stone bridges built in the seventeenth century. On the waterfront façades of palaces and on bridges many of them were tilted at an angle to be seen better from a gondola.

In 1630 a disaster befell Venice that changed the architectural face of the city as completely as the fires of the preceding century had been responsible for the emergence of a new school of painters. Ironically the catastrophe that transformed Venetian architecture was brought about by a carpenter. Five servants of the Mantuan ambassador, the Marchese di Strigis, were to be housed on the island of San Clemente during the statutory forty days (the *quarantina* or quarantine which Venetians invented) before they could enter the city with their master. Mantua was at that time afflicted with the infamous plague described by Manzoni in *I Promessi Sposi* and, unknown to the Mantuan ambassador, one of his suite was infected. This servant came into contact with the Venetian carpenter who was detailed to build the servants' huts on the island. The job quickly finished, the carpenter returned to his work and family in the parish of Sant'Agnese. Sixteen months later 46,490 Venetians were dead of the most terrible plague ever to ravage the island city. The hecatomb might have continued but one of the city's most treasured Byzantine icons, the *Nicopeia* was displayed in penitential processions and the slaughter abated. The relics of Venice's first patriarch, Saint Lorenzo Giustinian, had also proved efficacious and in gratitude the doge instituted an annual state visit to his tomb at San Pietro in Castello. The doge also sent a solid gold lamp to the shrine of the Madonna's house at Loreto and the Senate pledged on behalf of the entire population that an enormous votive church would be built and dedicated to Santa Maria della Salute, Saint Mary of Health. The twenty-first of November was proclaimed to be the date of the feast held in the Madonna's honour and the doge vowed to make an annual pilgrimage there with the Senate and Signoria. So seriously were these pledges taken that in 1631 a large wooden temple was built on the site chosen for the building in order that the vow of pilgrimage might be fulfilled.

The site was one of the finest in Venice and to a large extent determined the choice of the project for the shrine built there. In every other sense Longhena's design for the Salute was, like the city for which he built it, completely original, so much so that nothing like it had been built anywhere before, nor in fact would anything quite like it be built afterwards. This is not to say that it was not a success, for it was deemed so immediately; simply that it was and could only be unique. The church stands on a triangular shaped piece of land at the mouth of the Grand Canal. The old customs' depot surmounted with a fortified tower stood at the end of the point. The only other building on the island also served a diminishing aspect of Venetian maritime trade: the Hospice of the Trinity was where pilgrims were lodged before embarking for the Holy Land. With the Turkish occupation of the Levant and pirate raids in the Adriatic, seventeenth-century pilgrims ran the risk of being captured, held for ransom or sold into slavery; obviously fewer and fewer pilgrims attempted to reach the Holy Land by sea and the hospice was torn down to make way for the great votive church.

Longhena's project for the Salute was for an immense round church with a subsidiary domed chapel. The larger dome was not placed over a crossing, but incorporated the entire body of the church, the smaller dome covering the sanctuary where an elaborate high altar was planned. In the plan there was a certain resemblance to San Vitale at Ravenna. But a round church also recalled Marc' Antonio Barbaro's proposal in 1574 for an earlier votive church, the Redentore, and perhaps also Palladio's round Tempietto chapel built for the Barbaro villa at Maser. Scholars have even seen the influence of a woodcut depicting a round temple in the Aldine edition of the *Hypnerotomachia Poliphilo*. Whatever precedent may be discovered for this most original building, in the end it was the genius of Longhena and his sensitivity to the visual characteristics of Venice that are responsible for the success of the design. Longhena had studied Palladio's work and there are many elements of the building that suggest a clever manipulation and reinterpretation of his ideas. The Salute, designed from the outset like the Redentore as a pilgrimage church, is raised on a plinth of steps high above the canal. The chapels that radiate from the octagonal base have Paladian thermal windows in the upper order. The main entrance projection is more Sansovinesque in feeling with swags, garlands and outsize statuary crowded in niches between the giant orders of columns that frame the triumphal arch doorway. Atop all is the great dome with the smaller dome and twin belfries behind. Seen from the basin of San Marco – certainly one of the viewpoints Longhena had taken into consideration – the Salute takes up the motif of domes and small bell towers that appear to link all the other churches visible to the left of the Grand Canal: Palladio's San Giorgio, Zitelle and Redentore. The abundance of statuary and the splendid decorative volutes at the Salute added an extremely rich and theatrical silhouette to the Venetian skyline. The building took almost all of Longhena's long life to complete, and although he was forced to make compromises in the building materials to avoid too great a weight, he easily achieved the richness of visual effect he sought.

A decade later Longhena was commissioned to continue the Procuratie Nuove begun by Scamozzi. Longhena adopted a Palladian restraint in keeping with Venetian conservatism even though at variance with the spirit of the baroque age he had helped to inaugurate. Certain details of Venetian life suggest that patrician extravagance was unchecked even by the great plague. The portraits of donors in the narrative paintings of the day show Venetians dressed in sober black, but this was a matter more of following the latest fashion than of puritan restraint. Extravagance had reached such proportions that sumptuary laws were once again the frequent subject of legislative debate. The most famous of all was decreed in 1633 when the government announced that from thenceforth all gondolas must be painted black. The gondola of the early seventeenth century bore little superficial resemblance to the most distinctive of Venetian lagoon craft today. The sixteenth-century boat most often depicted by Carpaccio was a small single-oared boat with a flat-sided, flared hull more nearly resembling the modern *sandolo*. The seventeenth-century gondola was rowed by two men and was therefore longer: in profile its keel line followed more nearly a catenary curve from stem to stern post. The prominent bow post was curved forward with curious spike-like teeth pointing ahead; this unaccountable decoration eventually evolved into the distinctive iron bow-sprit or ornament about which much has been written. Much of the gondola's design was probably the result of practical considerations and possibly the bow-sprit helped the principal gondolier standing on the stern to judge the centre of the bridge under which he was guiding his long boat. Certainly that is one function of the modern gondola's *ferro*. The elaborate carved decoration and rich colours with which the patrician decorated his gondola before 1633 sur-vived only in the ceremonial gondolas used for the entry of an ambassador or head of state: occasions when most sumptuary legislation was suspended. The designs surviving for these gondolas and their depiction by various artists, especially in the eighteenth century, indicate that no matter how ornamented the bowsprit of the Venetian gondola became, it still kept its essential forward pointing shape and probably its function.

The early seventeenth century was definitely a period in which the use of the uniform gondola was becoming more and more widespread. Their exotic elegance often struck visiting foreigners, and Louis xiv ordered gondolas to decorate the *tapis d'eau* at Versailles. Painting them all black – incidentally not considered a funerary colour by the Venetians – curbed the extravagance and vanity of the individual patrician, but other regulations for their use were in-troduced at this period as well. The prostitutes of the city were not allowed a gondola with two oars, nor under other legislation were they allowed to have houses on the Grand Canal. The prostitutes had long played a prominent part in Venetian life. Over two hundred years before the government had sought to segregate them and regulate their activities; in the preceding century one of the foremost of her profession achieved such a reputation as a figure of learn-ing and wit that the king of France had asked to meet her. In the seventeenth century the city's prostitutes again played a role in the public amusements that attracted the war-weary of Europe to Venice.

Traditional Venetian public festivities of all sorts were increasingly popular with foreign visitors. The Bavarian Josef Heinz the Younger recorded the pre-Lenten *Giovedi Grasso* bull-baiting in the Campo San Polo in 1648 where the patricians and their guests looked on from specially constructed tribunes. In 1638 the Ridotto was opened for gambling and chocolate, imported from Egypt as a medicinal plant, was first sold in the city's pharmacies. Several of these shops survive with rich walnut boisseries, carved shelf brackets and fine majo-lica medicine jars; they provided comfortable meeting places for all classes and thus were the precursors of the city's innumerable coffee houses. The previous year the Teatro Nuovo di San Cassian was opened. It was one of the increasing number of theatres in the city although different from those owned by the patri-cians in that it was the first opera house in Europe open to the public. In 1637 a paying audience attended a performance of an opera by Francesco Cavalli. Two years later Cavalli was appointed second organist of San Marco, but his principal achievement in the history of Venetian music was his transformation of Monteverdi's dramatic spectacle into popular entertainment. He reduced Monteverdi's extravagant orchestra to more practical limits, he added melodious arias to his compositions and popular characters appeared in his libretti. He also introduced the broad and grotesque humour that was characteristic of Italian opera until the early eighteenth century.

In 1644 the attention of the Venetians was drawn away from the delightful distractions of their city. The Turks were on the rampage in the eastern Mediterranean and once again only the single fortress island of the Knights of Saint John with the scattered and weakened Venetian outposts remained as obstacles to a complete Ottoman conquest of the eastern sea and its trade routes. The Muslim forces chose to attack the richest and strongest of Venetian bulwarks, the island of Crete, which had been held by the Republic since its grant in fief within the Latin empire of the east. The Venetians were not caught entirely unprepared by the renewed hostility although the ferocious perseverance and determination of a previously ill disciplined enemy caused great alarm. Crete was defended by a series of impressive fortresses, some of which had been built by Sanmicheli, the foremost expert in sixteenth-century fortification. But despair at the strength of the enemy onslaught revealed itself almost immediately when Biagio Zuliani, captain of the great fortress of San Teodoro, blew up the whole complex rather than surrender it to the Turks. The fortified port of La Canea, one of the principal bastions of Crete – or Candia as it was known – was thus lost to the Turks. The Venetian forces regrouped to concentrate on the defence of the capital city, also called Candia.

In the year following the fall of La Canea the government solicited contributions from the wealthy merchant class for the defence of the island. For those who donated one hundred thousand ducats, a colossal sum, the Republic offered aggregation to the patriciate through inscription in the Golden Book. Sixty-seven families were admitted in 1646, many of them, like the Widman and the van Axel, foreigners from outside Italy. That such prodigious wealth was in the hands of non-Venetians, let alone men who were not patricians, gives the lie once again to the simple generalization that the riches of the Republic were exclusively in the hands of the patriciate. On the other hand the often repeated assertion that these families used the war and their contribution as a cynical pretext to obtain patrician privileges is belied by their additional voluntary contributions in kind for the war in Crete. Ships, arms and even troops were sent to Crete at private expense. This united war effort met with significant success at first and in the year 1650 what was left of the key fortress of San Teodoro was retaken.

In the following year there was a notable victory over the Turks at sea; the action was fought off Paros and the battle was the occasion for the debut of a new generation of Venetian military heroes. The *Capitano Generale* of the fleet at Paros was Alvise Mocenigo and two of his war galleys were commanded by Tommaso and Lazzaro Mocenigo. The key to containing the Turkish fleet in the eastern Mediterranean was obviously the Dardanelles, and the Mocenigos fought in three actions in those waters in the fifties. Alvise was killed in 1654; Lazzaro was wounded in 1656 and died in a third battle in the Straits in 1657. Lazzaro's replacement was Francesco Morosini, who eventually led the Venetians to triumphs unknown since Lepanto, becoming an almost legendary hero of the Republic. But Morosini's finest hour was yet to come. Meanwhile the outlook must have seemed desperate to the Venetians, especially to those under attack by Turkish forces on Crete. The siege of the capital, Candia, began in 1648 and was to prove the longest siege in western history, ending in defeat for the Venetians twenty-one years later.

Meanwhile a grandiose expression in the arts reflected the glorification of Venetian arms as well as the extraordinary prosperity indicated by the private contributions made for the War of Candia. A single most impressive funerary monument was typical of many that proliferated in the city's churches. The entire entrance wall of the church of San Lazzaro dei Mendicanti was given over to the glorification of Alvise Mocenigo who died in the first battle of the Dardenelles. Much traditional iconography for the commemoration of a *condottiere* or naval hero was revived in his funerary monument. There are over-lifesize allegorical statues signed by the Flemish sculptor Giusto le Court whose work decorates the high altar of the Salute; there are trophies of arms and columns of precious marbles; and high in the upper order, above the main entrance doorway of the church, stands the proud figure of Mocenigo himself dressed in costume that appears everywhere in Venetian seventeenth-century sculpture. Mocenigo wears the half armour of a seventeenth-century commander and carries the baton of his command in his right hand; the hat of his rank is a flat-topped round beret, but his silk sash and cape, a billowing mantle, his abundant peruke and his lace collar and cuffs afford the sculptor a chance to display his skill in carving as well as depicting the current taste in dress. Flanking the giant statue of Mocenigo are two large panels which illustrate the theatricality of the baroque taste as well as the cosmopolitan complexion of seventeenth-century Venetian workshops. In the convention of Venetian funerary monuments the two panels are meant to be bas-reliefs of battle scenes; instead the illusion of perspective is so cleverly handled as to seem fully realistic scenes carved in three dimensions and crowded with incident: on the one hand struggling bodies, cadavers and prisoners, and on the other several lines of ships engaged in complicated close manœuvres and broadside engagements between the type of frigates built in the Arsenal in the 1660s. The Mocenigo chose an Englishman, John Bushnell, to carve these panels, a reminder that these kinds of ships and this type of warfare had been introduced into the Mediterranean by the Dutch and English navies only at the beginning of the century. The depiction of crowded and confused naval battles figured not only on funerary monuments. The finest painters of the day were commissioned to paint the most recent victories for inclusion in the historical scheme of the decoration of the Scrutiny Hall of the Doge's Palace. The most highly regarded painter of the day, Pietro Liberi of Padua, who travelled widely and like Titian was ennobled by the emperor, enjoyed a handsome palace on the Grand Canal and numerous commissions including a huge painting of a naval battle in the Dardanelles. Lesser artists provided captains and commanders with the appropriate panoramic series of naval paintings to hang in their *palazzi*. It was in this period also that suits of armour, both antique and modern, trophies of captured arms and infidel banners were displayed in the watergates which were often lit by the giant *fanali da galere*, seventeenth-century flagship stern lanterns.

The Mocenigo's choice of the Mendicanti for Alvise's tomb is interesting in itself. This complex of church and hospice had been commissioned from Scamozzi early in the century not by a religious order, nor by patricians such as the Mocenigo, but by two merchants called Bontempelli and Biava. Neither man was ennobled for contributions to the War of Candia, but the church and hospice they built to house and care for beggars, impoverished old people and abandoned children represented not only the remarkable prosperity of the merchant class but the widespread private philanthropy still traditional in Venice and encouraged by a government hard pressed by the expenses of war. Other sections of the population were also enjoying considerable prosperity. Throughout the seventeenth century numerous investment and commercial partnerships were formed between Jews and patricians and in 1654 Longhena was commissioned by the Levantine community of Jews in the Ghetto to build them a new synagogue. Three years later the Jesuits were readmitted to Venice and obtained title to the suppressed monastery of the Crociferi in the northern quarter of the city where in the next decades their own astonishing contribution to Venetian baroque would be built.

But the outstanding monuments of seventeenth-century Venice were not only the result of the exceptional patronage of monastic orders, churches, scuole, merchants or even Jews; most of what was commissioned in this period was still based on the impressive prosperity of the patrician class. In the seventeenth century the relevant statistics are very often contradictory. The individual patrician may have been a rentier with part of his large income deriving from the vast mainland properties reclaimed and cultivated by his ancestors, but since the government was also determined to protect and develop those areas of commerce and industry which were safe from the Turkish menace, it created numerous opportunities for the patrician investor. At the mid-century the wool, silk and glass industries were placed under government protection, and although private banking at the Rialto was restricted, the patrician was, by virtue of his membership of the government, in a position to participate in the state's banking activities. Whatever the source of his wealth, the seventeenth-century patrician built imposing funerary monuments, endowed and decorated chapels, entered into investment partnerships with Jews and *cittadini* and hired the finest architects of the day to build his palaces.

The tremendous wealth of this proud and self-conscious class was recorded in Carlo Ridolfi's *Meraviglie dell' Arte* and Mario Boschini's *Carta del Navegar Pittoresco*, both of which provide extensive lists of the contemporary collections housed in the city's palaces. In 1658 a man who may be considered representative of his class, Giovanni Pesaro, was elected doge of the Republic. Giovanni's branch of his large family lived in the parish of San Stae and were known as the Pesaro del Carro. The Carro of their family sobriquet was the car on which lagoon boats and barges were once loaded near Fusina to haul them overland the short distance to the system of canals and waterways which were the commercial network of the mainland. The Pesaro's income from this essential part of Venetian river commerce was so great that eventually their monopoly on portage was taken over by the state, nonetheless compensation for their loss of revenue was massive. At San Stae they owned the large Veneto-Byzantine palace where the Republic had housed her most prominent guests including the emperor of Constantinople. In the early part of the seventeenth century the state again leased the house, this time as a *fondaco* or residence/emporium for the Turkish merchants of the city; for despite continual warfare with the sultan a colony of Ottoman merchants was allowed to live and trade in the city. Fifty years earlier, after the battle of Lepanto, this Turkish colony attracted the hostility of the populace and the Senate sought to segregate them for their own safety. As a result the Pesaro Palace at San Stae was converted to include a mosque, bath and a harem and became known, and is still known today, as the *Fondaco dei Turchi*. By the time Giovanni Pesaro was elected one hundred and third doge of the Republic he had bought a piece of land and had begun to demolish a number of houses to make way for a new palace on the Grand Canal near San Stae. The first construction work was begun on a courtyard well back from the Canal and when he died shortly afterwards the immense project was left to his nephew to complete. This nephew, a procurator of San Marco, was responsible for hiring Longhena to build the great Palazzo Pesaro and to design a vast tomb for his uncle near one of the family altars in the Frari.

Although the Doge Giovanni Pesaro had envisaged an immense new palace for his family, Longhena's building was not under way until 1676, seventeen years after the doge's death. In the meantime Longhena received a commission for a palace at San Barnaba from the Priuli Bon family. The construction of this palace, now known as the Cà' Rezzonico, was begun in more conventional fashion with the section on the Grand Canal. The courtyard, ballroom and monumental staircase wing at the back were added only long after Longhena's death. The Priuli Bon palace was an excellent example of patrician extravagance and Longhena created an impressive architecture for their pride and magnificence. However, neither of these two great palaces was finished in Longhena's

lifetime and in the case of the first the Priuli Bon virtually bankrupted themselves trying to realize their architect's splendid designs. Not only were the
great blocks of Istrian stone quarried and used in unprecedented abundance
in a private palace, but almost all of it was carved in high relief. The rustication
of the ground floor was massive; the upper floors were decorated with a richness
consciously derived from Sansovino's library. Shafts of columns were either
rusticated or fluted, there were Sansovino-type spandrel figures, river gods,
cherubs, garlands and trophies and each round arched window was capped with
a keystone carved to represent a head, no longer just a mask, but now a grim-
acing face encased in a visored helmet crowned with plumes and feathers.

Longhena was not the only architect to indulge in baroque extravaganza and
some of his work at this time, such as the building for the Scuola dei Carmini, was quite restrained. The much-excoriated, overloaded new façade of
San Moise, commissioned by the patrician Vicenzo Fini, was completed in
about 1668 on designs by the Paduan Alessandro Tremignon with the overall
sculptural decoration carried out by a Flemish pupil of le Court's. A few years
later, two of the most handsome baroque church façades in Venice were begun
by the architect Giuseppe Sardi, whose work reflects the contemporary taste
for the theatrical. Both façades are enriched with deep, elaborately framed
niches to contain the giant gesticulating statuary then in fashion. The façade
for the church of the Discalced Carmelites was begun in 1672, the year Longhena completed the building of the Salute. Sardi's façade for Santa Maria del
Giglio was commissioned by Antonio Barbaro who had been a *provvedditore*
of Candia during the siege of 1666 and who had held other high offices in the
colonial and mainland government until his death in 1679. In that year he left
a conspicuous legacy for the completion of the façade of Santa Maria del Giglio.
This represents the last great privately endowed extravaganza of family pride
on public display in Venice. In outline it followed the composition of the great
baroque funerary wall monuments, though this one covered the entire façade
of a church, not one of its interior walls. The glory was not individual, although
like Alvise Mocenigo, Antonio Barbaro is prominent in peruke, flowing robes,
half-armour with lace at the cuffs, and holding the baton of martial command.
The façade includes Antonio's four brothers as well, and the whole panoply
of their generation is embellished by trumpeting angels and lolling Virtues
crowned overall by a standing figure of Glory. There was no room left on the
façade of the church for the more conventional saint or angel. Even the less
important carving depicts either Barbaro's naval battles or delightful bas-relief
maps of fortresses commanded by Antonio and cities associated with his career.

The splendid pride and martial glory celebrated by Barbaro and other Venetian commanders of his generation rang somewhat hollow considering Venice's
true military position before the mid-eighties. Ten years before Antonio Barbaro's death the powers of Europe had become alarmed by the weakening of
Venice's besieged position in Crete. In 1669 Louis xiv sent reinforcements,

but the French ships and the fleets of the Germans, the pope and the Knights of Malta withdrew in the same year. The Venetians were forced to surrender to the Turks on 6 September, bringing to an end over four hundred and fifty years of continuous Venetian rule in Crete. By treaty Venice was allowed to keep the minute island of Gramvousa along with Souda, the port of La Canea, a kind of toe-hold on the northern side of the island. These concessions were obviously obtained with the desperate and displaced Venetian colonists in mind, but defence of their holdings or any profitable commerce with their own outpost was effectively cancelled by the loss of the capital city and the large fiefs of the island's interior.

In 1683 the tide seemed to turn miraculously against the Turks. The deadly thrust of the infidel hordes into the very heart of Christian Europe was successfully parried by the Habsburg emperor and King John Sobieski of Poland who managed to turn the siege of Vienna and put the Turks to rout. Venice's own brave and lonely role at sea against the powerful Muslim flotilla was acknowledged in her subsequent alliance with the heroic Christian sovereigns. The following year the Venetians took the initiative and struck back at the Turks in the Morea. The fighting that broke out in 1684 continued for fifteen years but resulted in some of Venice's finest hours under the leadership of her most talented commander Francesco Morosini. Within two years he had regained almost all of the Peloponnese and in 1687 he stormed and conquered Athens. His success in the islands of the former empire was remarkable and in 1687 he sent one of the famous lions of Delos as a trophy to the Arsenal. In the following year Morosini was elected doge in the field and his apotheosis was guaranteed. He entered the Venetian pantheon in the company not only of Sebastiano Venier, the Venetian commander at Lepanto, but also with the legendary Doge Enrico Dandolo, the conqueror of Constantinople. In fact the perspicacious and realistic Venetians, although exhilarated by Morosini's great victories on their behalf, did realize that Morosini's struggle to the death with the Turks was in many ways an inevitable consequence of Dandolo's dubious though heroic conquest four and a half centuries before.

Morosini's early victories, as well as those after his election, were facilitated by the financial support of the patriciate. The Golden Book had been opened at the outset of his campaigns in 1684 and forty-seven families were ennobled by the Republic on receipt of the statutory one hundred thousand ducats towards the war effort. But it must be observed that twenty fewer families qualified for this second aggregation than were admitted in 1646. Between the surrender of Candia and Morosini's election several building projects in the city were completed, notably the two splendid baroque façades by Sardi, and the long, low customs house surmounted by Fortune pirouetting on a gilded globe, which completed the setting of Longhena's Salute church. Ornate façades were merely façades just the same; the customs house was a superficial and rather slipshod remodelling, and the Palazzo Pesaro begun seven years before

Longhena's death in 1683 could not be completed until the next century for lack of funds.

The riches of the patriciate began to be lavished on other less enduring or monumental extravagances. In the year Candia surrendered Lorenzo Loredan left the state a legacy for the endowment of an anatomy theatre, but a more typical foundation was the Grimanis' private opera house built five years later. In 1675 one of the finest woodcarvers to work in Venice began his apprenticeship with the Genoese sculptor Filippo Parodi, although by the end of the century Andrea Brustolon's talent was turned from sculpture to the greater demand for elaborately carved furniture: chairs, ornamental blackamoors, torcheres and the like. At this same time the Senate instructed the *savii alle mercanzia* to levy a tax on the consumption of coffee and sorbets; but despite the tax the novelty proved so popular that in 1683 a coffee shop could open in the extremely expensive premises of the Procuratie Nuove; this café was the ancestor of today's Café Florian. But coffee drinking was a harmless extravagance compared with the gambling and ruinous luxury that the patriciate began to indulge in for pleasure. The state-sanctioned regattas and gala festivities in honour of visiting princes when sumptuary laws were suspended became the focus of a particularly lavish and conspicuous prodigality. There was a masked cavalcade held in the recently built riding school near San Giovanni e Paolo to honour the Duke of Mantua, but such exclusive spectacles never caught the most extravagant fancy of the patriciate; they spent more on the traditional regattas such as the one given for the state visit of the Duke of Brunswick in 1686. Elaborate preparation, especially in decorating the twelve-oared giant gondolas or peote, such as had been expended only for a legendary visit like that of Henri III, now became the order of the day with patrician clans vying for the hire of the finest artists to design and decorate for them. The floating tribunal or *macchina* for the judges of the gondola races became a permanent part of Venetian baroque iconography. It was an elaborate confection resembling one of the theatrical fantasies of the Bibbiena family of stage designers and early became a set piece of the view paintings made to commemorate specific regattas. By the early years of the following century, what had once been memorable spectacles of Venetian wealth now blurred in a continual haze of celebration and spectacular ceremonial.

Even by the time the Doge Francesco Morosini made his entrance to Venice as the conquering hero of the victorious empire and the ceremonies performed in San Marco took on the character of a combined coronation and canonization, the celebrations involved were just part of an elaborate round and did not capture the popular imagination the way the visits of the French king or Pope Alexander III had done. In fact reading between the lines Morosini was never an entirely popular hero. In typical baroque fashion he wallowed a bit too much in his own glory; his pronouncements from his camp when informed of his election as doge were pompous and he lost no time in sending off a request to Venice for the augmentation of his own personal coat of arms. This might seem a minor point of protocol were it not that every patrician was aware of the past ducal promises whereby a doge could neither devise nor display a personal coat of arms. But in the enthusiasm of the moment Morosini's requests were granted and he composed an heraldic nightmare in keeping with the taste of the day; reading the grant it seems his every achievement was squeezed into the compass of a multi-quartered shield. When Morosini entered the city in 1690 the celebrations were spectacular. There was the usual immense triumphal arch set in the Piazzetta for his debarcation from the *bucintoro*; by day the outside of the ducal palace was hung with rare materials and paintings, by night the courtyard was lit by torchlight; the ducal apartments were refurnished and rehung as richly as possible and the Morosini palace at Santo Stefano was the much-bedecked and garlanded scene of dancing and drinking by the populace and the patriciate.

In addition to all this acclaim the Senate commissioned Francesco Parodi to design a triumphal arch under which Morosini passed into the Hall of the Scrutiny before his acclamation by the Great Council. This arch, unlike all those that had been designed before for such occasions, subsequently became a permanent if rather ugly part of the decoration of the hall. When Morosini died in 1694 he was buried in Santo Stefano not in a great wall tomb, but beneath a more modest circular bronze tomb slab cast by his cannon makers. Only the year before he had redeemed his reputation for posterity with his re-election as *Capitan Generale da Mar* and with a number of victories in the Aegean. In these last years of the century there seemed to be fewer heroes to acclaim or to commemorate with elaborate monuments. Morosini's successor in the protracted and exhausting war against the Turks was imprisoned for his abandonment of Schio and even commanders bearing the proud name of Mocenigo were dismissed for incompetence earlier in the decade.

If Parodi's triumphal arch was one of the last *condottiere* memorials in the city, his most talented disciple realized the new turn in taste. Andrea Brustolon accepted commissions from the immensely rich Correr, Pisani and Venier families for elaborate suites of carved furniture. In the finest of his work the individual chair, torchere or plinth for the display of Chinese porcelain became as elaborate a piece of sculpture as had been seen in the city. Much of Brustolon's work surviving in Venice was executed in boxwood and ebony, exotic woods which were part of the new commerce of the East India companies. A number of Brustolon's sculptural motifs were also suitably exotic: ebony blackamoors or Nubian slaves in chains mingled with figures from classical mythology. The torchere or gueridon carved in the shape of a liveried blackamoor became one of the most widely known pieces of Venetian furniture in Europe. By the end of the seventeenth century and the early decades of the eighteenth furniture workshops had proliferated in Venice. Similarly a whole school of stuccoists from the traditional sources of Venetian sculptors – northern Italy and the Ticino – established themselves in Venice in the last two decades of the century. One of these, Abbondio Stazio, created an interior decoration like that of the Palazzo Albrizzi which was unrivalled for richness even by the apartments of the doge. The Albrizzi were not untypical of the richest families of the baroque period who set the fashion for the Venice of the following century. They were originally from the mainland; in Venice they prospered in trade and were admitted to the patriciate after contributing the statutory one hundred thousand ducats to the war effort in Candia. From their commerce in the Levant they were also able to provide and arm ships for the war fleet. Eventually the Albrizzi foresaw the diminishing role that sea trade was to play in Venetian prosperity and through advantageous marriages they managed to acquire vast tracts of land in the Veneto. In keeping with the honourable regard for commerce and industry in the Republic they also invested in a publishing house which soon became known as one of the finest in all Italy, not only for the quality of its printing but also for the splendour of each book's engraved illustrations.

The decoration of the Albrizzi palace at San Aponal is a fine example of the wealthy patrician's baroque taste. The stuccoists created an intricate array of figures, garlands, putti and billowing canopies for the walls and ceilings of each room. High relief compositions in stucco framed vast canvases set in the ceiling, a novel departure from the ceilings made of deep and heavily carved and gilded wooden frames. The walls too, especially those of the *portego* or central gallery of the palace, were treated lavishly by the stuccoists. Damask, silk or the older stamped, gilded leather hangings gave way to acres of fantastic figures and lush plant life running riot over the long walls. But here too space in the stucco walls was left for vast stretches of canvas, painted in a studio and bought and cut to fit the stuccoist's elaborate frames.

This decoration reflected several changes in taste and patronage. Painters were now executing large canvases, generally on mythological subjects, without a specific commission. On feast days the entire square in front of the church and *scuola* of San Rocco was frequently devoted to an open air exhibition of studio painting intended for a primarily decorative purpose. Paintings for churches were still the result of specific commissions although late in the century the idea of covering vast wall spaces with paintings of a more historical than religious significance was fully developed in the cycle of paintings at San Zaccaria by Antonio Zanchi, Niccolò Bambini, Andrea Celesti and Antonio Fumiani. The treatment of these subjects was derived from the quasi-historical-religious narrative canvases intended for the *scuole* as well as from the cycles commissioned for the ducal palace. Another development in church decoration appeared towards the end of the century and is best exemplified by Antonio Fumiani's masterpiece, the gigantic illusionist ceiling of San Pantaleone. The dizzying perspectives, cleverly observed foreshortenings and the conceit of an open sky above populated by saints and cupids owe much to the Rome of

The Ballroom of
Palazzo Albrizzi: the
richest interior of a
late seventeenth-
century private house
preserved in Venice.
The Albrizzi were rich
merchants originally
from Bergamo and
later important
publishers.

The Sleeping Venus
was commissioned,
perhaps as a wedding
gift, by Girolamo
Marcello from the
young Giorgione of
mainland Castelfranco.
In it the artist
established not only
the Renaissance canon
of feminine beauty,
but also a pose and
composition which
Titian frequently
copied.

Padre Pozzo and the Jesuits, although in Venice Veronese had shown himself a master, following the even earlier fashion of Mantegna, of such architectural illusion and *trompe-l'œil*. Fumiani's ceiling represented a temporary solution to an obviously difficult problem. Having abandoned the heavily carved frame with oil paintings for the ceiling decoration of a church, the new fashion for stuccowork ceilings was found unsuitable. For a stucco figure to be expressive if not visible from far below in the nave, it would have to be immense, and as Venetian stucco work could be supported only on iron armatures set in the false reed and plaster vaulting, a ceiling decorated with heavy stucco figures was too risky. Thus Fumiani's formula, though little copied, would partly contribute to the solution found in the first half of the following century when fresco work was widely used for ceiling decoration.

The last decade of the seventeenth century set the stage for all that was to follow, one of the most splendid periods of Venetian culture and civilization. A period which gave many artistic treasures to Europe but which gave Venice a reputation she has never lived down. The exaggeration of her fame as a pleasure capital in the eighteenth century was partially the fault of the seventeenth century which at certain moments was a time of vainglorious pride, pompous pretension and vulgar ostentation. The pride of the Republic in her martial and political accomplishments was too patently short-sighted and her richest patricians too often seemed anxious to neglect their abiding talent for commerce and industry. In the last year of the century Venice regained something of her old confidence and skill in diplomacy and successfully negotiated what is known as the Treaty of Carlowitz. The treaty brought an armistice with the Turks that was a sop to Venetian pride as by its terms the Republic was allowed to retain all Morosini had fought for in the Peloponnese. The new century opened on a note of peace, virtually the first that had been heard for the last one hundred years. Now the Venetians could turn their talents and their attention to the notorious business of the last century of the *ancien régime*: pleasure.

9

Carnival
and Collapse
1700-1797

Many of the things that distinguished Venetian culture and civilization during the eighteenth century were obviously the result of what had gone before. The Venetians remained the same basically conservative people their ancestors had been. In fact there is a good argument that the Venetian Republic could not have survived in the nineteenth century even if Napoleon had not wrought his work of destruction. The final years of the eighteenth century and the early nineteenth century favoured the extremes of revolution and reaction while the vital essence of the Republic had always been balance and a carefully wrought compromise and control. No matter how frivolous the eighteenth-century Venetian may have seemed to the rest of Europe, there can be no question of his innate pride in the institutions of his government. To a large extent this pride hampered much needed reform in the mechanism of the state. It was the self-assured, aloof attitude of the millennial government to the political struggles of Europe that preserved Venice as a haven of pleasure during these hundred years. The Venetians took much of what they had inherited for granted and thus were seen to fritter their inheritance away, while to the rest of Europe the city began to seem a wonder. When Venice collapsed in 1797 more than one writer spoke of the fall of the most ancient of all the world's governments. Europeans came to see this somewhat anachronistic marvel; Goethe was delighted to have a glimpse of the figure of the doge walking in a small procession in the streets. The doge had become a remote and legendary figure, leading a restricted life more hemmed in by ceremonial and his *promissione* than eighteenth-century monarchs whose palace door was frequently open to any who could afford the hire of a dress sword.

Foreigners came less and less to Venice to negotiate either political or commercial treaties. Goethe's countrymen could have assumed a special entrée and a greater familiarity with Venice than most Europeans, but in the eighteenth century the traditional commercial alliances and trade routes were being by-passed and the Germans in the city were merely tourists like the rest. The grandest of these were fêted with all the resources of an improvident government and often left with a highly developed taste for the delights of Venetian culture. Once returned to their homes they imported Venetian glassware, lace, lacquer furniture and hired the services of Venetian musicians, stuccoists and painters. Only slightly less splendid than these princely patrons were the ambassadors and grandees who commissioned views of the ancient and unique city or else had their portrait done in pastels by one of a school of fashionable artists. Venice began to trade on an unprecedented scale in her own culture and civilization. To a limited extent this had happened in every century in which Venice found herself pre-eminent in the arts, but generally speaking this commerce had taken the form of an extraordinary embassy sponsored by the state and addressed to a sovereign and his limited circle. Now Venetian art was exported everywhere and influenced the whole of an age in its taste.

Naturally it was the most exportable aspects of Venetian culture that exercised the widest influence, for example painting and the painters who were sent to every court and corner of Europe. Then came the exponents of Venetian patrician taste, the interior decorators of the day. Certain painters and frescoists, *ébénistes* and their furniture, and the glass blowers who not only supplied Europe's *surtouts de table* and mirrors, but whose elaborate chandeliers, thanks to the fact that they could be dismantled for shipment, were sent to glisten and illuminate every palace with any pretensions to the latest fashion. Venetian musicians and composers spread their arts far and wide. The sculptors in the city were like the painters of the preceding century, for the most part foreigners willing to work in the older traditions of the stonecutters who had supplied statuary for the decoration of a façade, a tomb or a high altar. The architects of Venice were also bound by local conventions so that their role in the eighteenth century was often to adapt the latest fashions from abroad – although it is typical of Venetian conservatism that neither the extreme Rococo nor the most severely correct neo-Classical gained a following in the city. However, through the media of printed books, published in Venice, some Venetian fashions and tastes in architecture were made available to be adopted elsewhere in Europe.

The earliest example of the influential, though seldom acknowledged, Venetian taste in architecture appeared in the very first year of the new century with Andrea Tirali's façade for the recently rebuilt church of San Vidal. The new façade was composed of superimposed temple pediments and can be described as the first neo-Palladian or neo-Classical façade built anywhere in Italy. The return to Palladio's precepts was not limited to ecclesiastical building; many eighteenth-century palace façades were ornamented with conservative details: by pilasters instead of fluted corinthian columns, small classical pediments above the windows instead of richly carved bays, or a sober Serlian window group for the *portego* or central hall. The Venetian classified this treatment as Palladian and, as a result, a large number of palaces in the city were erroneously attributed to Palladio. The most widely copied was the plain yet harmonious façade of the sixteenth-century Palazzo Papadopoli, only recently attributed correctly to Giangiacomo Grigi of Bergamo, the architect who had completed Sanmicheli's great palace for the Grimani at San Luca. That neither Palladio nor Serlio built palaces in Venice is an assertion of modern scholarship. Since Venetians did not see Palladio's work in Venice as limited to ecclesiastical commissions, they were already at home in the Palladian 'revival' that later became widespread throughout Europe.

Only six years later Tirali began another church façade that took Venetian neo-Palladianism further than any other building in the city. The porch of San Nicolo da Tolentino remained unique: it was in every detail a perfectly correct corinthian temple pronaos of the imperial Roman period. It does recall some of Palladio's villa façades and the formula was successfully adopted by church architects in other countries, but in Venice its classicism was obviously considered too extreme; the Palladian temple façade of superimposed pediments was more frequently copied as for most Venetian sites a flat façade was preferred to a deep porch. Another architect working in the first decades of the century designed façades for two other churches in the city: Domenico Rossi's work represented an adaptation of Roman baroque and one of his two commissions came from the Rome-based Jesuit order. The other, begun six years earlier in 1709, was the façade for the church of San Stae where the open and broken pediments are crowned by swooping, gesticulating angels and allegorical statuary carved by some of the best Venetian sculptors of these early decades; among them are works by the hand of the famous *ébéniste*, Antonio Corradini. Virtually all the pictorial decoration within the church belongs to the period in which Rossi and his colleagues were at work on the façade. The ceiling painting was executed in 1708 in commemoration of the purchase of a chapel in the church by the Scuola del Sacramento. There is also a later altarpiece by Sebastiano Ricci, works by Piazzetta and Gian Battista Tiepolo, all painted around 1717, as well as the work of more than a dozen other early eighteenth-century painters. A large part of the decoration and the commission for the façade was paid for by Alvise Mocenigo who had been elected doge in 1700.

San Stae was the parish church of his branch of the family and some of the artists employed there could be described as protégés of the Mocenigo. The sculptor-*ébéniste* Corradini or his workshop produced suites of gilded furniture for the Mocenigo Palace at San Stae while Sebastiano Ricci had been employed by another branch of the family at San Samuele in the decoration of their house. The work at San Vidal was also an example of patrician and ducal munificence, being the result of a legacy of the Doge Carlo Contarini. However, in its decoration it was less harmonious than that of San Stae. Altarpieces survived from the older church, such as a fine Carpaccio of San Vitale on horseback which was given the place of honour above the high altar built in 1704. Ricci and Piazzetta were represented at San Vidal too but not as well as at San Stae. The remarkable thing about these churches is that their decoration was provided for by two private legacies which reflect the patronage and prosperity of a supposedly impoverished and irreligious patriciate.

The baroque taste for elaborate ecclesiastical decoration continued throughout the century after the completion of a number of seventeenth-century building projects in the early decades. The church of the Discalced Carmelites was consecrated in 1705; its plan and façade remained typical of the preceding century. Its interior was subject to ever more elaborate finishing until the whole was a treasure house of precious marble sheathing, *marmi misti* inlaid in the Sicilian fashion, and great theatrical altars surmounted by pierced and cutout architecture to give the impression of infinite receding perspectives. Typically, the Jesuit church had one of the richest and most extraordinary schemes of interior decoration anywhere in Italy. The plan is based on the mother church of the order, the Gesù in Rome, where a broad nave accommodated the instruction of vast congregations. The Gesuiti's pulpit is an elaborate confection swathed in the heavy folds of a voluminous brocade curtain which had been drawn aside. This white curtain decorated in a handsome green damask pattern is in fact made of marble; all the walls of the church are covered with this same white and green imitation damask made of *verde antico* inlaid in slabs of white marble. The illusion is extraordinary. The wealth and power of the order did not exclude private patronage within the Church and, as at the Scalzi, the family of the last doge paid for some of the richest semi-precious stone decoration in the city: a lapis lazuli tabernacle.

The family of the last doge, the Manin, had been admitted to the patriciate during the wars against the Turks, but other older patrician families were also involved in major building projects. The Pesaro of San Stae hired Antonio Gaspari to complete Longhena's immense palace for them. Gaspari's tendency towards neo-Classicism hardly shows in his work at Palazzo Pesaro, although in the upper orders of the house he treated the Istrian stone decoration in a more restrained, two-dimensional way than Longhena would have done. At the end of the preceding century Gaspari had been commissioned by the Barbaro family of Santo Stefano to build an enlargement to their fifteenth-century

Gothic palace. The windows and balconies of the addition at Palazzo Barbaro were also borrowed from the vocabulary of Longhena, but it was the early eighteenth-century decoration of the ballroom that Gaspari designed for the second *piano nobile* that made his addition noteworthy. Elaborate stuccowork frames surround large stretches of canvas painted by Piazzetta and Sebastiano Ricci; there were once overdoors by Tiepolo as well as a ceiling of his depicting the *Glory of the Barbaro*, but this part of the decoration was only added later in the century.

The masterpiece of Venetian painting executed in the first decade of the century was Sebastiano Ricci's *Madonna and Child with Nine Saints* painted for San Giorgio. The composition in an acute triangle and the rich colours place Ricci's altarpiece directly in the particular Venetian tradition which began with Titian's Pesaro altarpiece, and was continued by Veronese in his *Enthroned Virgin Adored by Saints* painted for the sacristy of San Zaccaria and now in the Academy Gallery. At the very outset of the century Ricci's role as heir to Veronese is not only evident from his work in the traditions that influenced Veronese, but also in his commission to continue Veronese's fresco decoration at San Sebastiano. These youthful works are perhaps seventeenth century in inspiration but clearly set the fashion for the great generation of Ricci's followers who worked in Venice in the mid-eighteenth century. Ricci's role as precursor of eighteenth-century Venetian artistic taste as well as heir to some of her oldest traditions was transformed in 1712 into that of propagandist when he left Venice to spend five years painting in England. Ricci's nephew, Marco, his pupil Tiepolo, Canaletto and many others would eventually follow him abroad for longer or shorter periods. In these early decades the painters Pellegrini and Amigoni strengthened the traditional cultural links with Germany by working for patrons in the Palatinate and Bavaria.

The influence of Venetian artistic taste was spread abroad in other fields besides painting. The foundling hospital of the Pietà hired Antonio Vivaldi as its musical director in 1704 and only three years later the great Neapolitan composer Alessandro Scarlatti paid a brief visit to the recognized capital of baroque music and published in Venice his opera *Mitridate Eupatore*, which is considered by musical critics far in advance, both in technique and intellectual power, of anything he had written in Naples. Scarlatti placed the language of classical music on a firm foundation of modern harmony and tonality. His compositions show great power of thematic development as well as a wonderful sense of pure and serene melody.

A great number of foreign musicians visited Venice in the first years of the century. Handel was in Venice in 1709, the year the King of Denmark paid the Republic his state visit. Special theatricals accompanied by music were performed for the king, but the most memorable episode of his visit was the spectacular regatta staged in his honour and recorded by the protégé of the patrician Zenobio family, Luca Carlevaris. Carlevaris' view of the regatta was painted from the *volta del canal* looking up the Grand Canal to the Rialto; the great baroque *macchina* or floating tribunal is to the left in the foreground. Carlevaris' painting focuses on the wonderfully extravagant *peote* or many-oared ceremonial barges, in one of which sit the king and his suite, but equally important to the composition is the background, a theatrical tunnel-like perspective created by the palace façades lining each side of the Grand Canal. Carlevaris captured the scenographic quality of Venice so successfully that only rarely did an artist choose to record a regatta differently or from another vantage point. All the Canaletto paintings of the regatta repeat so many of the elements of Carlevaris' composition as to make critics wonder if Canaletto ever painted a regatta from direct observation. Carlevaris also established the iconography for another well-known set piece of Venetian view painting: the ceremonial entrance of an ambassador into the city. This scene was always set from a marvellously calculated viewpoint somewhere above the Rio del Palazzo looking the length of the Molo, with the domes of the Salute as the distant vanishing point of the perspective made by the ducal palace, mint and granary façades. The figures in the foreground, in the first case the Earl of Manchester and his suite stepping ashore in 1707, are the subject of the picture although a file of figures is obviously less arresting than the spectacular *peote* of the regatta pictures. Again Canaletto repeated Carlevaris' formula for pictures recording the arrival of embassies – always from the identical viewpoint – although he varied certain details and tried to add interest by inserting ceremonial barges in the foreground. Whatever the reasons behind the increasing popularity of Venetian scenic painting it was obvious to Carlevaris and to his followers and copiers that views of the city itself made interesting enough compositions for a wide variety of patrons who could not afford the special paintings typified by Lord Manchester's or the King of Denmark's commissions. As early as 1703 Carlevaris had produced a series of engravings which constituted the first inexpensive album of Venetian views.

Earlier view paintings were those recording special ceremonies and celebrations. In the preceding century foreign artists had often depicted the pre-Lenten bull baiting held in the city's squares, while paintings of official processions go back to the *teleri* of the *scuole*, as in the work of Gentile Bellini. The iconography of ceremonial arrivals is even more ancient, having survived in thirteenth-century mosaic work depicting the arrival of the relics of Saint Mark in 828. In the eighteenth century these festal occasions became more and more elaborate. When in 1705 the famous fist-fight cum tug-of-war between two rival parochial factions was prohibited its place in the Ascensiontide festivities was taken by regattas and the *Forze d'Ercole* or pyramids of acrobats known as Hercules's labours. These two popular factions, the Nicolotti and Castellani, elected their own doge for gala occasions. Throughout the eighteenth century he was dressed in scarlet shoes and socks with white gloves and a gentleman's beret. For the Marriage of the Sea he sat in his own ceremonial barge which followed astern the ducal *bucintoro*; the rest of the year his privileges included the collecting of a small tax on all fishing boats and the revenue from two fish stalls in the market.

The first decades of the eighteenth century were by no means given up entirely to pageantry and frivolity. In 1714 the Bailo of Istanbul, Andrea Memmo, was arrested by the Sultan Achmet III in an incident that was part of the Sublime Porte's move to reconquer the Morea from the Venetians. Within a year the Turks succeeded in re-taking all that had been won by the campaigns of Francesco Morosini. In 1716 Venice joined in league with the Emperor Charles VI against the Turks and sent reinforcements to the key bulwark of its system of defence, Corfu. The Turks promptly laid siege to Corfu but the island was well defended by heroic scions of the ancient Pisani, Loredan and Corner families along with their imperial ally, the Marshal Count Mattias von der Schulenburg, the last Venetian *condottiere*. In the next year Andrea Pisani, the Republic's *Capitan General da Mar* won battles off the Peloponnese and Venetian forces captured two ports in Albania. After the loss of the Morea these final victories against the sultan's forces gave Venice certain small advantages in the peace negotiations that took place at the Congress of Passarowitz in 1718. Venice was forced to surrender the Morea to the Turks but was allowed to keep uncontested certain of her possessions in Albania and Dalmatia. The Congress marked the end of Venice's active role in eastern Mediterranean politics and the settlements at Passarowitz represented the last of Venice's territorial losses or acquisitions until her total annihilation as a Republic eighty years later. Venice's once vast expanse of territory in the Levant, one quarter and one eighth of the Roman Empire, had been reduced to virtually nothing and she ended with the few scattered possessions which she had conquered almost eight hundred years before on the opposite shore of the gulf.

Nonetheless the decades following the Congress of Passarowitz until the middle of the century were full of artistic activity in the city. Much of it followed traditional patterns of patronage with the best work executed for either churches or for patricians while Marshal von der Schulenburg, who commissioned work for Sebastiano Ricci and Turkish fantasies from Gianantonio Guardi, briefly revived *condottiere* patronage. There were also innovations that were increasingly accepted and adopted as part of Venetian artistic convention. One was the foundation of an Academy of Painters in 1724. At first it enjoyed relatively little influence and was soon disbanded; the several traditions of Venetian painting were already well established and needed no authorization by an academic body. Eventually the Academy was reorganized, but more as a gallery administered by a club-like association of prominent local painters. The need for a gallery or museum of painting indicated another innovation that can be ascribed to this period, although hints of the development had appeared earlier. This was the increasing numbers of uncommissioned paintings, either views of the city or small mythological subjects. Some of the young

Tiepolo's work, such as the series of mythologies, including the *Rape of Europa* painted in the early twenties, belongs to this category. For a long time these splendid canvases were considered so close to the work of Sebastiano Ricci that their authorship was actually ascribed to Tiepolo's master. In the field of commissioned work Giambattista Piazzetta painted a magnificent *Glory of Saint Dominic* as a curved ceiling canvas for the Sacrament Chapel of San Giovanni e Paolo. A sketch of this same subject by Tiepolo shows the interest in major commissions shared by Venetian artists.

Frescoed ceilings were a considerable novelty in Venice where the only extensive work had been done in the sixteenth century on the solid walls of courtyards or palace façades. All Venetian ceilings which were not constructed à la Sansovino were false, being suspended beneath the original beams. This was true of coffered ceilings, frame and canvas ceilings and the stuccowork ceilings of the seventeenth century. The techniques used by the stuccoists for decorating these false ceilings were those adopted by the frescoists of the eighteenth century, when the fresco work was limited to a panel set in the ceiling, framed and surrounded by highly modelled stucco decoration. The plaster was laid on a surface made of reeds tied together and suspended from the beams above. The reeds could be bent or laid on a curve to counterfeit the coving or shallow vaulting considered a fashionable novelty appropriate to fresco work. Tiepolo was working on a fresco ceiling panel for the chapel of Santa Teresa in the Scalzi at the same time that Piazzetta painted his splendid canvas dedicated to San Domenico. There are several similarities in the two ceilings, especially in the pyramid composition of the figures used to heighten the suggestion of perspective depth in the open skies above. Only shortly before Tiepolo frescoed a salon of Domenico Rossi's sober Palazzo Sandi at Sant'Angelo, for which his small sketch in oils still exists. The subject of this early example of a frescoed palace ceiling was the *Power of Eloquence* and the four groups of figures on each edge provided suitable illustrations of the theme from classical mythology. Tiepolo's mastery of foreshortening, perspective and a convincingly ethereal heaven soon attracted ecclesiastical commissions such as the fresco panels he executed for the Carmelites and the Dominicans in 1739.

The more commonplace commissions for churches were for altarpieces. Piazzetta particularly excelled in creating the atmosphere of religious ecstasy or mystical revelation appropriate to these paintings. Much of their composition was determined by considerations other than the atmosphere required or the monastic order to which the saints portrayed belonged. The typical Venetian eighteenth-century church was lined with chapels, each opening into the nave through a tall bay. The restricted space in these side chapels was filled to overflowing with marble steps leading to an altar surmounted by ornate tabernacles, flanked by tall columns supporting an angel-burdened arch or pediment that crowned the chapel's architecture. The fashion became so popular that rich marble altars were installed in the side aisles of Gothic churches as well. Two, four, or even more tall columns of highly polished vari-coloured marble left little space for anything but a tall thin painting for the altarpiece. After the gradual disappearance of the polyptych altarpiece in the fifteenth century vertical altarpiece compositions had been quite commonplace. In the baroque period and especially with an artist like Piazzetta, the shape of the tall panel made a convention of etiolated figures and exaggerated compositions based on an elongated pyramid.

The church, which is still known by the name of the suppressed Gesuiti order, was typical of many of these eighteenth-century developments. Begun in 1726 by the architect Giorgio Massari, it took only ten years to complete. The façade is a local compromise between various traditional elements: in this case the giant corinthian order separated by niches with giant statuary suggests Palladian inspiration, whereas the interior is otherwise baroque in feeling and decoration. When it was finished there was not only the requisite theatrical high altar in a setting reminiscent of the Salute, but also frescoed ceiling panels by Tiepolo and altar paintings by Tiepolo, Piazzetta and Ricci. All the subjects depicted refer to the Dominican order which had purchased the church from the Gesuits at the end of the preceding century. Tiepolo's splendid ceiling represents not only the glory of the founder but refers to the Dominican Inquisitor's triumph over heresy and to their patronage of the cult of the Rosary. The tall side altar panels display Dominican saints including the recently canonized patron of South America, Saint Rose of Lima.

Other Venetian arts and crafts flourished in the twenties and thirties although in many cases novelties were introduced which reflected the increasing internationalism of baroque taste. Whereas details of ecclesiastical decoration were often borrowed from Rome, the crafts concerned with secular life frequently reflected older bonds between Venice and Germany on the one hand and Venice and the Orient on the other. For example, Germany had been responsible for the introduction of mirror-making to Murano two centuries earlier and now Germans were making Bohemian crystal which was imitated by the glass factories of the islands. It was also in the twenties and thirties that the Vezzi brothers, with the assistance of a former Meissen workman, established the first Venetian porcelain factory. Although this factory lasted only two decades, the existence of a Venetian porcelain represented a link between the tastes and wares of the Orient and the novelties and fashions already widely associated with Germany and the Saxon cities of Dresden and Meissen. The popularity of coffee drinking in the city was a result of Venice's continuing trade in the Levant and in 1720 one of the city's most prominent cafés, that in the Campo della Guerra, introduced the use of large coffee cups.

Another Venetian fashion with widespread repercussions was the increasing use of the small rooms of the mezzanine apartments as living quarters. The mezzanine floor had become a traditional part of Venetian palace architecture in the fifteenth century when these low-ceilinged rooms were furnished only with simple shelving for the storage of business records and family archives. In the larger palaces of the late seventeenth and the eighteenth century the mezzanine rooms were more suited to the new, intimate style of living and entertaining popularized by the French institution of the boudoir. To furnish these rooms, and eventually the rest of the palace as well, Venetian ébénistes like Corradini developed a whole range of furniture loosely based on the French *Régence* (1715–23) style. This style became more particularly Venetian than any of her furniture since the monumental carved pieces of Brustolon, from which the sculpted Venetian blackamoor derived. The long settee with an elaborate ribbon-patterned wooden back for the large *portego* was placed there more for show than comfort, but other pieces of Venetian furniture were smaller, more comfortable, and often extremely graceful. They were frequently finished in the pale green or yellow lacquers that were distinctively Venetian. The figure-eight-backed *fauteuil* and the '*pozzetto*' or Venetian *bergère* were popular pieces as were tripod tables and *bombée* chests of drawers; the highly decorated *trumeau* or *secretaire* were all typical pieces executed in lacquer. Highly carved gilt consoles, immense picture frames and unique pieces like the throne chair at the Ca' Rezzonico were destined for the larger state apartments. The walls of a Venetian palace were hung with silks or brocades sometimes framed by a thin strip of lacquer edging. Gilt or lacquer wall sconces were backed with Murano mirror glass, while a large pier glass stood over the simple marble-framed fireplace or above a rococo console table. The windows were crowned with a pelmet and two strips of material hung down on each side; the Venetians never used curtains that drew across, only the ruched translucent silk curtains that in Venice served to cut the water-reflected glare and abroad contributed an unmistakably Venetian element to interior decoration.

One of the most familiar contributions to Rococo decoration throughout eighteenth-century Europe were the vast, intricate chandeliers made at Murano. Curved and twisted jointed sections of glass were fitted together to make the baroque double curves of the fixture's branches. As part of the *tour de force* of the blower's art, there was no centre stem or support, but rather a hollow space to make these massive confections seem lighter. Typically Venetian was the profusion of coloured glass flowers and coloured edges on the fluted joints and *bobèches*. The fact that these extraordinary chandeliers were jointed and therefore could be dismantled for export must have contributed to their popularity throughout Europe, where they became an essential part of any eighteenth-century grand apartment.

Until the end of the century the Venetian mezzanine apartments were frequently decorated with delicate stucco work; that executed by Abbondio and Tencala in 1719 for the Sagredo at Santa Sophia was considered among the finest in the city. A number of proscenium alcoves were inserted in mezzanine rooms transforming them into bedrooms. The arch at the foot of the bed was often decorated with cherubs, garlands and other high relief stucco work.

Generally, however, Venetian stucco work in the mezzanine consisted of low relief flower and ribbon patterns with Rococo fronds and *cartouches* executed with a palette knife. Small pictures were commissioned from Venetian artists to hang in these rooms, and indeed to hang in the boudoirs of France, Germany and throughout Rococo Europe. Rosalba Carriera was acclaimed a celebrity in Paris in 1720 when she went there to make the numberless small pastel portraits for which she was so famous. Yet despite the reputation she earned for these delicate, psychologically profound portrayals and the fact that her pastel portraiture bred endless imitators, she assumed a craftsman's anonymity and virtually never signed any of her works.

In certain cases the exportation of Venetian taste became big business. Antonio Vivaldi travelled throughout Italy arranging for the production of his own operatic works. This aspect of his work, quite separate from his highly respected job as musical director of the Pietà hospice, was satirized by another composer, the patrician Benedetto Marcello in his *Teatro della Moda* of 1720; in fact, so pointed was Marcello's satire as to suggest that Vivaldi's role as fashionable theatrical impresario might have led him into some rather dubious business deals and financial manipulation. Apart from this show of pique Marcello's talent took the more high-minded direction indicated by the publication in 1726 of a setting for fifty of the *Psalms of David* which had been paraphrased by Giovanni Giustinian. Vivaldi did find time for more than promoting his operatic work; before his death in 1741 he had written some five hundred works for concert performance, not to number the endless oratorios and other works written expressly for the famous choir of girls he trained at the hospice.

The doge of this brilliant period for Venice was Alvise III Mocenigo, who had previously served as *provveditore* or military governor both on the mainland and overseas. His generosity was legendary and during his military career he had been known to pay from his own pocket not only the wages of his dependants, but of all the soldiers under his command as well. His years as doge were noted as a period of peace and for the improvements and restorations in the city. The old brick paving of the Piazza was replaced with the stone slabs and white marble that exist today. The thousand-year-old fabric of the Campanile was several times repaired as it was often being struck, as in 1745, by lightning. The basilica, too, required extensive maintenance and restoration: the Byzantine mosaics of the façades had long since become illegible and at least one of the lunettes had been remade in the preceding century. A mosaic of *The Venetian State Worshipping the Body of Saint Mark* designed by Sebastiano Ricci was installed over the second door in 1729. It is a striking composition with deep perspective and brilliant, rich colours, but although a masterpiece of its kind, it shows the degree to which the aesthetic principles of mosaic work were replaced by criteria more appropriate to painting.

It was also in Mocenigo's reign that Venice became the first city in Europe to have all its streets lit by lamps. In these years, too, the final and best known version of the *Bucintoro*, the doge's ceremonial barge, sparkling with the gilded decoration carved by Antonio Carradini, was launched. In this great hundred-oared ship the doge and Senate went to the Lido on the Feast of the Ascension for the annual Marriage with the Sea. The ancient ceremony had little significance in the eighteenth century except as the pretext for an elaborate fair in the Piazza though when Mocenigo died on the eve of the Ascension in 1732 the festivities were cancelled and the papier-maché arcade of shops in the Piazza hurriedly dismantled. The *Bucintoro* bearing Mocenigo's arms was widely known through the innumerable representations of it and of the *Sposalizio* by the popular view painters of the city. It was in Mocenigo's reign that Canaletto, the most successful and prolific of this school of Venetian painting, entered into partnership with the art dealer and English agent in Venice, Joseph Smith, later George III's consular representative to the Republic. This partnership resulted in a series of specially commissioned painted views of the city and later in a world-famous series of engravings made from these same views and published in 1744.

Smith's own taste in the arts was catholic. At the end of his long life he sold his collection to agents of George III and his pictures went to form a large part of the famous British royal collection while his books became a nucleus of the King's Library at the British Museum. When he decided to remodel the façade of his small Gothic palace at Santissimi Apostoli he and the engraver-architect Visentini settled on the restrained neo-Classical style then in vogue. This was the style which Frigimelica intended for the immensely theatrical double courtyard of the great Palazzo Pisani at Santo Stefano in 1728, or to take an extremely severe example, the style in which Tirali built the Palazzo Priuli-Manfrin on the Rio di Cannaregio in 1735. This façade with its lack of pediments, columns, pilasters or any other ornament remains the most apparently 'modern' and austere of all the palaces built in Venice. Venetian neo-Classicism was generally freer and more Palladian in spirit, as in the case of the Gesuiti church which Massari brought to completion in 1736, or the singularly tall-domed church of San Simeone Piccolo finished two years later with a corinthian temple pronaos set above a steep broad flight of stairs.

During the forties Venice managed to pursue the delights of her arts and culture by maintaining a policy of political and military neutrality in the face of widespread European upheavals. Thus she remained aloof from the War of the Austrian Succession, a conflict that otherwise managed to involve almost every European power. The government's neutrality was obviously a wise policy sanctioned by ancient tradition, but non-Venetian social historians have seen it as the Republic's licence for frivolity and decadence, an exaggerated reputation personified by Giacomo Casanova, who left Venice in 1743 to spread abroad his fantastic tales and adventures. Within the city the peaceful decade of the forties might be considered the period of Tiepolo. In the first year he

The arrival of the Bucentoro at the church of San Nicolò on the Lido for the Ascensiontide Marriage of the Sea. The ceremonial whereby the doge was rowed in state to espouse the sea was established in 1177 when Pope Alexander III presented the Republic with the marriage ring and granted her prince the rank and style of Serenissima. Francesco Guardi's painting of the ducal barge was part of a series recording twelve of the annual ducal solemnities.

executed the ceiling panel in fresco for the Dominican church of the Gesuiti and the canvases in oils set in the ceiling frames of the Scuola dei Carmini. Three years later he completed another fresco commission, a ceiling for the great baroque church of the Scalzi. This fresco, the *Translation of the House of Loreto*, was long considered one of his masterpieces, but it was destroyed when an incendiary bomb landed on the church roof in the First World War. Fortunately Tiepolo's oil sketch has survived and is a vivid testimonial to the sureness of the artist's touch. Vertiginous perspectives, dawn-dappled clouds supporting cavorting cherubim, swooping angels in a cerulean sky, all are gathered in a celestial composition around the glory of the Madonna and the miraculous flight of her house from Asia Minor to Loreto in the Marches.

Besides these ceiling frescoes, in 1740 Tiepolo painted the enormous *Christ Bearing the Cross to Calvary* for the church of Sant'Alvise. The composition showing Christ stumbling beneath the weight of the cross he dragged up the twisting path to the summit of Golgotha, owes a great deal to the similar zig-zag composition used by Tintoretto for his *Path to Calvary* in the Scuola di San Rocco. More often, however, Tiepolo's indebtedness to the Venetian traditions of painting derive from his use of Veronese as his model. The perspective point of view of his ceilings may be closer to that of his immediate master, Sebastiano Ricci, and his altarpieces often take their elongated form and sense to religious ecstasy from the atmosphere of similar paintings by Piazzetta, but his historical or mythological subjects have many attributes in common with Paolo. In 1745 he began what many consider the greatest of these. It was a private commission and the abundance of oil sketches and even large versions in oils shows the importance Tiepolo himself attributed to the two scenes from the encounter of Antony and Cleopatra which he executed in fresco for the ballroom of the Labia palace at San Geremia.

The Palazzo Labia standing at the mouth of the Cannaregio Canal where it joins the upper reaches of the Grand Canal, is a large palace with a richly modelled façade on the Canal completed by the beginning of the century along Longhenesque lines. When the palace was enlarged on the side away from the church of San Geremia a rear façade was added on more sober lines. The lateral enlargement provided space for a courtyard and a ballroom. It was this latter that Tiepolo decorated with the collaboration of the master *trompe-l'œil* frescoist, Menegozzi-Colonna. The hall was well lit from the courtyard and its regular shape gave endless possibilities for a dazzlingly illusory and theatrical scene. The ceiling apparently opens to reveal a sky crowded with a pantheon of cavorting mythological figures, but it is the two side walls, each pierced with two doors and two windows above (real and false), that provide Tiepolo with his canvas. On the one side he envisioned the banquet of Cleopatra, a scene worthy in its richness of any of Veronese's great supper paintings. It is a stately tableau given movement by the folds of Cleopatra's billowing gown, the highlights on gleaming armour and the antics of attendant dwarfs; the cut of Cleopatra's gown and the style of her hair were the artist's unmistakable homage to the cinquecento and to his master, Paolo Veronese. The essence of the room's success is the harmonious collaboration between the architect and Menegozzi-Colonna, who brilliantly counterfeited elements of the architecture creating a *trompe-l' œil* fantasy worthy of Tiepolo's visions and Tiepolo's own judgement in deepening those false perspectives with details of his own and adopting for the display of his own genius only that measure of wall space suited to the harmony of the whole. This was to remain the masterpiece of his secular decoration in his native city. Otherwise Tiepolo was also engaged on the more limited decoration of various Venetian palaces, often only ceiling panels, spandrel sections and overdoors. Around the mid-century he worked for the Barbarigo at Santa Maria Zobenigo, for the Barbaro at nearby Santo Stefano and for the Sagredo of Santa Sofia. In addition to Tiepolo's work, the Sagredo commissioned Pietro Longhi to cover their new stair hall with a nightmare fresco of the *Battle of the Giants*. In 1750 Tiepolo painted a splendid full-length formal portrait of a procurator of San Marco who has not been identified, but who seems the very image of the high official and shrewd patron of eighteenth-century Venice. Tiepolo's nostalgia for the cinquecento is represented by the Palladian arch in the background of the painting. The following year, 1751, he left to decorate the giant staircase and imperial chamber of the Prince Archbishop's Versailles-like palace at Würzburg. Tiepolo's work in Germany made his reputation as an international decorator and painter, and he became as sought after as Titian had once been.

The patricians who ordered fresco cycles and portraits were intensely conscious of the artistic heritage of their city. The ducal families of the century, for example, undertook large projects commensurate with their status and wealth: the Contarini and the Mocenigo rebuilt their parish churches; Alvise Pisani, a member of the richest banking family in the city, who was elected doge in 1735, enlarged his family house at Santo Stefano to the extent that the Senate forbade its continuation. Later ducal families joined the Barbaro, Barbarigo and Sagredo in merely redecorating their palaces, although the services of Tiepolo and Abbondio undoubtedly cost dear.

The immense building projects begun by ancient families in the preceding century were now being completed by the *arriviste* patricians. The Rezzonico hired Giorgio Massari to finish Longhena's great palace at San Barnaba for them. Two years earlier Massari presented a project to the Grassi family for a neo-Classical palace opposite the Cà' Rezzonico which was to be the largest private undertaking completed in the century. The façade is harmonious if severe, with the volumes owing something to Sansovino. Massari's most significant innovation was the courtyard built inside the building. More a colonnaded peristyle than a *cortile*, its principal function was to lead to a monumental staircase rising to the open loggias of the *piano nobile* – a most extravagant treatment of a limited building site in Venice. Massari had similarly grandiose ideas for the Rezzonico palace, but there he was restricted to what Longhena had already begun. Massari cleverly counterfeited a second *piano nobile* in Longhena's style but completed the attic in much lower relief. The extravagance of the Cà' Rezzonico is evident behind the main block of the palace, where the garden was filled in to provide a courtyard, and a monumental stair hall with a full-size ballroom above. An enlargement to provide a ballroom was frequent in the seventeenth and eighteenth centuries, but perhaps most like the Cà' Rezzonico was Palazzo Labia, where Massari was probably the architect of the ballroom space Tiepolo decorated. After his return from Würzburg Tiepolo worked at Cà' Rezzonico on a ceiling celebrating the marriage of a Rezzonico with an heiress of the Friulan house of Savorgnan. The ballroom had been decorated five years before with a fresco scheme by G. B. Crosato, a vast *trompe-l'œil* of columns and architecture on the walls, crowned by a heavenly vision of the popular *Four Parts of the World*, and often considered his masterpiece.

The architectural *trompe-l'œil* of large-scale fresco decoration partly derived from contemporary theatrical conventions. The Bibbiena family's designs for operatic performances in Europe's court theatres were usually based on classical architecture drawn in a baroque perspective. Flats and backdrops were painted with arches, arcades, colonnades and staircases, all sharply receding into an illusory distance. The Bibbienas' exercises in exaggerated perspective gained a wider audience through engraved versions of their designs. Besides influencing fresco *trompe-l'œil* these engravings inspired the young engraver, G. B. Piranesi, who left Venice in 1744 for Rome where six years later he published the haunting *Carceri* or prison etchings, a series of nightmare visions of vertiginous perspectives and architectural fantasies based on theatrical illusion.

In Venice the formal court theatre type of opera or oratoria was losing ground to comedy. Although there were sixteen theatres for the performance of opera by the mid-century, Venetians were turning now to the comedies of Carlo Goldoni, who was in partnership with the impresario of the theatre at Sant'Angelo. If the forties were the decade of Tiepolo for the student of Venetian art, to the average Venetian it was the dramatist, Carlo Goldoni, who dominated the city's culture in the fifties. Unlike *commedia dell'arte* productions which were often privately performed Goldoni's comedies were not improvisations, but used a fully written script with several masked characters speaking in dialect while the rest of the dialogue was in Tuscan. To meet the insatiable Venetian demand for new comedies, and also to save his partnership from bankruptcy, he promised sixteen plays for the season of 1749–50. The local theatre season lasted only through the Carnival; although in eighteenth-century Venice this was a notoriously long season which ran from October to 15 December and began again on Saint Stephen's Day, 26 December, lasting until Shrove Tuesday. Goldoni's promise meant producing a play each week throughout the entire Carnival. With some difficulty and a good deal of last-minute

Antony and Cleopatra executed in fresco by Giambattista Tiepolo for the ballroom of Palazzo Labia. Cleopatra's dress and various details of costume reflect Tiepolo's debt to sixteenth-century Venetian painting and especially to the work of Veronese. All the architectural details of the room are *trompe-l'œil* fresco work by Giambattista Menegozzi-Colonna.

writing this *tour de force* succeeded brilliantly, saving the partnership from ruin, although none of these particular plays is considered Goldoni's best work.

A quieter side of Venetian entertainments has been delightfully documented in the work of Pietro Longhi, who towards the mid-century was commissioned by the Sagredo and others to paint numerous charming genre scenes of Venetian life. There are the Carnival masks and dominoes, in which the patrician was permitted to circulate freely in public and to gamble at the Ridotto without regard for the sumptuary laws of the day. There are intimate scenes of patrician life, with the lady of the house dressing, receiving or singing for an elderly relation. Longhi also painted scenes of lower class life: laundresses and spinners, and peasants dancing together or eating polenta; and there are scenes in which the different classes mingle freely. There was the visit of a giant to Venice, and a rhinoceros put on display in the Piazza in 1751. All of these were painted with a charming naïveté suitable for a patrician boudoir and with little or no hint of the harsher realities of life.

Political realities were well removed from the average Venetian's concern, since the official policy of neutrality kept the Republic out of almost every European quarrel. A few matters of ecclesiastical reorganization affected Venice, but not seriously. For instance in 1751 the ancient benefice of the Patriarchate of Aquileia was suppressed and the remaining territories, which had usually been held by absentee Venetian prelates, were divided between the Archbishop of Gorizia and Tiepolo's patron, the Archbishop of Udine. In 1754 further ecclesiastical controversy was settled in favour of Venice and two years later a commission negotiated the borders between the Republic and Milan. Otherwise the greatest political episode of the fifties was the election of Carlo Rezzonico, Bishop of Padua, as Pope Clement XIII. Traditional hostility and suspicion of the papacy completely vanished in a display of popular enthusiasm and celebration. The wealth of the recently ennobled Rezzonico family had obviously paved the bishop's way to the papal election. In Venice this meant the completion and sumptuous decoration of their immense palace at San Barnaba, the conferment of the hereditary dignity of the knighthood of San Marco on the whole family, the dignity of the *procuratoria* for the pope's nephew and a return to excellent relations with Rome that remained virtually undisturbed for the next fifty years and culminated in 1800 in the election of a pope in Venice. In 1759 Clement XIII sent Venice the Golden Rose, and in 1761 he beatified the Venetian monk Gregoria Barbarigo. He also represented a new spirit in the arts; Papa Rezzonico was to become known as *Sua Scrupolosità* for the scrupulousness with which he had the private parts of every statue in the vast Vatican collection covered with a marble fig leaf. The pope's family became patrons of the young Venetian sculptor Antonio Canova. Canova has often been disparaged as a cold neo-Classicist, and there can be no doubt that he was more attuned to the imperial pretensions of Napoleon than he was at home in the city of Casanova or Goldoni.

In Venice, only the re-establishment of the Academy of Painters or a unique church like Temanza's round temple dedicated to the Magdalen, built in 1760, was in keeping with the severely academic aspects of the coming international neo-Classicism; generally Venetians still preferred Palladio as their classical model. In 1762 the parishioners of the ancient Byzantine church of San Giovanni Novo raised the money to rebuild completely their parish church. The funds ran out before the façade was completed, but the interior remains a perfect reproduction in miniature of a section of the interior of Palladio's San Giorgio Maggiore.

In 1759, the year Clement sent Venice the Golden Rose, the government fixed the number of cafés in the city at two hundred and six, as coffee houses had become centres of political comment and criticism. The following year, when Temanza was building the Maddalena, Gaspare Gozzi contributed to the liveliness of café discussions with the first Italian newspaper, *La Gazzetta Veneta*, a satirical weekly modelled on *The Tatler* and *The Spectator*. Three years earlier Gaspare's brother Carlo had made his debut on the literary scene with a spirited defence of the traditional *commedia dell'arte*. When Goldoni challenged this criticism of written as against improvised comedy Gozzi replied that anyone could write a comic play, and to prove his point he produced *The Love of Three Oranges*. To his astonishment this comedy based on a nursery tale was a great success, and for a while Venetian audiences were able to enjoy the fruits of the intense rivalry between the two. Goldoni created two of his masterpieces, the *Barruffe Chiozzote*, set in nearby Chioggia, and *I Rusteghi*. In both these plays Goldoni set the scene in the tiny gossipy society of the *campiello* or local square. Although the plots were the hackneyed entanglements of intrigue and misunderstanding popular in eighteenth-century comedy, the dialogue was the authentic voice of the people who then, as now, passed much of their time in the squares and streets of their parish. On the other hand the upper classes in Goldoni's plays were less parochial, and in many of his plays they include English milords, Frenchmen and others considered to be foreigners like Tuscans or Piedmontese. That Goldoni's comedies enjoyed a widespread fame was due in part to the collection of them printed in 1761 by Pasquali. A portion of the expense of this fine edition, with scenes from the plays represented in lively engravings, was borne by Pasquali's partner Joseph Smith. This partnership had been earlier responsible for an even wider acceptance of Venetian taste in the arts when the Pasquali press reprinted Palladio's *Four Books of Architecture*.

In 1762 Goldoni left Venice to seek a more secure future for his comedies in Paris. In the same year Tiepolo, only recently elected the first President of the revived Academy of Painters, went to Madrid at the invitation of the king, and there with his son Gian Domenico he worked on the decoration of the throne room of the royal palace until his death eight years later. Although Rosalba Carriera had died in 1762, the demand for Venetian taste was well served abroad by the Tiepolos in Spain and by Canaletto's nephew Bernardo Bellotto, who transferred the art of Venetian view-painting to central Europe and left us fascinating records of eighteenth-century Vienna, Warsaw and Dresden.

Eighteenth-century taste in music had gradually moved north, too, where both Bach and Handel acknowledged their debt to Venetian traditions and specifically to Vivaldi. The year before Vivaldi's death in 1740, Baldassare Galuppi, a young composer from the island of Burano, appeared on the Venetian musical scene and by 1762 was appointed *maestro di cappella* of San Marco. The musical traditions of the ducal chapel were still highly respected and throughout the city church organs remained an important feature of ecclesiastical furnishing. Organ makers restored many of the city's antique organs in the last decades of the century, and those constructed in the workshops of Gaetano Calido are highly prized today. In their own day, however, their more sensitive contemporaries may have shuddered at this wholesale renovation of antique instruments, as a result of which none of the pipes or mechanism behind organ doors painted by Veronese or the school of Titian is contemporary with their decoration.

On the other hand one of the most charming series of eighteenth-century paintings executed for the decoration of an organ case was that in the church of the Archangel Raphael, where in about 1750 Gianantonio Guardi painted small panels depicting the story of Tobias and the Archangel Gianantonio was the first and the least known of yet another family of painters who came to dominate the taste of a period in the art of Venice. Just as the Bellinis and Mantegna, Titian and Veronese's brothers and sons, Tintoretto, Palma and their sons, or the numerous painters of the family called Bassano spanned almost two hundred years, so the Guardi dynasty represented a particular aspect of Venetian taste in the eighteenth century. The sister of Gianantonio and Francesco Guardi was married in 1719 to Giambattista Tiepolo, and was therefore the mother of the painters Giandomenico and the lesser known Lorenzo. If the palette of Tiepolo's light celestial visions can be said to represent the shadowless atmosphere of the early eighteenth century, there is something equally appropriate to later years in Francesco Guardi's sombre depiction of the city. The mellow golden autumnal light of Canaletto's views seems to have departed from the city with his nephew Bellotto, who took it to illuminate and soften the Italianate outlines of buildings in northern capitals. Guardi's vision is darker, the clouds are heavier, his macabre carnival masks are no longer incidental figures but loom menacingly, tall and out of proportion to the scene. The buildings and perspectives are distorted like Greco's saints to heighten an unreal atmosphere. But Guardi's is not the heavenly city of El Greco, rather one sunk in a decaying worldliness. His Venice is no sparkling jewel set on the surface of a pristine pool, but a phantom ship with skeleton rigging, becalmed in troubled depths before a storm. The lagoon has a lurid cast, and the lone black gondola in one of his most famous compositions could easily have inspired the endless funerary metaphors that nineteenth-century writers associated with Venice.

But despite Guardi's intensely personal vision which seemed to prefigure the decline and death of the Republic, Venice in the sixties was still very much alive. In 1768, the year Canaletto died, Guardi himself completed a series of twelve canvases depicting the principal festivities of the doge's ceremonial calendar. The ducal ceremonies Guardi recorded were those presided over by Alvise IV Mocenigo who had been elected in 1763 and who was to reign for more than fifteen years. In his first year a long period of relative peace was abruptly interrupted by the attacks of pirates preying on Venetian convoys engaged in the revived spice trade with North Africa. Two years later negotiations were opened with the governments of North Africa and in 1766 Giacomo Nani forced the Bey of Algiers to ratify the treaties which would guarantee protection for Venetian commerce from the Barbary Coast pirates.

The renewed spice trade and the determination of the government to protect it with her navy was only one indication of a certain prosperity and vitality that returned to the Republic in the last years of her existence. Just as numerous artists had taken Venetian taste abroad, so now the products of the Republic's craftsmen and artisans were exported in increasing quantities. Venetian lacquer furniture became world famous, and 24,890 pieces were exported in the five years after Mocenigo's election; the workshop of Agostino del Bene alone produced almost nine hundred pieces of lacquer work in 1767. Before he left for Madrid Giambattista Tiepolo himself had contributed chinoiserie designs for a set of yellow lacquer doors for the Ca' Rezzonico. Despite the fact that much oriental trade had passed into the hands of the English and Dutch, enough still came through Venice to encourage expert imitation by local craftsmen. Chinoiserie enjoyed a brief vogue and took such forms as Gozzi's drama *Turandot* which was produced in 1765; otherwise its influence was limited to lacquer work, porcelain and oriental fans. In this same year a second Venetian porcelain factory, following Vezzi's abortive enterprise of thirty years before, was established by Geminiano Cozzi. Like Vezzi, Cozzi's short-lived manufactory imitated Meissen designs, but his soft paste porcelain was distinguished by a notably Italianate Rococo style and a freshness of colour.

Traditional Venetian entertainments attracted more and more foreigners, and in 1764 a great regatta was staged for King George III's brother, Edward, Duke of York. The Ridotto gambling rooms were remodelled by the architect Maccarucci a few years later and in 1773 there were over twenty hostelries registered in the city for housing foreign visitors. When the Emperor Joseph II came to visit Venice in 1775 he and his small suite stayed in the city's most famous hostelry, the Albergo del Leon Bianco, situated in the ancient da Mosto palace near the Rialto. The emperor was also entertained with a regatta and a series of balls given in private houses; but it was said that he found some of these entertainments too lavish and he left early for the comforts of his inn. By this time the government had obviously become concerned with patrician extravagance, and in keeping with the legislation that curtailed the proliferation of cafés in the city it closed the gambling house of the Ridotto in 1774, the year before the emperor's visit. Two years later the government sought to encourage decorous and profitable public festivity with the construction of Rococo trade stalls in the Piazza for the Ascensiontide Fair. But not all the public works undertaken towards the end of the century had this temporary character or served only the prolonged periods of official festivals and celebrations. Work was continued on the cyclopean Istrian stone sea walls at the Lido known as the *murrazzi* which had been begun in 1744. The quay near the prisons where the Slav merchants congregated and traded was widened in 1780 to provide more room for the unloading of merchandise. At the same time one of the more important patrician patrons in the city, Vettor Pisani, gave further impetus to the acceptance of the more severe and academic neo-Classicism by commissioning the well-known statue of *Daedalus and Icarus* from the young Antonio Canova.

In this same year another Pisani, Giorgio, was elected procurator of San Marco. He and Carlo Contarini represented the most outspoken proponents of reform within the government. A crisis had arisen earlier over the abuse of the powers of the Council of Ten and its examining magistrates, the Inquisitors of the State. Although the latter were found to merit official reprimand, the role of the former was confirmed by a large majority vote in the Great Council. Bonapartist liberal historians have dramatized and distorted the oppressive role of these committees of the government, but it was known locally that the Ten examined with great care any secret denunciation before proceeding to prosecute, and the populace also appreciated that the Council of Ten was often the only recourse of the humbler classes against wrongs suffered at the hands of arrogant patricians.

Although Giorgio Pisani and Carlo Contarini were radical voices in the councils of the government and often spoke of the overthrow not only of the Ten but of the Signoria, they did not represent so much the populace of Venice as a group of disaffected nobles known as the *Barnabotti* from the parish where they lived. Since the seventeenth century the government had undertaken to support its impoverished nobles and to provide them with free housing near the church of San Barnaba. In return these subsidized Venetians were subject to certain restrictions. Like their more prosperous brethren they had to maintain the dignity of wearing silk. They were also forbidden to marry, for the very good reason that their legitimate offspring would simply increase the financial burden on the state. Not surprisingly this wholly subsidized section of the patriciate became more and more demanding, until allowances were made for the support of their mistresses. In their notoriously cantankerous and arrogant frame of mind the *Barnabotti* were ripe for the propaganda of egalitarianism and its concomitant hatred of inherited wealth and power. By their vociferous criticism of the Republic's institutions, the scorn they poured on the traditions and conservatism of the patriciate and their mouthing of popular radical slogans, Pisani and the *Barnabotti* prepared the way for the complete moral paralysis of the government in the face of active hostility and attack.

It is a documented fact that the populace cheered loudly when the Great Council voted to preserve the powers of the Ten. A few years earlier Venetian morale had been even more uplifted when the news reached the city that Admiral Angelo Emo had fought a decisive action against the Barbary pirates. For a while the ancient institutions and glories of the Republic seemed assured of a new vitality; but soon frivolity asserted its sway again. In January 1782 the Grand Duke Paul, son of Catherine the Great, and his wife Dorothea of Württemberg, visited Venice under the thinly disguised if romantic incognito of the Counts of the North. The festivities were on a staggering scale, with the patriciate attending balls *en masse* in the city's theatres. When in May no less a visitor than Pope Pius VI arrived for a brief stay the state's reception was so grand that the Inspector of the Academy of Fine Arts commissioned Francesco Guardi, then in his seventies, to record the festivities for posterity. The most interesting of this series for the student of Venetian iconography is that depicting the Benediction Loggia built in the square in front of San Giovanni e Paolo. The Loggia was an enormous tribune constructed across the front of the ornate façade of the Scuola Grande di San Marco. The pope blessed the people from a box-like affair high above the principal door to the *scuola* and reached by a long double ramp of stairs. Guardi executed four canvases, though he chafed at Inspector Edwards' minute instructions as to how the scenes were to be composed and where the figures would be placed. His record of the Counts of the North was freer; it proved to be a veritable masterpiece and an invaluable record of eighteenth-century Venetian life. Of the four subjects, one depicted a ball at the Teatro di San Beneto and another the indispensable parade of allegorical chariots; but the finest of the series was undoubtedly the *Concert of the Ladies' Orchestra*, where Guardi captured not only the delightfully festive atmosphere, but also the flickering illumination of the candlelit hall.

When Baldassare Galuppi died only two years after the ladies' concert the generation of Venetian eighteenth-century composers which had begun with Benedetto Marcello and which included masters such as Giuseppe Tartini and Tommaso Albinoni, drew to a close. When Lorenzo da Ponte was banished from the territories of the Republic, he fled to the north where a career could be made in the service of princes who retained Italian musicians and local composers trained in the Italian mode; after an adventurous career da Ponte eventually became well known as Mozart's librettist. In 1784 the Swedish King Gustavus Adolphus, a knowledgeable patron of the arts who gained wider fame as the victim of the assassination that is the centrepiece of Verdi's *Ballo in*

Maschera, paid a state visit to Venice. Among the many treasures of the Republic, the king, a knowledgeable bibliophile, was shown the famous illuminated Grimani breviary – the young director of the Marciana got his first glimpse of it by joining the royal suite during their visit to the treasury of the ducal chapel. Almorò Pisani of Santo Stefano entertained the king at a lavish ball and later showed him his particular pride, an immense library collected by several generations of this rich banking family which was open to the general public on two days of every week in the year.

Such examples of the intelligent use of wealth and power were now rare, however, and the festivities of the *ancien régime* began to ring hollow. Andrea Tron, the *Inquisitore alle Arti* or Inspector of the Guilds, who had lavishly entertained the Emperor Joseph II, reported that wool work in the city was down from twenty-eight thousand pieces to only six hundred a year in 1784. Such depressing figures alarmed Tron and many responsible members of the patriciate. Antonio Cappello, the ambassador to Paris reported in 1788, with that objectivity and prescience for which Venetian ambassadors were famed and for which their *relazioni* are still prized by historians, that a serious upheaval in the French capital was imminent and inevitable. Much serious debate was held in the councils of the government and accurate predictions of doom were frequent; but the events of the next decade both abroad and in Venice reduced individual foresight and wisdom to irrelevance in the light of history. The two poles of debate that paralysed intelligent initiative were the combined voices of nihilistic defeatism and radical criticism on the one hand, and on the other slavish adherence to traditional policy. Unfortunately the proponents of the latter failed to realize that the strength of Venetian traditionalism had always lain in its flexibility, especially when the Republic had been threatened by the great powers of Europe, as it had been in 1509 and as it was to be in a few years' time. In the Levant and at sea a dogged determination was Venice's greatest asset; she struck back whenever feasible or whenever there were naval commanders capable of challenging Turkish harassment. By the eighteenth century trade in the Levant was only a shadow of what it had once been, but the Ottoman sultans were also less concerned with concerted war against insignificant merchant convoys than with keeping their vast territories in a state of proper subjection. The virtual independence of the Barbary pirates indicated the sultan's ineptitude in this part of his domain. Fortunately, Venice had in Angelo Emo a last great naval commander who continued to fight successful actions off the Barbary coast. His victories in the eighties were hailed throughout Europe and the Venetian navy seemed to have found a worthy captain.

The glorious traditions represented by Emo seemed forgotten in 1789 when for the first time in almost one thousand one hundred years a non-Venetian, Lodovico Manin, was elected doge; even the populace saw this choice as a scandal. To his electors Manin had two virtues: in a time of overwhelming inflation he was staggeringly rich, and in a government torn by acid debate, he had no enemies. His wealth derived from vast holdings and investments in the Friuli; astonishingly enough, his lack of enemies was simply because he had held no important office in the Republic before becoming doge. He had entertained Pope Pius VI during his state visit with some success, but that merely required a heavy purse. Manin can hardly be blamed for everything that came to pass during his reign but his generosity was neither matched by moral courage, determination, nor by a sense of history – nor even by panache. The admirer of Venetian culture and civilization turns from his words: 'We shall not be safe in our beds tonight', and seeks elsewhere for a worthy epitaph for the Most Serene Republic.

If the populace was outraged by Manin's election they were soon appeased by his largesse and by the splendid festivities that marked his coronation. On the other hand upheavals beyond the Republic's frontiers, such as the fall of the Bastille, were taking place that would have implications for Venetians far beyond their most prescient understanding. Yet in the following year a group of patrician investors commissioned the fashionable architect G. A. Selva to build them a large opera house at San Fantin. Rebuilt after the first of several fires, this splendid monument to one of the richest theatrical traditions in Europe took the apt name of the Phoenix, or *La Fenice*, by which it is still renowned throughout the world. La Fenice remains one of the finest examples of the special requirements of Venetian building. The site available was so extremely irregular that it was impossible to accommodate on anything like a symmetrical axis an adequate backstage area together with the stage itself, an orchestra pit, a raking floor for seats, five tiers of boxes as well as the foyer and reception rooms. However, all these separate spaces are so well designed and integrated that the theatregoer does not realize that he is in anything other than a conventional and particularly lovely eighteenth-century theatre. The theatre was opened in May 1792 with a comic opera by Paisiello.

Although the patriciate did not undertake any great palaces in this last decade of the century, their passion for decoration continued unabated with frescoed ceilings by second-rate disciples of the Tiepolo school. The Pisani at Santo Stefano hired Maccarucci, several times architect of the Ascension Fair booths in the Piazza, to remodel the interior of their gigantic house. More grandiose was the remodelling of Manin's palace near the Rialto, which had been designed by Sansovino for the Dolfin family. This was now enlarged by La Fenice's architect, Selva, to efface all trace of Sansovino's architecture save the façade, and the redecorated interior was fitted out at great expense with plaster casts of a great deal of the great sculpture of antiquity – a collection later sold to Tsar Alexander I. The extensive remodelling of Venetian interiors in the eighteenth century effaced almost all trace of earlier decoration in the city's palaces just as impoverishment in the nineteenth century resulted in the dispersal of Venetian furniture, china and plate.

By 1794 the full attention of the government and therefore the patrician class, if not the rest of the city, was focused on events in France. As these became more alarming, more complicated and increasingly involved for foreign powers, the Venetian state was obliged to adopt a line of policy. The principal government spokesman, and the man whom Napoleon blamed for accelerating the collapse of the Republic, was a kinsman of the doge, Francesco Pesaro. In 1794 his policy of armed neutrality was adopted by the doge's most intimate councillors, the six *savii grandi* or six great sages. The stipulation that Venetian neutrality should also be 'armed' was a show of bravado, as any of the mainland *provveditori* could have told the *savii grandi*. Nonetheless the traditional policy of neutrality had kept Venice out of the wars of the Spanish and Austrian successions, which were partly fought out on territory dangerously near the lands of the Serenissima. In 1795 this policy of neutrality, armed or not, was put at risk when the Count of Lille, the younger brother of Louis XVI and one of the prime enemies of the French revolutionary Republic, sought refuge in Verona. In June his ten-year-old nephew, briefly Louis XVII, died in the most sordid circumstances in the Temple, and the Count of Lille became *de jure* King of France as Louis XVIII. He then issued the ill-conceived Proclamation of Verona, in which he vowed to restore absolutism and punish his enemies with severity when he returned to his rightful throne. The emigrés were horrified by their king's proclamation and many declared it 'criminal' in the reprisals it was bound to provoke.

In the following year the twenty-six-year-old General of the French Republic took the revolutionary armies into northern Italy. The enemy Austrian army was chased from defeat to defeat at Montenotte, Millesimo and Lodi, and finally breached the neutrality of the Venetian Republic by passing through the fortress town of Peschiera on their retreat north to Austria. To secure their own retreat should the Austrians be reinforced and turn on their pursuers, the French besieged and captured the great lakeside fortress near Verona. By this time the attention of all Venice was fixed on the whirlwind progress of young Bonaparte, and with the capture of Peschiera an atmosphere of apprehension and alarm seized the city. Napoleon now began to make demands based on a mixture of motives. As a revolutionary his principles were offended by Louis XVIII's brief refuge in Venetian territory; as a strategist he was nervous about over-extending his lines of supply, especially if he pursued the Austrians further north. In addition he must provision his troops whether he moved or not, and provisioning and a secure base could be guaranteed only if the Venetian government allowed him to draw on the resources of nearby Verona. However, when the Venetian ambassadors continued to argue that the Republic was neutral, Napoleon flung at their heads the recent presence in Verona of Louis XVIII. He also pointed out that with the Austrian retreat across Venetian territory and his own occupation of Peschiera, Venetian neutrality no longer existed in fact.

By the end of the year a French garrison was established in the *Castelvecchio*

The rococo decoration of the interior of the Fenice theatre, one of the many opera houses built and owned by private patrons in eighteenth-century Venice. Its name, meaning the phoenix, refers to its reconstruction after several disastrous fires.

of Verona where provisions were secure for the while, although Bonaparte still had to consider the very real possibility of Austrian reinforcement and counter-attack. Early in 1797 he determined to secure a line of possible retreat across Lombardy by taking Bergamo and Brescia, both of which fell to him with the help of pro-revolutionary collaborators. Throughout these manœuvres he continued to negotiate with Venice for an armed alliance which would reinforce his own over-extended forces and protect him against a possible Austrian counter-attack. Over and over again the Venetians clung to the blindly inept policy of Francesco Pesaro, that as a neutral power Venice and her territory should be considered inviolate by both combatants. If the Venetian government refused to recognize the reality of Napoleon's presence and all it implied, the people of Verona did not. On Easter Monday, 17 April, the Veronese rose *en masse* against the French garrison. Their gesture was as futile as it was heroic and the bloody slaughter that ensued became known throughout all Italy as *La Pasqua Veronese*, the Veronese Easter. Before the end of the month Bonaparte had subdued Verona, and virtually unchallenged had marched on Padua. Not only was all negotiation with the Venetians at an end but Napoleon had shrewdly found another way to secure the freedom of his strategy in Italy against Austrian interference. At Leoben in Austria a secret treaty was being negotiated which would exchange Venetian liberty and territories for the unchallenged continuance of Napoleonic conquest in northern Italy.

This betrayal was as yet undiscovered in Venice and the approaching destruction of the Republic was only just beginning to seem a possible consequence of the government's incrèdible lack of realism and resolution. On 30 April the doge himself gave the *Pien Collegio*, the most powerful council of the state, a careful assessment of the situation, including an account of the attempt of a French ship to enter the lagoon only shortly before. The vessel had been fired on and stopped, and a potentially disastrous episode had been created by the death in the brief action of the ship's captain and five sailors. Manin's address also reflected the dismay of the Republic at Napoleon's capture of the impregnable fortress of Palmanova north of the city. According to eye-witness accounts, the councillors and the doge were visibly terrified throughout their nocturnal session by the noise of French guns close at hand on the mainland.

From the fortress of Palmanova on 1 May Napoleon issued a declaration of war against the Venetian Republic. Hoping to buy time, the government arrested the commander of the Venetian vessel that had fired on Captain Laugier and hastened to return the captured ship to the French representative in the city. But Bonaparte had already decided Venice's fate; she was only a pawn in his pragmatic game of military strategy and manoeuvre. Yet with his unfailing sense of history he realized that he had brought about something more than the mere conquest of territory. He is quoted as saying, in the Italian of his ancestors: '*Non voglio più Senato, non voglio più Inquisitori, io sarò un Attila per lo Stato Veneto.*' The Senate he would abolish represented not only patrician power and privilege, but also the self-deceiving temporizers who with blind pride had refused to recognize that they were vanquished; and his allusion to the Inquisitors of eighteenth-century Venice satisfied the requirements of revolutionary propaganda against these supposed oppressors of the people. In fact, when Napoleon's troops opened the prisons there were found to be no political prisoners, only common felons and petty criminals. It was Bonaparte himself who filled the notorious Pozzi and the Piombi prisons with political prisoners after the liberation of Venice. The literalness with which Napoleon later proved an Attila for the Venetian state could not have occurred to the young general in 1797.

Epilogue

The government collapsed suddenly and completely with the pathetic abdication of Doge Lodovico Manin, an act that signalled the end of one thousand one hundred years of continuous ducal reign over the Venetian Republic. If the more ancient foundation of Venice is dated from Attila's arrival in the Roman province of Venetia, the agonizing decline and death of her millennial culture and civilization began with the coming of Napoleon. Attila stood in relation to the culture and civilization of ancient Rome much as Napoleon stood in relation to the culture and civilization of Venice. Neither single-handedly destroyed what he challenged and confronted with his power, but both have often been accused of administering the *coup de grâce*. Such generalizations can be qualified endlessly, but one thing is certain: Napoleon in person demanded the abolition of the institutions that had been part of the unique character of Venetian civilization for centuries. As a student of history he anticipated the inevitable comparison with the Hunnish commander when he said, '*Saro un Attila per lo stato Veneto*' – 'I shall be an Attila for the Venetian State.'

By the terms of his treaty of Campoformio there was little time before the Austrian troops assumed the duties of occupying power, but what Napoleon's agents managed to accomplish at the expense of Venice in eleven months was remarkably thorough. They collected the booty, spoils and trophies of war for the victorious young general to display before his superiors: treasures to impress the people of Paris whose approval he considered essential to the acquisition of power in France. His agents uncovered talented collaborators in Venice. The enigmatic Pietro Edwards, who had commissioned Guardi to record the most splendid moments of the Republic's last years now compiled very thorough inventories of works of art to be confiscated and sent to Paris: in the first month alone he catalogued and considered over twelve thousand paintings. The extent of his success and the standard of his taste is reflected in the reputation of the Louvre as a gallery of painting. Many of its finest treasures arrived in Paris with this first Venetian hoard. In order to reach Paris, the great Veronese supper scene that covered the end wall of the Palladian refectory at San Giorgio Maggiore was cut into sections. At the Louvre it was decided that the best way to display this largest single item from the extensive Venetian lists was to let it into a specially constructed wall: its permanent place among the treasures of France was thus secured for posterity.

Other collaborators of less exalted talents than Edwards were found for the culling of Venetian riches. Women of the populace were employed in the tedious work of picking precious stones out of their ancient settings; the ceremonial robes and ducal cap or *corno* were picked threadbare and vanished entirely. Of course only the grandest ceremonial vestments, the most precious jewel-encrusted Byzantine bindings or Gothic reliquaries were stored in the Marcian treasury and thus subjected to this meticulous despoliation. Settings were generally melted down, but the Pala d'Oro escaped this sad fate because it was believed to be made of gilded base metal. After his abdication Manin handed his personal *corno* to his valet who later sold it. For a generation it was displayed by its patrician owners, until Teodoro Correr bought it; it is now housed in the museum of his collections.

If these incidents of the systematic sack of Venice represent the partial dispersal of Venetian riches, other acts can be taken as symbolic of the spirit behind these depredations. Napoleon had insisted on the abolition of various offices of the government and especially that of the Inquisitors of State. These infamous and powerful investigators were supposed to have kept the Venetian people submissive through a reign of fear based on secret denunciation. The prisons of the Republic were rumoured to be full of Venetians secretly arrested and held without trial or any recourse to principles of justice. When the prisons were open this was seen to be patently untrue. In a very short time these same prisons were well filled, full to overflowing with men who disagreed with the high-minded idealism of the French. Eventually the doge's ceremonial barge, the *bucentoro*, was used as a supplementary prison, but before that, in the very last days of this first military occupation, French soldiers broke into the shed where it was kept in the Arsenal and in act of gratuitous vandalism stripped the golden state barge of its gilded carved ornaments and velvet hangings.

Before the French left, and they stayed in Venice less than a year, they made one last confiscation that eventually symbolized all the depredations, humiliation and impoverishment Venice suffered after the collapse of her millennial government: Napoleon removed the four golden horses from San Marco and brought them to Paris to adorn the *Arc du Carrosel*. The horses, trophies from the conquest of Constantinople, had stood in the place of honour overlooking the Piazza for seven hundred and ninety years. By the time the eighth centenary of the presence of Constantine's horses in Venice was reached Napoleon had returned in imperial guise to begin in earnest his work as self-proclaimed Attila of the Venetian state.

On their departure in January 1798, the French left behind them a provisional government that was soon disbanded by the Austrians; they also left illusions of liberty, fraternity and equality that had to be accommodated to the pragmatic world view of the Holy Roman Empire into whose hands Napoleon had betrayed the Venetians and finally, besides high-flown sentiments and grandiose ideals, the French left their usual legacy of custom and especially costume. The Barnabotti and their richer colleagues had immediately adopted so-called revolutionary dress for their dance around the Tree of Liberty in the Piazza. Hardly different from the years when masked aristocrats flocked to the Merceria to see *La Piavola da Franza*, the porcelain doll just arrived from Paris wearing miniature versions of the latest fashions of the court at Versailles.

The first Austrian occupation had little or no effect on the city save to inflict the one suffering that would most humiliate it, while paradoxically preserving its unique beauty: the Austrians simply ignored and neglected Venice. The imperial government at Vienna was far too preoccupied with the continual threat represented by Napoleon at large in Europe; and from a practical point of view, the port of Trieste was more convenient to their capital and hinterland. Venice was garrisoned and governed as the Austrians ruled other parts of their vast, heterogeneous and multilingual empire: with a surprising degree of fairness and a considerable respect for local autonomy. Nonetheless this period was a time of war for the empire and perhaps the first brief period of Austrian military government was not as lenient as it later proved to be. In the end the empire itself did not long survive its occupation of Venice. After an astonishing series of military successes throughout Europe Napoleon forced the abdication of the Emperor Francis II and replaced the Holy Roman Empire with a rump Austrian one. From his negotiations Napoleon gained the emperor's daughter as a bride, and Venice was returned to the French for incorporation in the *Regno Italico*.

In 1807 Napoleon returned to Venice, not like the successful young general anxious to follow his star to greater glory, but now very much the emperor he had made himself. He moved impressively through spectacular public ceremony and devised grandiose schemes stretching decades into the future to reinforce the illusion that his empire would endure for many generations and

The Four Horses, brought to Venice after the Sack of Constantinople in 1204, were taken
from San Marco by Napoleon's troops in 1798. The removal of these fourth-century, gilded
copper-bronze masterpieces came to symbolize, more than any other defeat or loss, the death
of the Venetian Republic.

be spoken of for ever. He was still determined to destroy the old order, but he did not delude himself with any ambition to efface it completely. Had he suffered such an illusion he would never have undertaken the projects he had in mind for Venice where, perhaps more than any city in his domains, every stone existed as a reminder of what had gone before. Certain of his policies were intended solely for Venice while others, such as the closure of monasteries and convents and the sequestration of their riches, had wider application. His intelligent viceroy, Eugène de Beauharnais, who sought advice from the most talented remnants of the Republic, re-established the old Academy of Painters as a picture gallery to house the riches of the religious houses. The *scuole* were disbanded as potential breeding grounds of political discontent and sub-version and one, the Scuola Grande della Carita', was chosen to house the new Academy.

Just as the foundation of the Academy Gallery was based on the abolition and despoliation of ancient Venetian institutions, so other of Napoleon's projects revealed both strongly negative and positive aspects for Venice. The viceroy was seen to need a suitable palace; the doge's private apartments were not considered nearly grand enough. Thus the separate apartments of the pro-curators in the Scamozzi-Longhena building on the Piazza were knocked together to make an impressive enfilade for the viceregal household during its occasional residence. Since the viceroy might also enjoy a view over the basin of San Marco, the ancient state granary that stood on the Molo behind the Procuratie Nuove was thrown down. Gardens were planted and an elongated private terrace or promenade made on the site for the viceroy's pleasure. This was decorated at one end in the Viennese fashion with a small *kaffeehaus* or pleasure pavilion. The granary which Napoleon had razed was certainly no architectural masterpiece. Its façade was a blank brick wall behind which the grain was stored to be distributed in times of poor harvest or when sources of supply were cut off. Its only ornament was a large bas-relief of the winged lion of Saint Mark. Napoleon had already ordered the defacement of all such Marcian emblems in Venice; but besides blocking the view the granary symbo-lized the paternalism of the Venetian welfare state and as such was a suitable target for destruction.

Still the viceregal apartments lacked a requisite of nineteenth-century grandeur: a ballroom and an imposing staircase. To provide for this Napoleon ordered the demolition of the western continuation of the two procuratie, old and new, along with the church of San Geminiano that Sansovino had designed between them. This particular depredation has provoked more outrage than any other of Napoleon's attempts to 'rationalize' the city's buildings. Actually the *Ala Napoleonica* which he had built to close the western end of the Piazza and to house a staircase and a ballroom is quite in keeping with the arcaded prospect of the rest of the Piazza. Its tall attic was ornamented with statues of the twelve Caesars: admittedly an inappropriate motif in Venice, but inoffensive enough since the central statue of the frieze, a double life-size representation of Napoleon draped in a toga, was never put in place. When he visited Venice for ten days in 1807 Napoleon commented that the Piazza was '*le seul salon au monde lequel le ciel seul est daigne d'être la voûte*', but no memorable artist found his improvements to its ballroom-like character worthy of record. The numerous canvases of Canaletto, Guardi and others showing San Geminiano and the western end of the Piazza are an aesthetic rebuke to Napoleon's architectural schemes.

The fate of San Geminiano is often described as outrageous barbarism. Only recently has an accurate catalogue been compiled of the extensive destruction accomplished in the few years of the Napoleonic *Regno Italico*: more than forty churches and over eighty palaces were razed to the ground. But Napoleon's work represented more than the sum total of the buildings which were pulled down. By abolishing the institutions of the millennial Republic he destroyed the *raison d'être* of an entire people. Of this people we have always known more about the patrician class because they were carefully registered at birth. The statistics recorded after the fall of the Republic reveal one of the most extraordinary sociological phenomena of modern European history. More than one third of all the families inscribed in the Golden Book in 1797 were extinct within the space of a generation. The ancient Contarini family, for example, flourished in the last years of the Republic with eighteen active branches; by 1836 there was not a patrician Contarini left on the face of the earth. The mystery suggested by these figures has inspired all sorts of romantic explanations. The most often repeated is that the patriciate drew up family suicide pacts in which it was agreed that none of the offspring would marry. What is true is that very few children of any Venetian noble family ever married. Primogeniture did not exist within the patriciate so it was never incumbent on the first-born son to marry and beget an heir; the eldest often entered the Church while the richest families provided large dowries to secure their daughters suitable rank in the city's convents. When the economic basis of Venice was destroyed in 1797 young noblemen obviously found it increasingly difficult to make a match and many girls with insufficient dowries could not attract a husband. Whatever the reasons, the astonishing fact remains that a large number of the patrician families, rich and poor alike, simply vanished. It is in this tangible if indirect sense as well as in many other ways that Napoleon can be blamed for the death not only of the Republic, but of Venice herself.

When, after the downfall of Napoleon, the Austrians re-occupied Venice by the Treaty of Paris, they brought back the golden horses and the little the Louvre would surrender of the looted possessions of the Republic. But by this time the impoverishment of the Venetians was so great that many treasures in private hands were already dispersed. More than one hundred important paintings belonging to the Barbarigo family alone had been sold off and eventually found their way to the Hermitage; even the Manins' plaster copies of

antique statuary were deemed worthy of purchase by the tsar. When the last
Contarini died in 1836 he bequeathed over one hundred paintings to the
Academy Gallery, his books to the Marciana and the splendid Brustolon suites
of furniture now in the Cà' Rezzonico to the municipal government. By availing
himself of the institutions Beauharnais had established Contarini was contributing to the development of museums of Venetian culture and civilization.
It was also in this period that the patrician Teodoro Correr made his extensive
collections of memorabilia of the Republic. Correr lived in the small palace
he had inherited from his ancestors and spent a large part of his patrimony
collecting everything he could lay his hands on that reflected life in the Venice
of the Republic. The personal *corno* and portraits of the last doge; the ballots
and voting balls used in a ducal election; paintings depicting ducal audiences
and public festivities; the robes of procurators and samples of rare lace, stuffs,
glass and coins; furniture, printed ephemera and books all crowded together
in his small house. Today Correr's wonderful collections are suitably displayed
in the former viceregal, later royal, apartments of the Procuratie Nuove.

   Under the Austrians tourists began to arrive not only to enjoy the beauty
of the city but to imbibe the romantic atmosphere of her past. Byron and Turner
were among the first after the fall of Napoleon. In his letters Byron described
the few proud survivors of the Republic he met and took up a life *en grand
seigneur* as he imagined it lived by the ancient patriciate. But he appeared little
interested in the city's buildings and merely referred his correspondents to the
current guide books for descriptions of what he saw. Though he tried to live,
deplorably or not, in Venice as a Venetian and though he gave instructions
to be buried there, he understood the city merely through contemporary guide
books. When he came to write two tragedies based on Venetian subjects, he
dabbled in the archives, but his opinions were mostly received from Napoleonic
liberal historians. In much the same way Turner painted Venice as he painted
the Thames; he was interested in capturing an atmosphere reflected in water
as it could be expressed in light. While his Venetian canvases and water colours
say a great deal that is interesting about Turner they say remarkably little about
Venice. The last great native artist, Antonio Canova, found his patrons outside
Venice in the popes of the day and at Napoleon's *arriviste* court. His neo-Classicism was copied throughout Europe and nowhere more successfully than in
Denmark, a country hardly Venetian in its cultural heritage or outlook.

   All the great nineteenth-century artists associated with Venice brought their
own culture to it. Wagner and Verdi drew inspiration from its atmosphere
as did D'Annunzio, Proust and Henry James, but their work was nonetheless German, Italian, French or Anglo-American and could hardly be thought
of as Venetian. Whistler, Sargent and Monet found Venice a suitable subject
for paintings in their own fully developed manner. The only one of these nineteenth-century artists who kept his vision firmly focused on the great civilization whose ghost still haunted Venice was John Ruskin. As a result he is to

a large extent responsible for our modern approach to Venice. Ruskin came with many of the prejudices of his protestant industrial nation, but he rightly argued for its preservation and restoration and for the correct understanding of the Venetian past in order better to accomplish these undertakings.

Ruskin had first arrived in Venice when it was still an island; when he returned less than a decade later the railway causeway had been built. The twentieth century has demonstrated what an aesthetic, if not economic, disaster this link with the mainland had been for the city, but even by the mid-nineteenth century its destructive potential was apparent. It was from this causeway, during the abortive revolt led by Daniele Manin in 1848, that the Austrians bombarded and subdued Venice, the only successful siege recorded since men first sought refuge in the lagoon. The failure of Manin's revolt set the seal on the Venetians' bankruptcy for the rest of the nineteenth century. A large number of the remaining patricians had supported Manin by contributing what treasures and jewels they still possessed. The victorious Austrians made a bonfire of the paper money printed by Manin's Republic and for many ruin came at a stroke. Henceforth the Austrian artillery garrison on the island of San Giorgio Maggiore, which fired its cannon at noon, symbolized the city's subjugation.

Venice was finally rescued from Austrian occupation by the House of Savoy who forcibly joined it to the Kingdom of United Italy, but her neglect and impoverishment as a useless outpost of the Austrian Empire was already complete. It was not until the period after the First World War that businessmen of the kingdom realized that industrial development and expansion could be carried out cheaply on land reclaimed from the marshes that surrounded the lagoon. The industrial port and refinery complex at Mestre-Marghera was established in the spirit of the assembly line and mass production; yet the very founders of the Mestre-Marghera industrial complex also demonstrated what might be done not only to preserve Venice's artistic and cultural legacy but to integrate it into the twentieth century. This was the case with the monastery island of San Giorgio Maggiore which was entirely restored shortly after the Second World War. A foundation was established there under whose auspices a wide range of cultural activities have been organized. In addition the refectory and former conventual rooms of the Palladian cloister have been adapted as conference centres. The international private committees formed to help Venice after the disastrous high waters of 4 November 1966 have met at San Giorgio several times. With the additional sponsorship of UNESCO they have been able effectively to put their case for Venice's special requirements to the appropriate ministries of the Italian Republic.

The problems these committees, the UNESCO and the Italian Government have recognized are of an immense complexity. The cleaning of a painting or an Istrian stone façade, the strengthening of larch piling foundations or the insulation of a brick wall against rising damp involve problems with implications far beyond Venice: intricate chemical analysis, atmospheric pollution studies, questions of oceanography and even the larger mysteries of the earth's surface movements. Much is being done today to make Venice a laboratory and study centre of this intricate interplay of forces that may either preserve or destroy the unique city.

Venice is an entirely man-made city; even the lagoon itself, thanks to four-teenth-century and later engineers who diverted the silt-bearing rivers that emptied into it, is a result of natural phenomena manipulated and rearranged to suit man. This delicate balance and harmony between nature and what the Venetians created is perhaps the most valuable legacy of her thousand-year civilization. Much of the Venetian past has already been preserved if not en-shrined in the museums of the world, but those who seek to discover the living source and spirit of these great masterpieces must first understand the mil-lennial existence and survival of Venice herself, the most beautiful city in the world. How and to what purpose her great legacy should be preserved will undoubtedly be debated for decades to come, but even were the city to dis-appear beneath the waters tomorrow, the name of Venice would still echo for ever in the consciousness of those who value what the west understands as culture and civilization.

Select Bibliography

J. Ackerman *Palladio*, London, 1966.

E. Arslan *Gothic Architecture in Venice*, London, 1971.

E. Bassi *Palazzi di Venezia*, Venice, 1976.

B. Berenson *Italian Pictures of the Renaissance: Venetian School*, 2 Volumes, London, 1957.

H. Brown *Venice: An Historical Sketch of the Republic*, London, 1895.

P. Burke *Venice and Amsterdam: A Study of Seventeenth Century Elites*, London, 1974.

G. Casanova *Memoires*, 6 Volumes, Paris, 1967.

R. Cessi *Storia della Repubblica di Venezia*, 2 Volumes, Milan, 1968.

D. Chambers *The Imperial Age of Venice 1380–1580*, London, 1970.

Classici dell'Arte Rizzoli *Antonello da Messina*, Milan, 1967

Giovanni Bellini, Milan, 1969

Bernardo Bellotto, Milan, 1974

Antonio Canaletto, Milan, 1968

Vettor Carpaccio, Milan, 1967

Albrecht Dürer, Milan, 1968

Giorgione, Milan, 1968

Francesco Guardi, Milan, 1974

Pietro Longhi, Milan, 1974

Andrea Mantegna, Milan, 1967
Sebastiano Ricci, Milan, 1976
Giambattista Tiepolo, Milan, 1968
Jacopo Tintoretto, Milan, 1970
Tiziano Vecellio, Milan, 1969
Paolo Veronese, Milan, 1968.

M. Crawford   *Salve Venetia*, 2 Volumes, London, 1905.

A. Da Mosto   *I Dogi di Venezia nella Vita Pubblica e Privata*, Milan, 1966.

C. Davis   *The Decline of the Venetian Nobility as a Ruling Class*, Baltimore, 1962.

J. Hale, ed.   *Renaissance Venice*, London, 1974.

D. Howard   *Jacopo Sansovino*, New Haven, 1975.

H. Inalcik   *The Ottoman Empire, The Classical Age 1300–1600*, London, 1973.

F. C. Lane   *Venice: A Maritime Republic*, Baltimore, 1973.

O. Logan   *Culture and Society in Venice 1470–1790*, London, 1972.

G. Lorenzetti   *Venice and Its Lagoon*, Rome, 1961.

P. Molmenti   *Venice: Its Individual Growth from the Earliest Beginnings to the Fall of the Republic*, trans. H. F. Brown, 6 Volumes, London, 1906.

J. J. Norwich   *Venice: The Rise to Empire*, London, 1977.

G. Perrocco and A. Salvadori   *Civiltà di Venezia*, 3 Volumes, Venice, 1973–1976.

T. Pignatti   *Venice*, London, 1971.

M. Polo   *The Travels*, trans. R. Latham, London, 1958.

J. Pope-Hennessy   *An Introduction to Italian Sculpture*, 3 Parts, London, 1955–1963.

B. Pullan   *Rich and Poor in Renaissance Venice: The Social Institutions of a Catholic State to 1620*, Oxford, 1971.

J. Ruskin   *The Stones of Venice*, 3 Volumes, London, 1925.

J. Steer   *A Concise History of Venetian Painting*, London, 1970.

Storia della Civiltà Veneziana, 8 Volumes, Florence, 1955–1962.

G. Tassini   *Curiosità Veneziane*, Venice, 1863.

F. Thiriet   *Histoire de Venise*, Paris, 1969.

UNESCO   *Rapporto Su Venezia*, Milan, 1966.

A. Vasiliev   *History of the Byzantine Empire*, 2 Volumes, Madison, 1952.

I Vedutisti Veneziani del Settecento, Catalogue of the Exhibition, Venice, 1967.

Venezia e Bizanzio, Catalogue of the Exhibition, Venice, 1974.

V. de Villhardouin   *Conquest of Constantinople*, trans. M. Shaw, London, 1963.

R. Wittkower   *Architectural Principles in the Age of Humanism*, London, 1949.

A. Zorzi   *Venezia Scomparsa*, Milan, 1971.

Index

Page numbers in *italic* refer to the illustrations and their captions.